The

BEATLES

BOOK OF LISTS

The BEATLES

BOOK OF LISTS

Stephen J. Spignesi

A CITADEL PRESS BOOK ▪ PUBLISHED BY CAROL PUBLISHING GROUP

A Citadel Press Book
Published by Carol Publishing Group
Citadel Press is a registered trademark of Carol Communications, Inc.

Editorial, sales and distribution, and rights and permissions inquiries should be
addressed to Carol Publishing Group, 120 Enterprise Avenue, Secaucus, N.J. 07094.

In Canada: Canadian Manda Group, One Atlantic Avenue, Suite 105, Toronto,
Ontario M6K 3E7

Carol Publishing Group books may be purchased in bulk at special discounts for
sales promotion, fund-raising, or educational purposes. Special editions can be
created to specifications. For details, contact Special Sales Department, Carol
Publishing Group, 120 Enterprise Avenue, Secaucus, N.J. 07094.

Title page and page xi photos courtesy of Photofest

Manufactured in the United States of America
10 9 8 7 6 5 4 3 2 1

Library of Congress Cataloging-in-Publication Data

Spignesi, Stephen J.
    The Beatles book of lists / Stephen J. Spignesi.
        p.   cm.
    "A Citadel Press book."
    ISBN 0–8065–1972–X (pb)
    1. Beatles—Miscellanea.   I. Title.
ML421.B4S66   1998
782.42166'092'2—dc21
    [b]   97–42461
                                                                    CIP
                                                                    MN

From me to . . .

My cousin Dan Fasano, a totally devoted Beatles fan who completely understands why Paul's bass line in "Dear Prudence" is a subject worthy of at least a half hour's discussion—even if the phone's ringing, the kids are screaming, it's starting to rain, and all the windows are open.

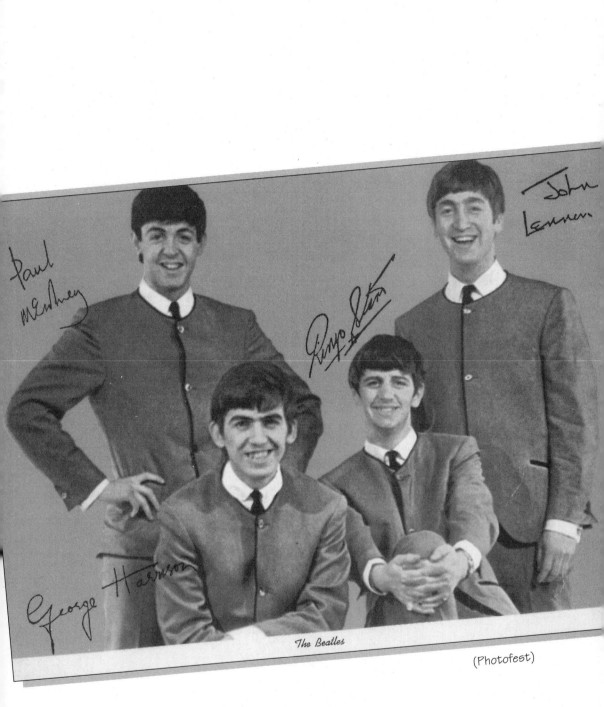

Paul McCartney

Ringo Starr

John Lennon

George Harrison

The Beatles

(Photofest)

Contents

The Singer's Gonna Sing a Song . . .

Rocking Horse People . . .

Look What You're Doing . . .

The Life That We Once Knew . . .

He Blew His Mind Out in a Car . . .

Then We Will Remember . . .

The Greatest of Them All . . .

Nice Apple Tart . . .

Everything Money Could Buy . . .

It Took Me Years to Write . . .

Singing Songs for Everyone . . .

They've Been Going in and out of Style . . .

Sit Back and Let the Evening Go . . .

I Saw a Film Today, Oh Boy . . .

48 Beatles Facts from Beatles Photo Cards From the Mid-sixties

JOHN

BIRTHDAY	October 9, 1940
BIRTHPLACE	Liverpool
HAIR	Brown
EYES	Brown
HEIGHT	5'11"
WEIGHT	159
FAVORITE COLOR	Green
FAVORITE FOOD	Corn Flakes
HOBBY	Writing
FAVORITE SINGER	Shirelles
LIKES	Cats
FAVORITE TYPE OF GIRL	His Wife
BROTHERS AND SISTERS	2 Stepsisters

PAUL

BIRTHDAY	June 18, 1942
BIRTHPLACE	Liverpool
HAIR	Dark Brown
EYES	Brown
HEIGHT	5'11"
WEIGHT	158
FAVORITE COLOR	Blue
FAVORITE FOOD	Roast Beef
FAVORITE SINGER	Little Richard
FAVORITE ACTRESS	Sophia Loren
LIKES	Sleeping
FAVORITE TYPE OF GIRL	Any Kind
BROTHERS AND SISTERS	1 Brother

GEORGE

BIRTHDAY	February 25, 1943
BIRTHPLACE	Liverpool
HAIR	Dark Brown
EYES	Hazel
HEIGHT	5'11"
WEIGHT	142
FAVORITE COLOR	Purple
FAVORITE FOOD	Hamburgers
LIKES	Drive-in Movies
FAVORITE TYPE OF GIRL	Friendly
BROTHERS AND SISTERS	2 Brothers, 1 Sister

RINGO

BIRTHDAY	July 7, 1940
BIRTHPLACE	Liverpool
REAL NAME	Richard Sharkey [sic]
HAIR	Dark Brown
EYES	Blue
HEIGHT	5'8"
WEIGHT	136
FAVORITE COLOR	Red
LIKES	Science Fiction
FAVORITE TYPE OF GIRL	All Types
BROTHERS AND SISTERS	None

(Photofest)

Preface: Roll Up

A Liverpool rhythm group the Beatles, made their debut at Neston Institute on Thursday night when north-west promoter, Mr. Les Dodd, presented three and a half hours of rock 'n' roll.

The five strong group, which has been pulling in capacity houses on Merseyside, comprises three guitars, bass, and drums.

John Lennon, the leader, plays one of the three rhythm guitars, the other guitarists being Paul Ramon [Paul McCartney] and Carl Harrison [George Harrison]. Stuart Da Stael [Stu Sutcliffe] plays the bass and the drummer is Tommy Moore. They all sing, either together, or as soloists.

Recently they returned from a Scottish tour, starring Johnny Gentle, and are looking forward to a return visit in a month's time.

Among the theaters they have played at are the Hippodrome, Manchester; the Empire, Liverpool, and Pavilion, Aintree.

—*Birkenhead News and Advertiser*
Saturday, June 11, 1960

John Lennon and Paul McCartney were two of the greatest popular song-writers of the twentieth century and the Beatles were the greatest pop group in the history of music. The music of the Beatles is, so far, the most important music of our century. Since, at this writing, we've got only a couple of years to go before the twentieth century bids us adieu, it's a safe bet that my admittedly effusive evaluation of John, Paul, George, and Ringo will undoubtedly hold up.

The Beatles were unique for many reasons, not the least of which was that they were a rock band that was taken *seriously,* something that, let's face it, before our boys came along was totally unheard of. There was something emotionally ethe-real and supremely transcendent about the Beatles music. The first time they all heard "Hey Jude," a palpable frisson went through the cultural sensibility of people in their late teens and early twenties.

There was a sense that John, Paul, George, and Ringo had somehow captured all the angst, confusion, sadness, and disillusionment that permeated the shared experiences of growing up *and* of growing up in the sixties, and transmuted them—*transformed* these emotional battlefields—into a simple, joyous expression of optimism: "Take a sad song and make it better." Indeed. That's exactly what they did: They took an ostensibly sad song and made it a whole lot better, a whole lot happier.

I have been a Beatles fan since 1963. I was ten years old when I first heard "I Want to Hold Your Hand" and "Please Please Me" on the radio. "Please Please Me" especially intrigued me since I had never heard a descending harmony vocal line in a pop song before. You know the line I'm referring to: "Last night I said these words . . ." etc. This sounded, well, *new*. It *was* new.

I followed the Beatles from that point and bought all their 45s and albums. I can remember the Christmas of 1968 as though it was yesterday. I was fifteen and, thanks to Santa, I found the *White Album* (along with, of course, the requisite socks and shirts) under the tree. We were still living on Elizabeth Ann Drive in the Annex section of New Haven and my mother's sister and her family lived on the first floor of our big two-family house.

We were having Christmas dinner downstairs that year and I can remember hearing all the noise and commotion as I sat upstairs making a list of the *White Album* songs that I wanted to learn how to play on the piano or guitar. My guitar songs included "Dear Prudence," "Blackbird," "Mother Nature's Son," "Rocky Raccoon," "Julia," "I Will," and "Cry Baby Cry." My piano songs were "Martha My Dear" (of course), "Piggies," "Sexy Sadie," "Ob-La-Di, Ob-La, Da," "Why Don't We Do It in the Road?," and "I'm So Tired."

I felt that all these tunes were within my modest playing and singing capabilities and I planned a post-Christmas trip to a music store to see if the sheet music for the album was available yet. I was so excited about actually *doing* these songs that I did not want to take the time to figure them out off the record.

To cut to the chase, the sheet music *was* available and I learned every one of the songs that I had written down on my optimistic list. To this day, I can still do Paul's piano part for "Martha My Dear" note-perfect and, until an unfortunate finger amputation put an end to my guitar-playing days in 1984, I could also play his "Blackbird" guitar-picking flawlessly.

The point is that there were no other artists whose work I would look to as a source of songs to *learn*. Oh sure, once in a while I'd pick out a Doors organ riff ("Light My Fire" was a favorite) or a Mamas and Papas chord sequence (I especially liked the changes in "California Dreaming"). When it came to the Beatles, however, I had a sense of awe about their songs and I dove head first into learning exactly *how they did it*.

I was not alone in considering the Beatles songs as something more than just pop songs. During the long school Christmas vacation that year, a bunch of guys and I went to what used to be euphemistically called "mixers." These were dances where kids could meet and maybe hit it off and start dating. Since many kids went to all-boys or all-girls high schools in my area, this was one of the few ways for teens to meet each other.

Back then, live bands still played at these dances. Today, DJs own the high school dance turf, but in the late sixties, if you went to a mixer (or even a club for that matter—but we were too young for that, of course) you got to hear a live band, usually local, and occasionally good.

During the week between Christmas and New Year's, this particular "holiday mixer" was held in the church basement of St. Mary's Roman Catholic Church just off the Yale University campus. The band playing that night was the Wildweeds, a local favorite fronted by Al Anderson, a brilliant guitarist and songwriter who would go on to form the group NRBQ. In fact, the Weeds (as they were affectionately known locally) were an early incarnation of the terrific NRBQ and the caliber of their playing and writing was an early indicator of their later, nationally known work.

This night, the Weeds did their usual playlist of Rolling Stones, Doors, and Beatles covers, as well as some Motown and Crosby, Stills, and Nash stuff. Then everyone except Al Anderson and a percussionist left the stage and Al said they would like to do a new Beatles song. He and the percussionist did an absolutely flawless rendition of "Blackbird," complete with tapping and bird sounds.

The White Album had been out only about a month, remember, and many in the audience had not even bought it yet. Nonetheless, Al Anderson had learned Paul's guitar part and vocal for the song perfectly and had added it to the group's playlist almost before the record had stopped spinning on his turntable. The Beatles tended to bring out this kind of obsessive attention in people. Today, thirty years later, this attention is as gloriously rabid as ever.

The Beatles Book of Lists is a really fun way of looking at the many facets of the Beatles universe. It contains some lengthy and extremely comprehensive lists such as "78 Important People From Across the Beatles Universe" and "78 'Toppermost of the Poppermost' Moments From *The Beatles Anthology*." Then there are brief "mini-lists" (list titles notwithstanding!) such as "The 4 Slogans Used to Describe Each of the Beatles in Revell's Official 1964 Plastic Model Kits of the Group," and "The 5 Members of Paul McCartney's Imagined Supergroup."

The book concentrates mainly on the Beatles as a group, but there are several lists about some of the Fabs' solo work and a couple of features on John Lennon's assassination. In conclusion, we hope you will enjoy the show . . . and a splendid time is guaranteed for all!

(Photofest)

Acknowledgments

First and foremost I'd like to thank Tom Schultheiss for his Beatles knowledge, his "Popular Culture, Ink." Beatles books, his advice and guidance, and his enduring friendship.

Mike Lewis, my Citadel Press editor, is next on my "Thank You" list. Mike is as avid a Beatles fan as I am and he has a huge Fab Four collection that he would regularly look through, searching for things he knew I'd be able to use for this book. Mike has been my editor on several Citadel Press books and his talent and skills have been extremely helpful on all of them, but *The Beatles Book of Lists* brought out his best. It is a wonderful feeling to be working on a project with a guy who knows who I'm talking about, when I mention people like Ivan Vaughan or Pete Shotton! Mike's editorial guidance on this book was invaluable and it is due to him that I toned down my remarks about John Lennon's murderer, using the words *sick, twisted individual* to describe that creep instead of my original choice.

My agent, John White, deserves combat pay and I am sorry I cannot afford to give it to him. He has been my staunchest advocate over the past few years, steadfastly looking out for my interests during a time when every article about the book business uses the adjective *beleaguered* to describe the publishing industry. Thanks, John, for taking sad songs and making them better.

My friend, screenwriter Jim Cole, was always on the lookout for Beatles-related stuff and would never fail to come through with a tape, an article, or just an encouraging word. Jim's scripts will someday catapult him into the "Land of Extreme Busyness" and so his days as my West Coast advance guard may be numbered, but I appreciate (and will take shameless advantage of!) his help until then.

My publisher, Steven Schragis, was the guy who believed in this project and who gave it the green light—even though there are enough Beatles books in print to build a pulp bridge (by a fountain?) to Liverpool. He had faith that I'd write something the fans would want to read and for his belief in me and my work, he has my fond appreciation.

Rounding out the list, I would like to say thank you on behalf of the group and myself to Pam and Carter Spignesi, Dan Fasano, Lee Mandato, Mike Streeto, and Dolores and Tony Fantarella.

Paul performing in his 1984 film *Give My Regards to Broad Street*. (Photofest)

A Few Words From Paul

The one thing that I'm really proud of with the Beatles is that I'm glad of the content of the songs, of what we said in them. Because if you listen to Beatles songs, we're saying good things—we're saying love and peace, Let It Be, there will be an answer . . . Hey Jude, don't make it bad—looking back on it, none of it says go and screw your brother.

🍎

Our songs weren't anthems of rebelliousness, we weren't saying "Come on kids, hate your parents." Although we could have done, we had that power—we could have stood for Satanism instead of love—and if we had chosen to use that power, the whole thing could have gone a very different way.

🍎

I thought spreading love was important then and I still do now. I really do think that's all there is. I don't think you need much else and a lot of the problems in society that you're getting now is because there isn't enough love, especially between families. Kids are just not getting it.

🍎

But I think the overall impression that the Beatles left people with was an affectionate feeling. Most people I talk to say, "Aah, great days." They've got lovely memories of it. And if there is any residue of love for the Beatles, I think it's because we had that very honest, loving attitude and our message still remains a very positive, loving message.

🍎

PAUL MCCARTNEY
From the official "Real Love" press release
February 1996

"Music by The Beatles, full orchestra."

Notice on a card found while tearing down a house in Clyde, New York, in 1965. The card said that a dance would be held at Perkins Hall. The date of the dance—with music by "The Beatles"—was Tuesday, April 9, 1878.

The BEATLES

BOOK OF LISTS

(*Left to right*) George Harrison, Paul McCartney, Pete Best, John Lennon. This is one of the few surviving photos of this early sixties incarnation of the band. (Photofest)

You Became a Legend . . .

1. The Beatles Timeline: 18 Steps to a Legend

We were four guys. I met Paul and said do you wanna join me band, you know? And then George joined. And then Ringo joined. We were just a band who made it very very big, that's all.

—John Lennon

This is a look, from skiffle to *Sgt. Pepper* and beyond, at the early bands the lads played in who would, in August 1962, become the final incarnation of the Beatles. (English "skiffle" groups were similar to the American amateur folk revival groups popular in the late 1950s. The music was characterized by an "old-timey" sound, which included jug band music, circa 1920s Preservation Hall jazz, and novelty songs from the 1930s and 1940s, all of which was played on unusual instruments such as jugs, kazoos, washboards, and washtub basses.)

1. **Early 1956, the Blackjacks**   This was a skiffle group consisting solely of 16-year-old John Lennon and his friend Pete Shotton. (This two-man incarnation lasted approximately one week before John and Pete added other members.)
2. **March 1957–June 1957, the Quarry Men**   John came up with this name in honor of the school he was attending at the time, Quarry Bank. The lineup consisted of 16-year-old John on guitar and vocals, Colin Hanton on drums, Rod Davis on banjo, Eric Smith on guitar, Pete Shotton on washboard, and Bill Smith on tea-chest bass. Ivan Vaughan and Nigel Whalley also joined the group during this period, alternating on tea-chest bass.
3. **June 1957–July 1957, the Quarry Men**   This group comprised essentially the same lineup except for the addition of Len Garry on second tea-chest bass.
4. **July 1957–January 1958, the Quarry Men**   This incarnation is notable for the addition of Paul McCartney on guitar and vocals. This seven-month period was the first musical collaboration ever between the songwriting team that would change the world culture and redefine popular music.
5. **February 1958–June 1958, the Quarry Men**   The lineup of the group changed yet again during this period, most dramatically by the addition of George Harrison to the group. The Quarry Men now consisted of John Lennon on guitar and vocals, Paul McCartney on guitar and vocals, George Harrison on guitar and vocals, John "Duff" Lowe on piano, Eric Griffiths on guitar, Colin Hanton on drums, and Len Garry on tea-chest bass.

6. **June 1958–January 1959, the Quarry Men**   During this period, the group was down to five guys: John, Paul, and George, John Lowe on piano, and Colin Hanton on drums.

7. **January 1959–August 1959, the Quarry Men**   The history of the group is sketchy during this period, but it seems that the basic five-man lineup of the band, with the occasional addition of other players for certain gigs, played in clubs in Liverpool and its environs.

8. **August 1959–October 1959, the Quarry Men**   During this two- or three-month period, the Quarry Men performed in what might be their oddest configuration. They were now down to four players, John, Paul, and George, all on guitar and vocals; as well as Ken Brown, who also played guitar and sang. They had no drummer and performed as an all-guitar band.

9. **October 1959–December 1959, Johnny and the Moondogs**   This was the first ever "all-Beatles" musical group. For a brief period at the end of 1959, John, Paul, and George worked as a trio, still playing without a drummer.

10. **January 1960–April 1960, the Beatals [sic]**   This still-drummerless quartet was the first incarnation of the Beatles as we would come to know them. The four-man lineup consisted of John, Paul, George, and the ill-fated Stuart Sutcliffe on bass guitar. (Stu died in 1962 at the age of twenty-one from a cerebral hemorrhage. Stu's brief life—with an emphasis, of course, on his career as a Beatle—was dramatized in the 1994 film, *Backbeat*.)

11. **May 1960–June 1960, the Silver Beetles**   A quartet briefly became a quintet with the addition of drummer Tommy Moore to the group's lineup. John and Moore didn't get along and his tenure with the band was subsequently very shortlived.

    According to Beatles authority Bill Harry, Moore didn't show up for a gig and when Allen Klein and the other members of the band went to Moore's house looking for him, his girlfriend shouted out the window at them, "You can go and piss off! He's not playing with you anymore; he's got a job at Garston Bottle Works on the night shift."

    Moore died of a stroke in 1981.

12. **June 1960–July 1960, the Silver Beatles**   This once-again drummerless version of the group was back to John, Paul, George, and Stu Sutcliffe due to Tommy Moore's departure. By this time they had changed "Beetles" to "Beatles" because a musician friend of theirs named Brian Casser had told them he didn't like "Beetles."

13. **July 1960–August 1960, the Silver Beatles**   This brief version of the group consisted of John, Paul, George, Stu, and Norman Chapman on drums.

14. **August 1960–November 1960, the Beatles**   This was the first incarnation of the group using the name the Beatles and it consisted of John, Paul, George, Stu, and Pete Best on drums.

15. **November 1960–January 1961, the Beatles**   In November of 1960, Stu Sutcliffe left the band and Chas Newby signed on as their new bass guitarist. Newby had been with the Blackjacks before John joined the group.

16. **January 1961–June 1961, the Beatles**   This version of the Beatles had the same lineup as the August 1960 crew. In January of 1961, Chas Newby left the band and Stu Sutcliffe returned.

17. **June 1961–August 1962, the Beatles**   When Stu Sutcliffe left the band in June of 1961 to study art in Hamburg, Germany, he was not replaced and John, Paul, George, and Pete Best played together for over a year as the Beatles.

18. **August 1962–April 1970, the Beatles** In August of 1962, John, Paul, and George replaced Pete Best with former hairdresser Ringo Starr. Ringo had previously been playing with Rory Storm and the Hurricanes but told reporters that he had followed the Beatles for years and was thrilled that he had been asked to join the group. The August 23, 1962, edition of the newspaper *Mersey Beat* broke the news:

BEATLES CHANGE DRUMMER!

Ringo Starr (formerly drummer with Rory Storm and the Hurricanes) has joined the Beatles, replacing Pete Best on drums. Ringo has admired the Beatles for years and is delighted with his new engagement. Naturally he is tremendously excited about the future. The Beatles comment, "Pete left the group by mutual agreement. There were no arguments or difficulties, and this has been an entirely amicable decision."

On Tuesday, September 4th, the Beatles will fly to London to make recordings at EMI Studios. They will be recording numbers that have been specially written for the group, which they have received from their recording manager George Martin (Parlophone).

(The *Mersey Beat* report about the Fabs recording songs "specifically written" for them was actually a bit of journalistic hyperbole. The truth is, the "songs" referred to turned out to actually be just *one* new song, Mitch Murray's "How Do You Do It?" which George Martin strongly felt should be the A-side of the Beatles' first single. The boys reluctantly recorded the song (after rearranging it to better suit their own style) but ultimately succeeded in not allowing it to be released. Gerry and the Pacemakers went on to have a number one hit with the song (ironically, using the Beatles' new arrangement). In 1995, the Beatles released their version of "How Do You Do It?" on *The Beatles Anthology 1*.)

Immediately following the article about Ringo's new gig was the following short piece:

THE BEATLES TO PLAY CHESTER

As a result of the phenomenal Box Office success of the Beatles during their 4-week season of Monday nights at the Plaza Ballroom, St. Helens, the directors of Whetstone Entertainments, controllers of the ballroom, have engaged the Beatles for a series of four Thursday night sessions at the Riverpark Ballroom, Chester, which commenced on 16th August.

This lineup of John, Paul, George, and Ringo lasted seven years and eight months. In April 1970, the Beatles were no longer a group, but there was still the possibility they could someday reunite and make new music. In December 1980, that thrilling possibility became an impossible dream.

2. 40 Beatles Personality Traits

A popular gimmick used in teen magazines in the sixties was to ask their readers who their favorite Beatle was, such was the familiarity fans had with each of the boys and their personalities. This feature is a personality quiz that can determine the Beatle you are most similar to. From the following list of forty Beatle personality traits, you can see how many individual "John," "Paul," "George," and "Ringo" personality traits you possess!

(The personality traits for the Beatles were arrived at by analyzing interviews, comments, and behaviors of each of the Beatles, as well as factoring in the accepted perception of each Beatles' dominant personality traits. This is, of course, not a scientific study, so don't write me because you're mad that I called George "prickly.")

John	*Paul*	*George*	*Ringo*
Artistic	Ambitious	Difficult	Accommodating
Brilliant	Deliberate	Enlightened	Considerate
Defensive	Devious	Iconoclastic	Cooperative
Earthy	Devoted	Intelligent	Friendly
Honest	Diplomatic	Prickly	Funny
Interested	Entrepreneurial	Realistic	Jolly
Obsessive	Frugal	Reclusive	Naive
Passionate	Good-natured	Reluctant	Quiet
Philanthropic	Nostalgic	Spiritual	Self-effacing
Profane	Optimistic	Taciturn	Subdued

3. 5 Posters That Hung on the Walls During John and Yoko's 1969 Bed-in for Peace

These five posters were all seen in suite 1742 of the Queen Elizabeth Hotel in Montreal during the media coverage of the Bed-in. (Most of these posters can be glimpsed in *Imagine: John Lennon,* the video documentary about John.)

1. "Grow Your Hair"
2. "Hair Peace"
3. "Remember Love"
4. "Bagism—Love and Peace"
5. "L'amour et La Paix" ("Love and Peace")

4. The First Report to Break the News of John Lennon's Assassination

Most Beatles fans remember precisely where they were when they learned of the murder of John Lennon. I was asleep in a recliner in front of the TV and was awakened by a phone call from my cousin Danny (the guy to whom this book is dedicated). Danny had been watching the Monday Night Football game during which the shooting was announced as breaking news, and I was the first person he called.

From that moment on, everything changed for Beatles fans. Here is the complete text of the original United Press International wire report that broke the horrible news to the world.

876G

URGENT

LENNON—SUB

(NEW YORK)—NEW YORK POLICE SAY FORMER BEATLE JOHN LENNON IS IN CRITICAL CONDITION AFTER BEING SHOT THREE TIMES AT HIS HOME ON MANHATTAN'S UPPER WEST SIDE. A POLICE SPOKESMAN SAID "A SUSPECT IS IN CUSTODY," BUT HE HAD NO OTHER DETAILS. A HOSPITAL WORKER SAID—QUOTE—"THERE'S BLOOD ALL OVER THE PLACE. THEY'RE WORKING ON HIM LIKE CRAZY."

UPI 12–08–80 11:35 PES

(Photofest)

(Upper left) George at the age of twelve; (Upper right) Paul at eight; (Lower left) John at eight; (Lower right) Ringo at nine. (Photofest)

Waiting to Take You Away . . .

15 Lists That Chronicle the Magical Mystery Trip of the Beatles From 1930 to the Present

Beatles' Magical Mystery Trip

The twentieth century's greatest romance or "just a band that made it very very big"? The latter view is John's, in hard-hatted post-Beatles myth-demolition mode; the former is mine, rose-coloured, with long and loving hindsight.

—Derek Taylor, Beatles' Publicist

We reckoned we could make it because there were four of us. None of us would've made it alone, because Paul wasn't quite strong enough, I didn't have enough girl-appeal, George was too quiet, and Ringo was the drummer. But we thought that everyone would be able to dig at least one of us, and that's how it turned out.

—John Lennon

I can hear you: "Who is Spignesi kidding?" How in the name of Mother Mary can he reduce the entire history of the Fab Four to around six hundred events? What is he, barmy?"

Well, perhaps, but that's *another* story.

Beatles fans, fear not: This feature and its 15 lists, when read in its entirety, *will* provide you with an accessible, comprehensive history of the Beatles from the marriage of their parents through the release of the *Anthology* series.

Honest.

It includes details on all the releases of the Beatles' music, as well as anything and everything else that can be considered important in their lives and careers. Because this is, of course, the history of the Beatles, the boys' solo work is not chronicled unless it was a landmark release, such as John's weenie-wagging *Two Virgins;* Paul's irrevocable (in light of the breakup of the band) solo album *McCartney;* or his 1997 tribute to John's wit, *Flaming Pie.*

The history of the Beatles is unquestionably the history of the sixties. That's a given. Their impact has been too wide-ranging and too far-reaching to get away with being too glib about their overall importance. Of course they changed music. There isn't a pop musician working today who does not, in some way, owe a "thank you" to John, Paul, George, and Ringo.

The Beatles also changed the culture in ways that are still being felt today. They may have contributed to bringing the disastrous Vietnam War to an end and they crystallized the concept of world peace and made it their own—while showing the world that it was entirely possible for people to *live* in peace. All they had to do was—all together now—give peace a chance. How do we do that? All you need is love.

The Beatles saw music and art as something more than entertainment. They saw it—and unashamedly *used* it—as a bully pulpit for the ideals of a greater good, for the hope of an enlightened race.

That's enough analysis. Here comes the sun and since I am a paperback writer, I've got to get back to my day in the life of working like a dog. Enjoy this revealing look at the Beatles in their time here, there, and everywhere.

Why?

Because.

5. 14 "Pre-Beatles" Events 1930–1943

1930 May 20   George Harrison's parents, Harold Harrison and Louise French, were married.

1933 February 18   Yoko Ono (the future Mrs. John Lennon) was born in Tokyo, Japan.

1934 September 19   Brian Epstein, the future manager of the Beatles, was born in Liverpool, England.

1936   This year, Ringo Starr's parents, Richard Starkey and Elsie Gleave, were married.

1938 December 3   John Lennon's parents, Alfred "Freddie" Lennon and Julia Stanley, were married.

1939 September 10   Cynthia Powell (the future Mrs. John Lennon) was born in Blackpool, England.

1940 June 23   Stuart Sutcliffe was born in Edinburgh, Scotland.

1940 July 7   Ringo Starr—nee Richard Starkey Jr.—was born at Royal Liverpool Children's Hospital in Dingle, Liverpool, England.

1940 October 9   John Lennon was born at Oxford Street Maternity Hospital in Liverpool, England. A German Luftwaffe air raid on Liverpool took place at the time of John's birth.

1941   This year, Paul McCartney's parents, James McCartney and Mary Patricia Mohin, were married.

1941 November 24   Pete Best was born in Madras, India.

1942 June 18   James Paul McCartney was born at Walton Hospital in Liverpool, England.

1942 September 24   Linda Louise Eastman (the future Mrs. Paul McCartney) was born in Scarsdale, New York.

1943 February 24   George Harrison was born at 12 Arnold Grove, in Wavetree, Liverpool, England.

An eight-year-old John with his beloved Aunt Mimi, his mother Julia's sister, who raised him as if he were her own. This photo was taken outside of Mimi's house (known locally as Mendips) on Menlove Avenue in Woolton. (Photofest)

6. 13 Beatles-Related Events of the Fifties

1. **1956**   Early this year, John formed a skiffle group called the Blackjacks with his longtime friend Pete Shotton. They quickly, however, change their name to the Quarry Men.

2. **1956**   This year, Paul McCartney wrote his first song, "I Lost My Little Girl." He was all of fourteen.

3. **1957 June 9**   The Quarry Men auditioned for *TV Star Search* (*not* the Ed McMahon Show!) at Liverpool's Empire Theater. They bombed and were beaten for the TV gig by the Sunnysiders.

4. **1957 July 6**   John Lennon and Paul McCartney met for the first time at a summer concert at St. Peter's Church Hall in the Woolton suburb of Liverpool. John's group, the Quarry Men, was performing at the concert and Ivan Vaughan (a friend of both John and Paul's) invited Paul to attend the show. After the performance, Ivan introduced Paul to John. After the concert, Paul jammed with the Quarry Men and impressed John with his ability to tune a guitar and memorize all the lyrics to rock-and-roll songs. They jammed to "Long Tall Sally," "Tutti Frutti," and other songs of the period. Two weeks later, John invited Paul to join the band.

5. **1957 July 20**   Through Pete Shotton, John Lennon invited Paul McCartney to join the Quarry Men. Paul, who was away at summer camp with his younger brother Michael, did not accept until he returned, thus delaying his debut with the band until October 18.

6. **1957 August 7**   The Quarry Men (without Paul) performed at the Cavern Club. The band played rock-and-roll standards (Elvis, Chuck Berry, etc.) and were quickly ordered to stop since The Cavern Club at the time only allowed jazz and skiffle. Rock-and-roll was verboten.

7. **1957 October 18**   Paul made his debut with the Quarry Men at the Conservative Club's New Clubmoor Hall in Back Broadway, Liverpool. Even though the addition of his talent immediately improved the band and would ultimately result in more and better bookings, on this night he was nervous and screwed up his guitar solo in the old Arthur Smith classic, "Guitar Boogie." The reason he messed up was because he was left-handed and was playing a right-handed guitar upside down and backwards because he still hadn't learned how to restring a guitar so he could play it properly.

8. **1958 February 6**   Paul McCartney's school friend George Harrison met John Lennon and the other Quarry Men at a gig at Wilson Hall.

9. **1958**   Mid-year, the Quarry Men recorded "In Spite of All the Danger," a Lennon/McCartney composition (actually a Paul McCartney song).

10. **1958 July 15**   John Lennon's mother Julia was killed when she was run down by a car driven by a drunken off-duty police officer.

11. **1958**   Late this year, the Quarry Men failed an ABC-TV audition.

12. **1959 August 29**   George Harrison performed with the Quarry Men at the opening of Mona Best's Casbah Coffee Club in West Derby, Liverpool. This club was actually in Pete Best's basement and the Quarry Men would play there every Saturday night, through October 1958.

13. **1959**   By the end of this year, John Lennon and Paul McCartney have collaborated on at least one hundred songs including: "In Spite of All the Danger," "Looking Glass," "Catswalk," "Winston's Walk," "Thinking of Linking," "The

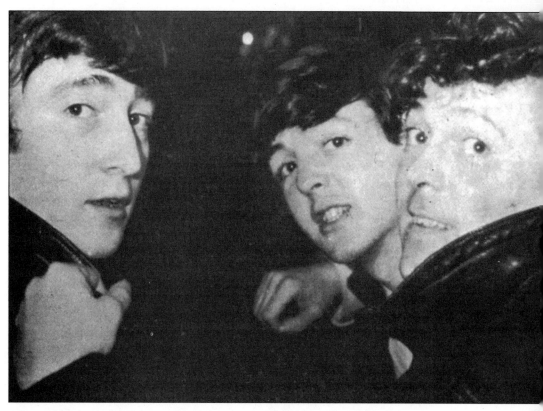

John and Paul, with their rock hero Gene Vincent in the Cavern Club, early 1961. (Photofest)

One After 909," "Years Roll Along," "Keep Looking That Way," "I Lost My Little Girl" (now counted as a Lennon/McCartney composition), "That's My Woman," "Just Fun," "Too Bad About Sorrows," "Love Me Do," "Hello Little Girl," "When I'm Sixty-Four," and "Hot as Sun." A decade later, "The One After 909" would ultimately appear on the *Let It Be* album as "One After 909," and *almost* a decade later, "When I'm Sixty-Four" would end up on the *Sgt. Pepper's Lonely Hearts Club Band* album.

7. *20 Important Beatles Events 1960–1961*

1. **1960 January**   Stuart Sutcliffe joined the Quarry Men.
2. **1960 August 12**   John, Paul, and George auditioned Pete Best as the drummer for their group, now known as the Beatles. They accepted him and he accompanied them to Hamburg, Germany, for a lengthy tour.
3. **1960 September**   In Hamburg, the Beatles met and became friends with Klaus Voorman, the artist who would eventually design the cover of their *Revolver* album.
4. **1960 October**   Still in Hamburg, the Beatles became friends with Ringo Starr, who was then touring with Rory Storm and the Hurricanes.
5. **1960 October 15**   John, Paul, and George agreed to play as a backup band for Lou Walters, one of the players in Rory Storm's group. Ringo sat in on drums instead of Pete Best, and thus, the first ever recording session with all four final members of the Beatles took place.

6. **1960 December 17** Paul began playing bass in the band.
7. **1960 December 31** Neil Aspinall quit accounting school to take a job as the Beatles' chauffeur. He would ultimately become a personal assistant and confidant to the boys and managing director of Apple. His close relationship with the Fabs would earn him the honored sobriquet of the "Fifth Beatle."
8. **1961 February 9** The Beatles returned to the Cavern Club for an afternoon gig. The Cavern finally began to allow rock and roll and the Beatles became one of the acts who played for Liverpool workers on their lunchbreak. (It was at one of these afternoon gigs that future manager Brian Epstein first caught a glimpse of the band.)
9. **1961 April** Sometime between April and the summer, Astrid Kirchherr "designed" the moptop hair look that would ultimately become known around the world as the "Beatle Cut." All of the Fabs—except for, tellingly, Pete Best—adopted the new look.
10. **1961 June 22** For a few days, the Beatles played backup for vocalist Tony Sheridan, playing on six songs for Sheridan. They also used this time in the studio as an opportunity to record two songs themselves, the standard "Ain't She Sweet" and the Lennon/McCartney composition "Cry for a Shadow." These two songs are considered the Beatles' first professional recordings.
11. **1961 July** This month, Tony Sheridan's single "My Bonnie"/"The Saints" was released in Germany on the Polydor label. The Beatles were credited on the label as the "Beat Brothers."
12. **1961 July 6** The first issue (Volume 1, Number 1, July 6–20, 1961) of the Liverpool music newspaper, *Mersey Beat*, was published. Its editor was Bill Harry, who would later write several authoritative books about the Beatles. This first issue of *Mersey Beat* was notable because it included one of John Lennon's earliest published essays, a satirical piece titled, "Being a Short Diversion on the Dubious Origins of Beatles," which was "translated from the John Lennon."
13. **1961 July 14** The prodigal sons were welcomed home from Germany. The Cavern Club held a "Welcome Home" night for the Beatles.
14. **1961 August 17** Fan letters to the Beatles were published for the first time in *Mersey Beat*. Also on this day, a poem by John Lennon titled "I Remember Arnold" appeared in *Mersey Beat*.
15. **1961 September 14** John Lennon began writing a regular column in *Mersey Beat* entitled "Around and About." He wrote under the pseudonym "Beat Comer."
16. **1961 November** This month, the Beatles performed twenty shows at the Cavern Club.
17. **1961 December 3** The Beatles met with Brian Epstein for the first time to discuss the possibility of Epstein managing the group. The Beatles could not decide on whether or not to sign on with Epstein at this meeting and a second was scheduled.
18. **1961 December 6** The Beatles met with Brian Epstein for the second time and John spoke for the group and accepted Brian as their new manager.
19. **1961 December 10** The Beatles told Brian Epstein that they would sign a management contract with him if he could get them a recording contract. Brian agreed to the conditions and persuaded a Decca representative to hear the Beatles perform at the Cavern Club.
20. **1961 December 13** Mike Smith of Decca Records attended one of the Beatles' shows at the Cavern Club. Based on what he heard, he agreed to a formal, recorded audition of the Beatles in London the following January.

8. 22 "Ready, Steady, Go!" Beatles Events 1962

1. **January 1** The Beatles auditioned in London for Mike Smith of Decca Records. They recorded the following songs:

"Love of the Loved"
"Money (That's What I Want")"
"Sure to Fall"
"Take Good Care of My Baby"
"Three Cool Cats"
"Like Dreamers Do"
"Crying, Waiting, Hoping"
"Searchin'"
"Till There Was You"
"Memphis"
"Hello Little Girl"
"Besame Mucho"
"September in the Rain"
"Sheik of Araby"
"To Know Her Is to Love Her"

Of these fifteen songs, "Love of the Loved," "Like Dreamers Do," and "Hello Little Girl" were Lennon/McCartney compositions.

Even though Mike Smith had been optimistic about the group's potential after attending their Cavern Club performance, he was less than thrilled with their audition tape and was actually the one who ultimately made the decision not to offer them a recording contract. At first, Smith sent out what seemed to be mixed signals. Shortly after their New Year's Day audition, Tony Dow wrote in the *Liverpool Echo*, "Decca disc producer Mike Smith tells me he thinks the Beatles are great. He has a continuous tape of their audition performance, which runs for over thirty

George in 1958 at the age of fifteen. (Photofest)

minutes, and he is convinced his label will be able to put the Beatles to good use."

The Beatles Decca audition tapes were saved and were released in the United States in 1981 on the albums *Dawn of the Silver Beatles* and *Lightning Strikes Twice*. The cuts "Searchin'," "Three Cool Cats," "The Sheik of Araby," "Like Dreamers Do," and "Hello Little Girl" were also included on *The Beatles Anthology 1*.

2. **January 4**   A *Mersey Beat* poll of five thousand readers ranked the Beatles as Liverpool's most popular group.

3. **January 5**   Tony Sheridan's single "My Bonnie"/"The Saints" was released in the United Kingdom. The Beatles—credited as the "Beat Brothers"—were Sheridan's backup group on this single.

4. **January 24**   The Beatles signed a contract making Brian Epstein their manager. His commission was a staggering twenty-five percent of the Beatles' earnings.

5. **February 12**   The Beatles auditioned for BBC Radio in Manchester. They performed "Like Dreamers Do," "Till There Was You," "Memphis," and "Hello Little Girl."

6. **March 24**   The Beatles began wearing suits on stage.

7. **April 10**   Stu Sutcliffe died of a brain hemorrhage.

8. **June 6**   The Beatles auditioned for George Martin at EMI Studios on Abbey Road in London. Martin did not like the Beatles repertoire and he also felt that Pete Best was unsatisfactory as their drummer. This was the beginning of the end for Pete Best.

9. **June 23**   Brian Epstein formed NEMS Enterprises (named for his family's furniture business NEMS, which was short for North End Music Stores). The sole function of NEMS Enterprises was to attend to the ever-expanding business affairs of the Beatles.

10. **June 24**   The Beatles performed for the last time at Mona Best's Casbah Coffee Club.

11. **July**   This month, George Martin offered the Beatles a recording contract with Parlophone Records. Their royalty was one cent per double-sided record. The Beatles and Brian Epstein did not tell Pete Best about the contract and John, Paul, and George began to pressure Brian to fire Pete.

12. **August 15**   Pete Best performed for the last time with the Beatles at the Cavern Club.

13. **August 16**   Brian Epstein fired Pete Best and he is replaced by Ringo Starr, who decided to leave Rory Storm and the Hurricanes to join the Beatles.

14. **August 18**   Ringo Starr made his first appearance with the Beatles.

15. **August 19**   Ringo Starr made his first Cavern Club appearance with the Beatles. Pete Best's fans heckled the band and George Harrison ended up with a black eye when he was punched by a "music lover" who was not happy about Pete Best's departure.

16. **August 23**   John Lennon and Cynthia Powell were married in Liverpool. Also, John's poem "Small Sam" appeared in that day's issue of *Mersey Beat*. ("Small Sam" began "Once Upon a Tom" which is the identical opening to John's *In His Own Write* short story, "The Wrestling Dog." "Small Sam" was originally scheduled to appear in John's 1965 collection *A Spaniard in the Works*. For

some unknown reason it was cut, and it remains today one of John's uncollected pieces.)

17. **September 4**   The Beatles' first official recording session with George Martin took place. They recorded "Love Me Do" and "How Do You Do It?" As mentioned earlier, sensing that Ringo's drumming might not be up to snuff, Martin hired session drummer Andy White to back the group on "Love Me Do."

    Even though the Fabs did not want to record the Mitch Murray song, "How Do You Do It?" (which ultimately became Gerry and the Pacemakers first number-one hit), they did so because George Martin insisted.

18. **October 2**   The Beatles formalized their somewhat haphazard agreement with Brian Epstein by signing a five-year, legally binding contract designating Epstein their manager. His 25-percent commission was now "carved in stone," so to speak and Brian set out to make the Beatles an enormous success.

19. **October 5**   The Beatles' first single "Love Me Do"/"P. S. I Love You" was released in the United Kingdom. Brian Epstein personally bought ten thousand copies, thereby assuring that the Beatles would have a Top 20 hit.

20. **November 23**   The Beatles failed an audition for BBC Television.

21. **November 30**   Brian Epstein retained Dick James as the exclusive publisher for original Beatles songs.

22. **December 31**   According to John Lennon, by the end of this year, true cocomposition of songs by Lennon and McCartney stopped. Each lad was by now concentrating on writing his own songs, with occasional contributions from the other.

9. 49 "Beatlemania Begins"
Beatles Events 1963

1. **January 11**   The single "Please Please Me"/"Ask Me Why" was released in the United Kingdom.
2. **January 13**   The Beatles were interviewed and reviewed for the first time in the London papers, a major step toward increasing their reputation and public awareness of their music.
3. **January 21**   Vee Jay Records signed the Beatles for U.S. record releases.
4. **February 2**   On this day, the Beatles began their first nationwide U.K. tour. Helen Shapiro headed the bill and the Fabs received the grand sum of £80 per week. The Helen Shapiro Tour lasted until March 3 and included the following fifteen gigs: February 2, Bradford, Gaumont; February 3, Doncaster, Gaumont; February 4, Bedford, Granada; February 7, Wakefield, Odeon; February 8, Carlisle, ABC; February 9, Sunderland, Odeon; February 10, Peterborough, Embassy; February 23, Mansfield, Granada; February 24, Coventry, Coventry Theater; February 26, Taunton, Odeon; February 27, York, Rialto; February 28, Shrewsbury, Granada; March 1, Southport, Odeon; March 2, Sheffield, City Hall; and March 3, Hanley, Gaumont. The other acts on the bill were Danny Williams, Kenny Lynch, the Honeys, the Kestrels, and the Red Price Band.
5. **February 22**   Dick James formed Northern Songs Ltd. as the exclusive publishing company for Beatles compositions.
6. **February 23**   The single "Please Please Me" reached the number-one spot on *Disc* magazine's U.K. chart.

7. **February 25**   The single "Please Please Me"/"Ask Me Why" was released in the United States on the Vee Jay label. It did not chart.

8. **March 1**   "Please Please Me" reached the number one spot on *New Musical Express* magazine's U.K. chart.

9. **March 2**   "Please Please Me" reached the number one spot on *Melody Maker* magazine's U.K. chart.

10. **March 2**   The Beatles were interviewed live on ABC-TV's U.K. show, *ABC at Large*.

11. **March 22**   The LP *Please Please Me* was released in the United Kingdom.

12. **April 8**   Cynthia Lennon gave birth to John Lennon's first child, Charles John Julian Lennon.

13. **April 11**   The single "From Me to You"/"Thank You Girl" was released in the United Kingdom.

14. **April 14**   The Beatles attended a performance by a new group called the Rolling Stones at the Crawdaddy Club in Richmond.

15. **May 5**   The single "From Me to You" reached the number-one spot in the Top 20 of *Music Week* magazine. It remained at number one for seven weeks.

16. **May 18**   The Beatles began the first tour on which they were the top billed act. The tour was called the Beatles' Tour and it began this day at the Adelphi in Slough, Granada. The other acts on the bill were Roy Orbison, Gerry and the Pacemakers, David Macbeth, Louise Cordet, Erkey Grant, Ian Crawford, the Terry Young Six, and Tony Marsh.

17. **May 27**   The single "From Me to You"/"Thank You Girl" was released in the United States on the Vee Jay label. Its highest position on the *Billboard* charts was a pathetic 116.

18. **July 12**   The EPs *My Bonnie* and *Twist and Shout* were released in the United Kingdom.

19. **July 21**   Tickets went on sale for the Beatles' final performance at the Cavern Club. The tickets were sold out within a half hour.

20. **July 22**   The LP *Introducing the Beatles* was released in the United States.

21. **August 1**   The first issue of *The Beatles Book* was published in the United Kingdom. This monthly fan publication was entirely devoted to the Beatles.

22. **August 3**   The Beatles performed for the 275th—and last—time at the Cavern Club (the club was torn down ten years later). Reportedly, after the show, Brian Epstein promised the Cavern Club's emcee, Bob Wooler, that the Beatles would return one day to the Cavern and perform again for their hometown fans. The enormous worldwide popularity of the Beatles made that impossible, however, and they never again played at the club where they had gotten their start.

23. **August 11**   The Beatles met Mal Evans for the first time at Manchester Airport. Mal became one of the boys' good friends and worked as assistant road manager for Neil Aspinall when the Beatles still worked as a group.

24. **August 23**   The single "She Loves You"/"I'll Get You" was released in the United Kingdom. Advance orders for the single totaled 500,000 copies, guaranteeing that it would enter the charts in the number-one position.

25. **September 6**   The EP *The Beatles Hits* was released in the United Kingdom.

26. **September 10**   John and Paul visited the Rolling Stones at a rehearsal and offered them the Lennon/McCartney composition, "I Wanna Be Your Man," even though they hadn't actually completed writing the song. When the Stones

Brian Epstein (Photofest)

expressed interest in recording it, John and Paul reportedly finished writing it in ten minutes. In 1980, John told *Playboy* that he and Paul considered "I Wanna Be Your Man" somewhat of a "throwaway." John also bluntly admitted, "We weren't going to give them anything *great*, right?"

27. **September 11** *Melody Maker* announced that the Beatles were voted the most popular recording artists in Great Britain.

28. **September 16** The single "She Loves You"/"I'll Get You" was released in the United States on the Swan label, having been turned down by Capitol Records. Also around this time, George Harrison became the first Beatle to visit the United States when he traveled to Benton, Illinois, with his brother Peter to visit their sister Louise.

29. **October 4** The Beatles made their first live appearance on the British TV show, *Ready, Steady, Go!* They lip-synched to "Twist and Shout," "I'll Get You," and "She Loves You."

30. **October 11** The single "She Loves You"/"I'll Get You" became the Beatles' first U.K. gold disc, having sold in excess of one million copies.

31. **October 13** The term "Beatlemania" was born. The term was apparently used in press coverage of the Beatles' live appearance on *Val Parnell's Sunday Night at the London Palladium*. The Fabs garnered an audience of fifteen million viewers and "Beatlemania" was the term the media came up with to describe this kind of phenomenal success.

32. **October 17** The Beatles used 4-track recording equipment for the first time to record "I Want to Hold Your Hand" and "This Boy." (Prior to this session, the Fabs had only double-tracked their recordings. Four-track allowed them to do more with their trademark harmonies and add more instruments.)

33. **October 31** The Beatles returned to London after a successful Swedish tour and were met by hundreds of hysterical fans at Heathrow Airport. This "home-town" response to the group dramatically illustrated to the Beatles just how enormous their popularity had grown. Ed Sullivan had flown to the United Kingdom to witness the Beatles' return and upon seeing the reaction of the crowds, booked the group to appear on *The Ed Sullivan Show* in the United States in early 1964.

34. **November 1** The EP *The Beatles (No. 1)* was released in the United Kingdom.

35. **November 4** The Beatles performed at the Royal Variety Show at the Prince of Wales Theater in London. This was the fabled "command performance" before the British Royal Family at which the Beatles performed "From Me to You," "She Loves You," "Till There Was You," and "Twist and Shout." This was also the

performance at which John Lennon snidely asked those in the cheap seats to join by clapping for "Twist and Shout" and the others to "rattle your jewelry."

36. **November 5** Brian Epstein traveled to New York to begin promoting the Beatles in the United States. He successfully wangled them top billing on their forthcoming *Ed Sullivan Show* appearance by committing the boys to two shows, February 9 and February 16, 1964. Brian was able to negotiate fees of $3,500 per Beatle per show, plus a $3,000 taping fee. *The Ed Sullivan Show* received 50,000 ticket requests for the Beatles' performances. (The theater had 700 seats.)

37. **November 9** George Harrison signed a five-year music publishing contract with Northern Songs, Ltd.

38. **November 19** ABC-TV ran its first U.S. feature on the Beatles.

39. **November 21** A television milestone was achieved this day when all three U.S. TV networks—CBS, ABC, and NBC—covered with film footage and interviews the Beatles November 13, 1963, concert in Bournemouth, England.

40. **November 22** The LP *With the Beatles* was released in the United Kingdom. Advance orders totaled 250,000 copies.

41. **November 29** The single "I Want to Hold Your Hand"/"This Boy" was released in the United Kingdom. Advance orders totaled one million copies, instantly placing it at the number-one position on the music charts.

42. **December 4** The Beatles Film Productions Ltd. was formed.

43. **December 13** Capitol Records, the shortsighted company that had earlier rejected the Beatles single "She Loves You"/"I'll Get You" apparently finally saw the light and signed an agreement which gave Capitol first refusal to all future U.S. Beatles releases.

44. **December 20** Britain's *New Musical Express*'s 12th Annual Popularity Poll ranked the Beatles as the United Kingdom's number-one group and their single "She Loves You" as Record of the Year.

45. **December 24** The Beatles formed their second film company. This one was called Subafilms Ltd.

46. **December 26** The single "I Want to Hold Your Hand"/"This Boy" was rush released in the United States. Capitol was so swamped with advance orders they decided to push the release date from January 13, 1964, to this day.

47. **December 27** John Lennon and Paul McCartney were named "Outstanding Composers of 1963" by the music critics of the *London Times*.

48. **December 29** Richard Buckle, the music critic for the *London Sunday Times*, effusively described John Lennon and Paul McCartney as "the greatest composers since Beethoven."

49. **December 31** By this date, seven million Beatles records had been sold in the United Kingdom. EMI generously increased the Beatles royalty rate from one cent per single to two cents per single.

10. 74 "America Comes Down With Beatlemania" Beatles Events 1964

1. **January 20** The LP *Meet the Beatles* was released in the United States by Capitol Records.

2. **January 27**   The Tony Sheridan single (costarring the previously mentioned "Beat Brothers") "My Bonnie"/"The Saints" was released in the United States on the MGM label.

3. **January 30**   The single "Please Please Me"/"From Me to You" was released in the United States by Vee Jay Records.

4. **February 3**   The LP *The Beatles with Tony Sheridan and Their Guests* was released in the United States on the MGM label.

5. **February 4**   The Beatles appeared on the cover of the U.S. edition of *Newsweek* magazine.

6. **February 7**   The Beatles arrived in New York. Close to five thousand fans greeted them at JFK Airport. The Beatles held their first U.S. press conference. Also, the EP *All My Loving* was released in the United Kingdom this day.

7. **February 9**   The Beatles made their first appearance on *The Ed Sullivan Show*. They performed five songs: "All My Loving," "Till There Was You," "She Loves You," "I Saw Her Standing There," and "I Want To Hold Your Hand." Their appearance was watched by 73 million viewers, an astonishing 60 percent of all U.S. TV viewers.

8. **February 11**   The Beatles performed their first U.S. concert at the Washington Coliseum in Washington, D. C. They played before seven thousand fans and they were hardly heard over the screams. They performed "Roll Over Beethoven," "From Me to You," "I Saw Her Standing There," "This Boy," "All My Loving," "I Wanna Be Your Man," "Please Please Me," "Till There Was You," "She Loves You," "I Want to Hold Your Hand," "Twist and Shout," and "Long Tall Sally."

9. **February 12**   The Beatles performed at two sold-out concerts at Carnegie Hall in New York City.

10. **February 15**   For the first time ever, *Billboard* magazine listed five singles and three LPs by the same group on their charts. The five Beatles songs on the charts were "I Want to Hold Your Hand," "I Saw Her Standing There," "She Loves You," "Please Please Me," and "My Bonnie." The three Beatles LPs were *Meet the Beatles* (number one on the albums charts), *Introducing the Beatles,* and *The Beatles with Tony Sheridan.*

11. **February 16**   The Beatles made their second appearance on *The Ed Sullivan Show*. Their appearance was watched this time by close to seventy-five million viewers, the single largest television audience ever. They performed six songs: "I Saw Her Standing There," "I Want to Hold Your Hand," "From Me to You," "Twist and Shout," "Please Please Me," and "She Loves You."

12. **February 26**   The LP *Jolly What! The Beatles and Frank Ifeld on Stage* was released in the United States by Vee Jay Records.

13. **February 28**   The single "Why"/"Cry for a Shadow" was released in the United Kingdom.

14. **March 1**   Wax effigies of the Beatles were placed on display in Madame Tussaud's Wax Museum in London. The Beatles were the first pop musicians to be so honored.

15. **March 2**   The Beatles began shooting their first feature-length film, *A Hard Day's Night*. Filming lasted until April 24. The movie, directed by Richard Lester and written by Alun Owen, was a huge success.

On *The Ed Sullivan Show* (Photofest)

16. **March 2** The single "Twist and Shout"/"There's a Place" was released in the United States on the Tollie label.

17. **March 13** By this date, U.S. sales of the LP *Meet the Beatles* had reached a record-breaking 3.5 million copies. Beatles singles comprised an astonishing 60 percent of the U.S. singles market.

18. **March 16** The single "Can't Buy Me Love"/"You Can't Do That" was rush released in the United States. Advance orders for the single totaled two million copies.

19. **March 20** The single "Can't Buy Me Love"/"You Can't Do That" was released in the United Kingdom.

20. **March 21** The single "She Loves You" reached number one on the U.S. charts.

21. **March 23** The Beatles were awarded the prestigious Carl-Alan Award for Best Beat Group of 1963 and Best Single for "She Loves You." The awards were presented to the boys by Prince Philip.

22. **March 23** John Lennon's first book, *In His Own Write*, was published in the United Kingdom. It received good reviews.

23. **March 23**   The single "Can't Buy Me Love" reached number one in both the United Kingdom and the United States.
24. **March 23**   The EP *The Beatles: Souvenir of Their Visit to America* was released in the United States on Vee Jay Records.
25. **March 23**   The single "Do You Want to Know a Secret"/"Thank You Girl" was released in the United States on Vee Jay Records.
26. **March 27**   The single "Why"/"Cry for a Shadow" was released in the United States.
27. **March 27**   By this date, six of the Top Ten singles in Australia were by the Beatles.
28. **April 1**   John Lennon reunited with his father Freddie Lennon after not having seen him for seventeen years.
29. **April 4**   The top five singles on *Billboard*'s Hot 100 list were by the Beatles, the first time in history this was ever achieved by a single group or artist. The five singles were "Can't Buy Me Love," "Twist and Shout," "She Loves You," "I Want to Hold Your Hand," and "Please Please Me."
30. **April 10**   The LP *The Beatles Second Album* was released in the United States.
31. **April 11**   By this day, the Beatles have a record-breaking fourteen singles on *Billboard*'s Hot 100 list.
32. **April 23**   John Lennon received the prestigious U.K. Literary Prize for his book, *In His Own Write*. John's acceptance speech consisted of one sentence: "Thank you very much, and God bless you."
33. **April 27**   The single "Love Me Do"/"P. S. I Love You" was released in the United States.
34. **April 27**   Lennon's *In His Own Write* was published in the United States.
35. **April 30**   John and Paul formed a Beatles music publishing company called LenMac Enterprises Ltd.
36. **May 2**   *The Beatles Second Album* reached number one in the United States.
37. **May 11**   The EP *Four by the Beatles* was released by Capitol Records in the United States. This EP, not to be confused with the February 1, 1965, Capitol Records EP *4 by the Beatles,* included four cuts from *Meet the Beatles* and *The Beatles Second Album.*
38. **May 21**   The German-language version of "She Loves You," "Sie Liebt Dich"/"I'll Get You" was released as a single in the United States.
39. **May 29**   The single "Ain't She Sweet"/"If You Love Me Baby" was released in the United States.
40. **May 30**   The single "Love Me Do" reached number one in the United States.
41. **June 1**   The single "Sweet Georgia Brown"/"Take Out Some Insurance on Me Baby" was released in the United States.
42. **June 4**   The Beatles began a world tour that included a staggering 77 performances from this date until November 10. This 1964 marathon began in Denmark and included dates in Hong Kong, Australia, New Zealand, Sweden, the United States, England, and Scotland. The Beatles, of course, topped the bill everywhere they played, and some of the other acts that appeared with them included Jackie DeShannon, the Righteous Brothers, and Mary Wells.

(*Left to right*) Paul, George, Ringo, and John in a scene from *A Hard Day's Night.*
(Photofest)

43. **June 19**   The EP *Long Tall Sally* and the LP *The Beatles First* were released in the United Kingdom.
44. **June 26**   The LP *A Hard Day's Night* was released in the United States on the United Artists label.
45. **July 6**   The Beatles' first feature film, *A Hard Day's Night,* had its world premiere at the London Pavilion at Picadilly Circus in London. The premiere was attended by all four Beatles as well as Princess Margaret and Lord Snowdon. Huge crowds of screaming Beatles fans had to be kept behind police-guarded barriers. The film was met with enormous acclaim and wonderful reviews.
46. **July 6**   The single "Ain't She Sweet"/"Nobody's Child" was released in the United States.
47. **July 10**   The LP *A Hard Day's Night* was released in the United Kingdom. This album was markedly different from the U.S. version and included songs not in the film. The U.K. album also did not include George Martin's orchestral versions of certain Beatles songs that were added to the U.S. release.
48. **July 10**   The single "A Hard Day's Night"/"Things We Said Today" was released in the United Kingdom.
49. **July 13**   The single "A Hard Day's Night"/"I Should Have Known Better" was released in the United States.
50. **July 18**   The LP *A Hard Day's Night* reached number one in the United Kingdom.
51. **July 20**   Two new Beatles singles were released in the United States: "I'll Cry Instead"/"I'm Happy Just to Dance With You" and "And I Love Her"/"If I Fell." Also, the LP *Something New* was released in the United States.

52. **July 25** The LP *A Hard Day's Night* reached number one in the United States. The single "A Hard Day's Night" reached number·one in the United Kingdom.

53. **August 11** The film *A Hard Day's Night* opened in the United States to excellent reviews.

54. **August 23** The Beatles performed their first Hollywood Bowl concert. George Martin recorded their performance, which was released as *The Beatles at Hollywood Bowl* in 1977.

55. **August 24** The single "Slow Down"/"Matchbox" was released in the United States.

56. **September 11** George Harrison formed his own music publishing company called Mornyork Ltd.

57. **September 20** A taped performance by the Beatles was seen on *The Ed Sullivan Show*.

58. **September 25** Brian Epstein was offered $3.5 million for the Beatles by a group of American businessmen. He turned down the offer (which would have netted him personally $875,000).

59. **October 1** Brian Epstein's memoir, *A Cellarful of Noise,* was published in the United Kingdom.

60. **October 1** The LP *The Beatles vs. the Four Seasons* was released in the United States by Vee Jay Records.

61. **October 12** The LP *Songs, Pictures, and Stories of the Fabulous Beatles* was released in the United States by Vee Jay Records.

62. **October 25** The Beatles received five British Music Industry Ivor Novello Awards for 1963. They were awarded Most Outstanding Contribution to Music in 1963, Most Broadcast Song for "She Loves You," Top-Selling Record for "She Loves You," Second Top-Selling Record for "I Want to Hold Your Hand," and Second Most Outstanding Song for "All My Loving."

63. **November 4** The EP *Extracts From the Film A Hard Day's Night* was released in the United Kingdom.

64. **November 6** The EP *Extracts From the Album A Hard Day's Night* was released in the United Kingdom.

65. **November 13** The film *What's Happening! The Beatles in the U.S.A.* was aired on CBS-TV. The film documented the Fabs' February 1964 visit.

66. **November 23** The LP *The Beatles Story* was released in the United States.

67. **November 23** The single "I Feel Fine"/"She's a Woman" was released in the United States.

68. **November 23** The Beatles taped their final appearance on the show *Ready, Steady, Go!*

69. **November 27** The single "I Feel Fine"/"She's a Woman" was released in the United Kingdom.

70. **December 4** The LP *Beatles for Sale* was released in the United Kingdom.

71. **December 7** George Harrison changed the name of his music publishing company to Harrisongs Ltd.

72. **December 12** The LP *Beatles for Sale* and the single "I Feel Fine"/"She's a Woman" both reached number one in the United Kingdom.

73. **December 15** The LP *Beatles '65* was released in the United States.

74. **December 26** The single "I Feel Fine" reached number one in the United States.

11. 52 "The Beatles Juggernaut Rolls On"
Beatles Events 1965

1. **January 9**   The LP *Beatles '65* reached number one in the United States.
2. **January 27**   The music company Maclen Music Ltd. was formed with John Lennon, Paul McCartney, and Brian Epstein named as its directors.
3. **January 29**   The single "If I Fell"/"Tell Me Why" was released in the United Kingdom.
4. **February 1**   The EP *4 by the Beatles* was released in the United States by Capitol Records. This EP, not to be confused with the May 11, 1964, Capitol Records EP *Four by the Beatles,* included four cuts from the *Beatles '65* album.
5. **February 11**   Ringo Starr and Maureen Cox married at Caxton Hall Register Office in London. John Lennon, George Harrison, and Brian Epstein attended the ceremony. Paul McCartney, who was on vacation in North Africa with Jane Asher, did not.
6. **February 15**   The single "Eight Days a Week"/"I Don't Want to Spoil the Party" was released in the United States.
7. **February 18**   Public sale of shares of Northern Songs Ltd., the Beatles' music publishing company, began on the London Stock Exchange.
8. **February 23**   The Beatles began filming their second feature film, *Help!,* in the Bahamas. Shooting continued until May 13. Richard Lester again directed the Beatles; Walter Shenson served as Producer; and the script was by Marc Behm and Charles Wood from a story by Behm. Unlike *A Hard Day's Night, Help!* was filmed in color and was filmed on location in several countries.
9. **March 13**   The single "Eight Days a Week" reached number one in the United States.
10. **March 17**   The Beatles issued a press release announcing the tentative title of their new film as *Eight Arms to Hold You.*
11. **March 22**   The LP *The Early Beatles* was released in the United States.
12. **April 6**   The EP *Beatles for Sale* was released in the United Kingdom.
13. **April 9**   The single "Ticket to Ride"/"Yes It Is" was released in the United Kingdom.
14. **April 11**   The single "Ticket to Ride" reached number one in the United Kingdom.
15. **April 14**   The Beatles rejected *Eight Arms to Hold You* as the title of their next movie. They all agreed to call the film *Help!*
16. **April 19**   The Beatles received 1964 Grammy Awards for Best Vocal Performance by a Group for "A Hard Day's Night" and for Best New Artists.
17. **April 19**   The single "Ticket to Ride"/"Yes It Is" was released in the United States.
18. **May 9**   The Beatles attended a Bob Dylan performance at London's Royal Festival Hall and they (especially John and George) were immediately captivated by his writing and style. Dylan's work had a lasting impact on their own writing and recording.
19. **May 13**   The Beatles completed filming *Help!*

Ringo, with first wife Maureen, 1972. The two were married in 1965. (Photofest)

The Fabs in a scene from *Help!* (Photofest)

20. **May 22**   The single "Ticket to Ride" reached number one in the United States.
21. **May 22**   The Beatles appeared on an episode of *Dr. Who* in the United Kingdom.
22. **June 4**   The EP *Beatles for Sale* was released in the United Kingdom.
23. **June 12**   Harold Wilson, the Prime Minister of Great Britain, announced that the Beatles would each receive the MBE (Membership of the Most Excellent Order of the British Empire), one of the ceremonial honors awarded in the United Kingdom. An MBE is below knighthood and life peerage on the Royal awards scale. (See October 26, 1965, January 19, 1994, and January 13, 1997.)
24. **June 14**   The LP *Beatles VI* was released in the United States.
25. **June 24**   John Lennon's second book, *A Spaniard in the Works,* was published in the United Kingdom.
26. **July 1**   *A Spaniard in the Works* was published in the United States.
27. **July 11**   The LP *Beatles VI* reached number one in the United States.
28. **July 13**   Paul McCartney accepted five Ivor Novello Awards for the Beatles at a luncheon at the Savoy Hotel in London.
29. **July 19**   The single "Help!"/"I'm Down" was released in the United States.
30. **July 25**   The single "Help!" reached number one in the United Kingdom.
31. **July 29**   The world premiere of *Help!* was held at the London Pavilion. As they did for *A Hard Day's Night,* Prince Margaret and Lord Snowdon attended the screening.
32. **August 6**   The LP *Help!* was released in the United Kingdom.
33. **August 8**   Two days after its release, the LP *Help!* reached number one in the United Kingdom.
34. **August 15**   The Beatles performed their first concert at Shea Stadium. They played before fifty-six thousand screaming fans and performed twelve songs in thirty minutes.
35. **August 23**   The film *Help!* opened in the United States.
36. **August 29**   The Beatles performed the first of two concerts at the Hollywood Bowl.
37. **September 4**   The single "Help" reached number one in the United States.
38. **September 12**   The LP *Help!* reached number one in the United States.
39. **September 13**   The single "Yesterday"/"Act Naturally" was released in the United States.
40. **September 25**   *The Beatles,* a half-hour animated cartoon series about the Fabs, began airing in the United States on ABC-TV on Saturday mornings from 10:30 to 11:00 A.M. The series ran for four years until September 7, 1969. Paul Frees did the voices of John and George and Lance Percival did Paul and Ringo. Two Beatles songs were "performed" in each episode. Notably, this was one of the few cartoon series ever produced about living people.
41. **October 9**   The single "Yesterday" reached number one in the United States.
42. **October 26**   The Beatles were presented with their MBE awards by Queen Elizabeth at Buckingham Palace. The legend survived over the years that the Beatles smoked pot in the royal loo before the presentation. The truth is that they smoked cigarettes and the story evolved over the years until the cigarettes transformed into joints. In *The Beatles Anthology 4,* George confirmed that they all smoked cigarettes and revealed that John (probably mischievously in typical Lennon style) later told a reporter that they had gotten high.

Perhaps the final word was Ringo's. When he was asked about the tobacco/pot story he responded that he was too stoned to remember.

In 1995, Paul reminisced to *Newsweek* magazine about receiving the MBE: "It's the lowest honor you can have from Britain. It's the lowest. George Martin's got a higher one than we have. There's a guy who's a deejay called Jimmy Savile. There's Andrew Lloyd Webber. All these people are sirs. Sir Cliff Richard. But you can't sit around saying, 'God, I wish they'd make me a sir.'" (See January 13, 1997.)

43. **December 1** John Lennon's short story, "Toy Boy," was published in *McCall's* magazine.

44. **December 3** The groundbreaking LP *Rubber Soul* was released in the United Kingdom. This was the first Beatles album to show the previously mentioned influence of Bob Dylan, as well as the first record on which they used a sitar. Later, the Beatles admitted that this album was greatly influenced by their use of marijuana.

45. **December 3** The single "Day Tripper"/"We Can Work It Out" was released in the United Kingdom.

46. **December 3** The Beatles began their final British tour in Glasgow, Scotland, at the Odeon. The tour ran nine days and nine performances and concluded in Cardiff at the Capitol Theater. The other acts on the bill were the Moody Blues, the Paramounts, Koobas, Beryl Madsen, and Steve Aldo. The Beatles performed twelve songs on this tour: "Dizzy Miss Lizzie," "I Feel Fine," "She's a Woman," "If I Needed Someone," "Ticket to Ride," "Act Naturally," "Nowhere Man," "Baby's in Black," "Help!" "We Can Work It Out," "Day Tripper," and "I'm Down."

47. **December 5** In the midst of their final British tour, the Beatles performed for the last time in their hometown of Liverpool at the Empire Theater.

48. **December 5** The single "Day Tripper"/"We Can Work It Out" became the Beatles first two-sided, number-one hit in the United Kingdom.

49. **December 5** The LP *Rubber Soul* reached number one in the United Kingdom.

50. **December 6** The LP *Rubber Soul* was released in the United States.

51. **December 6** The single "We Can Work It Out"/"Day Tripper" was released in the United States. Even though "Day Tripper" was the A-side in the United Kingdom, "We Can Work It Out" was thought to be the stronger cut for the U.S. market and the sides were reversed.

52. **December 6** The EP *The Beatles Million Sellers* (also known as *The Beatles' Golden Discs*) was released in the United Kingdom.

12. 34 "The Troubles Begin" Beatles Events 1966

1. **January 8** The single "We Can Work It Out" reached number one in the United States.

2. **January 8** The LP *Rubber Soul* reached number one in the United States.

3. **January 21** George Harrison and Pattie Boyd were married at Esher Register Office in Surrey, England.

4. **February 21**   The single "Nowhere Man"/"What Goes On" was released in the United States.

5. **February 28**   The Cavern Club closed.

6. **March 4**   A profile of John Lennon titled "How Does a Beatle Live? John Lennon Lives Like This" by Maureen Cleave appeared in the London *Evening Standard*. In the article, John was quoted as saying the following: "Christianity will go. It will vanish and shrink. I needn't argue about that; I'm right and I will be proved right. We're more popular than Jesus now; I don't know which will go first—rock 'n' roll or Christianity. Jesus was all right but his disciples were thick and ordinary. It's them twisting it that ruins it for me."

7. **March 4**   The EP *Yesterday* was released in the United Kingdom.

8. **May 1**   The last Beatles U.K. performance took place at the Empire Pool in Wembley. They performed at the *New Musical Express Poll Winner's Concert*. The other acts on the bill included the Small Faces, Spencer Davis, Roy Orbison, the Yardbirds, Cliff Richard, the Who, and the Rolling Stones. Befitting their stature as the world's most successful and important rock band, the Beatles were the final act on the high-power bill.

9. **May 23**   The single "Paperback Writer"/"Rain" was released in the United States.

10. **June 10**   The single "Paperback Writer"/"Rain" was released in the United Kingdom.

11. **June 15**   The LP *Yesterday and Today* was released in the United States. This release had the infamous "butcher" cover showing the Beatles in white coats covered in blood and draped with slabs of meat and dismembered baby dolls. Fans were shocked and the cover was quickly withdrawn. A new photo of the Beatles was pasted over already-printed sleeves of the offensive cover until new sleeves could be produced.

12. **June 20**   The LP *Yesterday and Today* with the new cover was released in the United States.

13. **June 23**   The Beatles' final tour began in Hamburg, Germany.

14. **June 25**   The single "Paperback Writer" reached number one in the United States.

15. **June 25**   The single "Paperback Writer" reached number one in the United Kingdom.

16. **July 3**   John Lennon was quoted in the *New York Times Sunday Magazine* as saying, "Show business is an extension of the Jewish religion." The article was written by Maureen Cleave, the journalist who published John's "Christianity will go" comments a few months earlier.

17. **July 8**   The EP *Nowhere Man* was released in the United Kingdom.

18. **July 23**   In response to protests from Beatles fans, the Cavern Club reopened under new management. British Prime Minister Harold Wilson presided over the ceremony.

19. **July 29**   The American magazine *Datebook* reprinted Maureen Cleaves's article from the London *Evening Standard,* and John's caustic remarks about Christianity were not dismissed in the United States as they were in the United Kingdom. This began a wave of anti-Beatles protests that included the burning of Beatles' records and the banning of their music on some American radio stations (see August 11, 1966).

20. **July 30**   The LP *Yesterday and Today* reached number one in the United States.

21. **August 5**   The LP *Revolver* was released in the United Kingdom. This was one of the most important albums the Beatles had yet produced and their creative development continued with songs such as "Tomorrow Never Knows," "Love You Too," "Eleanor Rigby," and, of course, the monumentally influential and popular ballad, "Yesterday." The Beatles would later admit that *Revolver* was greatly influenced by their experimentation with LSD while working on it.

22. **August 5**   The single "Eleanor Rigby"/"Yellow Submarine" was simultaneously released in the United Kingdom and the United States. "Yellow Submarine" was the A-side in the United States.

23. **August 8**   The LP *Revolver* was released in the United States.

24. **August 8**   South Africa banned all radio airplay of Beatles records.

25. **August 11**   At a press conference in Chicago, John Lennon apologized for offending Christians around the world for his flip comment that the Beatles were more popular than Jesus and that Christianity would fade away. "I'm sorry I said it, really," he told the assembled media. "I never meant it as a lousy, antireligious thing. I wasn't saying whatever they're saying I was saying. I was sort of deploring the current attitude towards Christianity. From what I've read or heard, [Christianity] just seems to me to be shrinking, to be losing contact." The next day, John again spoke to the press about his inflammatory comments from the previous March. "I suppose if I had said television was more popular than Jesus, I would have got away with it. I am sorry I opened my mouth," he told the media. "I'm not anti-God, anti-Christ, or anti-religion," he continued. "I was not knocking [religion]. I was not saying we are greater or better." John's bandmate George Harrison then commented, "I know [John]. He believes in Christianity. But I do agree with him that Christianity is on the wane." Regarding the recent burning of Beatles records, John said, "I think it's a bit silly. If they don't like us, why don't they just not buy the records?"

26. **August 13**   The LP *Revolver* reached number one in the United Kingdom.

27. **August 14**   The Longview, Texas, radio station KLUE sponsored a public bonfire for the burning of Beatles records. Shortly after the bonfire, the station's broadcast tower was struck by lightning, knocking the station off the air. The lightning ruined some of the station's electronic equipment and knocked the news director unconscious. Beatles fans around the world felt vindicated.

28. **August 20**   The single "Eleanor Rigby"/"Yellow Submarine" became the Beatles second two-sided, number-one hit in the United Kingdom.

29. **August 29**   The last scheduled concert the Beatles performed took place at Candlestick Park in San Francisco, California. They performed eleven songs: "Rock and Roll Music," "She's a Woman," "If I Needed Someone," "Baby's in Black," "Day Tripper," "I Feel Fine," "Yesterday," "I Wanna Be Your Man," "Nowhere Man," "Paperback Writer," and "I'm Down." Following this concert, the boys never toured as a group again.

30. **September 5**   John began filming *How I Won the War* in Germany for Richard Lester, becoming the first Beatle to work professionally as a solo artist. (Refer to feature "16 Non-Beatle Movies in Which a Beatle Appeared.")

31. **September 10**   The LP *Revolver* reached number one in the United States.

George and Indian sitarist extraordinaire Ravi Shankar—the two remain good friends today. (Photofest)

32. **September 14** George Harrison began a vacation in India during which he met sitarist Ravi Shankar and began to study this ancient Indian stringed instrument.

George had been introduced to the sound of the sitar while filming *Help!* (A sitar had been used in the song "Help!" on the American *Help!* album.) In London, George went out and bought what he described as a "crummy sitar" and used it on "Norwegian Wood (This Bird Has Flown)" on the *Rubber Soul* album in 1965. Musician David Crosby later introduced George to the music of Ravi Shankar and when George finally met the master sitarist, he used the opportunity to devote himself to studying and mastering the difficult Indian instrument.

33. **November 9** John Lennon met Yoko Ono for the first time at the Indica Gallery in London during a preview of her exhibition, *Unfinished Painting and Objects by Yoko Ono.*

34. **December 10** The LP *A Collection of Beatles Oldies* was released in the United Kingdom.

13. 46 "Sgt. Pepper Rules the World" Beatles Events 1967

1. **January 27** The Beatles signed a new, 9-year contract with EMI Records. Under the terms of this new deal, the Beatles' royalty rate was 10 percent of the wholesale price in the United Kingdom and 17.5 percent of the wholesale price in the United States.

2. **February 13** The single "Penny Lane"/"Strawberry Fields Forever" was released in the United States.

3. **February 17**   The single "Penny Lane"/"Strawberry Fields Forever" was released in the United Kingdom.

4. **March 11**   The Beatles received three Grammy Awards for their work in 1966: Best Contemporary Pop Vocal Performance, Male, for Paul's performance of "Eleanor Rigby"; Best Album Cover for *Revolver;* and Song of the Year for "Michelle" (which had never been released as a single).

5. **March 18**   The single "Penny Lane" reached number one in the United States.

6. **March 23**   The Beatles received three British Music Industry Ivor Novello Awards for 1966 for "Michelle," "Yellow Submarine," and "Yesterday."

7. **April 19**   The four Beatles signed a new ten-year partnership agreement. They created the entity The Beatles and Company.

8. **May 15**   Paul McCartney met Linda Eastman for the first time at London's Bag O'Nails nightclub during a Georgie Fame show.

9. **May 20**   Before it is officially released, the BBC banned the song "A Day in the Life" from the Beatles' forthcoming *Sgt. Pepper's Lonely Hearts Club Band* album, contending that lyrics such as "I'd love to turn you on," and "had a smoke," encouraged drug use.

10. **May 26**   The LP *Sgt. Pepper's Lonely Hearts Club Band* was rush released in the United Kingdom.

11. **June 1**   The LP *Sgt. Pepper's Lonely Hearts Club Band* was officially released in the United Kingdom. The album sold 250,000 copies within the first week and entered the charts in the number-one position. Within a month, sales of the album hit 500,000 copies and the album hit the one million copy sales mark in the United Kingdom in April of 1973. *Sgt. Pepper* became the largest-selling album in Britain of all time—until January 1971 when another Beatles album, *Abbey Road,* ended its run. In May 1977, the *London Times* critic Kenneth Tynan called *Sgt. Pepper* "a decisive moment in the history of Western civilization."

12. **June 1**   The first credits given to the Beatles' production company, Apple, appeared on the sleeve of the *Sgt. Pepper* album. Apple, which was still simply an *idea,* would not officially come into existence until February 1968 when the Beatles formally changed the name of their existing company, The Beatles Ltd., to Apple Corps.

13. **June 2**   The LP *Sgt. Pepper's Lonely Hearts Club Band* was released in the United States. In a gushing and adulatory review, the *New York Review of Books* called the album "a new and golden Renaissance of song." Thanks to its enormous population (and equally enormous contingent of Beatles fans), U.S. sales of the album far outpaced sales in the United Kingdom. Advance orders alone were 1 million copies and 2.5 million copies were sold within the first 90 days of the album's release. The album immediately reigned in the number-one position on the *Billboard* charts and remained there for 15 weeks. The album remained a presence on the *Billboard* Top 100 for an astonishing 85 weeks.

14. **June 4**   This may be the most telling anecdote in the history of the Beatles and was without a doubt a moment that truly illustrated the regard with which the Beatles and their work was held by other musicians of their time. On this day, following the release of the *Sgt. Pepper* album, Paul and the other Fabs went to a London concert by legendary American rock guitarist Jimi Hendrix

An unusual photo of (*from left*) George, John, Brian Epstein, and Paul, goofing around while preparing for the June 25, 1967, "All You Need Is Love" live broadcast. And you thought they only played guitars and keyboards! (Photofest)

and his band the Jimi Hendrix Experience. At that performance, Jimi opened his show with a flawless cover version of the song "Sgt. Pepper's Lonely Hearts Club Band." Jimi had learned the song off the record within a couple of days after the album had become available and liked it so much he used it to open his show. (He did a typically kick-ass "Hendrix-ish" version of the rocker.) This show of respect and admiration so moved Paul McCartney that in 1997, thirty years after the concert, Paul related the story in volume 6 of the eight-video set of *The Beatles Anthology*.

15. **June 5**   The LP *Sgt. Pepper's Lonely Hearts Club Band* reached number one in the United Kingdom.

16. **June 15**   Paul McCartney told a reporter for *Life* magazine that he had taken LSD. He was the first of the Fabs to publicly admit to drug use. John, George, and Brian Epstein were next to publicly own up to drug use.

17. **June 25**   The Beatles performed John's brilliant new song, "All You Need Is Love," live at EMI Studios in London for the satellite-feed TV show *Our World*. Accompanying them for the performance were Eric Clapton, Graham Nash, members of the Rolling Stones, and other notables of the music world. Their

performance was seen by an estimated four hundred million people worldwide and "All You Need Is Love" immediately became the young people's anthem of the sixties. Paul's lighter "Hello Goodbye" was rejected by the producers of the show and the other Beatles in favor of John's more sweeping and uplifting song.

18. **July 3**   The LP *Sgt. Pepper's Lonely Hearts Club Band* reached number one in the United States.

19. **July 7**   The single "All You Need Is Love"/"Baby You're a Rich Man" was released in the United Kingdom.

20. **July 17**   The single "All You Need Is Love"/"Baby You're a Rich Man" was released in the United States.

21. **July 17**   The single "All You Need Is Love" reached number one in the United Kingdom.

22. **July 24**   The Beatles and Brian Epstein took out an ad in the *London Times* urging the British government to legalize marijuana. All five signed the ad.

23. **August 19**   The single "All You Need Is Love" reached number one in the United States.

24. **August 24**   The Beatles met the Maharishi Mahesh Yogi for the first time. They attended one of the guru's lectures on transcendental meditation at the Hilton Hotel in London. This was the beginning of the Beatles short-lived infatuation with the Maharishi and his teachings.

25. **August 26**   Two days after meeting the Maharishi for the first time, the Beatles held a press conference at which they announced that they had become followers of the guru and had quit using drugs in lieu of meditation and study. They were initiated into the International Meditation Association and would ultimately travel to India in February 1968 to study with the Master.

26. **August 27**   The Beatles' manager, confidant, and dear friend, Brian Epstein was found dead of an accidental drug overdose in his home in London. The Beatles, who were with the Maharishi at the time, were told not to mourn Brian because death is only a transformation. The Beatles then became members of the Maharishi's Spiritual Regeneration Movement. As part of their initiation, they each donated one month's earning to the group.

27. **August 29**   Brian Epstein's funeral was held in Liverpool. The Beatles did not attend.

28. **September 8**   Brian Epstein's death was ruled accidental by the U.K.'s Coroner's Court. It was revealed that Brian died from the accidental buildup of bromide in his bloodstream from his ongoing ingestion of a narcotic drug called Carbitral. (There was the equivalent of six Carbitrals in Brian's stomach at the time of his death, a dosage that would have been lethal to nonusers, but which Brian had built up to with his regular usage of the barbiturate.)

29. **September 11**   The Beatles began shooting the short film *Magical Mystery Tour* without a script. (This lack of focus and direction was evident in the final result.)

30. **September 27**   The Beatles appeared as papier-mâché caricatures on the cover of *Time* magazine. The inside article reported on the backlash against the group for their quickly recalled "butcher cover" version of their *Yesterday and Today* album. *Time* wrote that the original cover demonstrated "a serious lapse of taste" by the Beatles.

31. **October 7**   Concert promoter Sid Bernstein offered the Beatles $1 million to perform one more concert. (Bernstein had promoted the Beatles 1964 Carnegie Hall concert.) The Beatles declined the offer.
32. **October 17**   All four of the Beatles attended a memorial service for Brian Epstein at the New London Synagogue on Abbey Road in London.
33. **October 18**   John's first "non-Beatles" feature film, *How I Won the War,* had its world premiere at the London Pavilion.
34. **November 3**   The Beatles completed filming of *Magical Mystery Tour.*
35. **November 8**   *How I Won the War* premiered in the United States.
36. **November 24**   The single "Hello Goodbye"/"I Am the Walrus" was released in the United Kingdom. John Lennon was reportedly upset that his "I Am the Walrus" was not released as the A-side of the single.
37. **November 27**   The LP *Magical Mystery Tour* was released in the United States.
38. **November 27**   The single "Hello Goodbye"/"I Am the Walrus" was released in the United States.
39. **December 5**   The Beatles' Apple Boutique opened at 94 Baker Street, London. John's childhood friend, Pete Shotton (author of *John Lennon in My Life*), was manager of the shop.
40. **December 8**   The EP *Magical Mystery Tour* was released in the United Kingdom.
41. **December 9**   The single "Hello Goodbye" reached number one in the United Kingdom.
42. **December 21**   The film *Magical Mystery Tour* premiered at a party given by the Beatles at the Royal Lancaster Hotel in London.
43. **December 25**   Paul and Jane Asher announced their engagement.
44. **December 26**   The BBC aired *Magical Mystery Tour* in black and white. It flopped.
45. **December 26**   The BBC banned airplay of "I Am the Walrus," claiming its lyrics were drug-related.
46. **December 30**   The single "Hello Goodbye" reached number one in the United States.

14. 38 "Things Get Tense" Beatles Events 1968

1. **January 5**   The film *Magical Mystery Tour* aired in color on the BBC.
2. **January 6**   The LP *Magical Mystery Tour* reached number one in the United States.
3. **January 12**   The Beatles changed the name of their music company from Apple Music Ltd. to Apple Corps Ltd.
4. **January 22**   The Beatles officially opened the Apple offices at 95 Wigmore Street in London.
5. **February 16**   John and Cynthia Lennon and George and Pattie Harrison were the first of the Beatles to fly to Rishikesh, India, to study transcendental meditation with the Maharishi Mahesh Yogi.

6. **February 19** Paul and Jane Asher and Ringo Starr and Maureen Starkey joined John, George, and the rest in India to study with the Maharishi.

7. **March 9** The Beatles received four Grammy Awards for their 1967 album *Sgt. Pepper's Lonely Hearts Club Band:* Album of the Year, Best Contemporary Album, Best Engineered Recording, and Best Album Cover.

8. **March 15** The single "Lady Madonna"/"The Inner Light" was released in the United Kingdom.

9. **March 18** The single "Lady Madonna"/"The Inner Light" was released in the United States.

10. **March 30** The single "Lady Madonna" reached number one in the United Kingdom.

11. **April 16** The Beatles formed Apple Publicity Ltd. to promote Apple-sponsored projects.

12. **April 20** Apple Music ran ads soliciting music submissions from unknown artists. Apple eventually signed and produced a wide range of acts, including Badfinger, James Taylor, Mary Hopkin, Jackie Lomax, Steve Miller, Billy Preston, Plastic Ono Band, Yoko Ono, Ronnie Spector, Ravi Shankar, and Elephant's Memory.

13. **May 11** John and Paul, now totally disillusioned with the Maharishi and his teachings, publicly denounced him to the press. John scathingly attacked the Maharishi in the song "Sexy Sadie" on the Beatles yet-to-be released *White Album.*

    The Beatles became disenchanted with the Indian holy man for many reasons, some of which included John's belief that the Maharishi had the "answer" and was holding out on him. John also believed the Maharishi's espousal of spiritual delights instead of physical pleasures was hypocritical. The rumor making the rounds in India suggested that the guru had expressed an interest in Mia Farrow that ignored her mind and soul and focused on her more "earthly" parts.

14. **May 14** John and Paul appeared together on *The Tonight Show.* An utterly clueless Joe Garagiola, guest-hosting for Johnny Carson, asked John and Paul which one of them was Ringo. John later described this appearance as one of the most embarrassing moments of his career.

15. **May 16** The Beatles officially created the legal entity Apple Management Ltd.

16. **June 21** Apple Corps Ltd. purchased office space at 3 Saville Row in London.

17. **July 17** The Beatles' animated film *Yellow Submarine* had its world premiere at the London Pavilion. All four Beatles attended.

18. **July 20** Paul and Jane Asher broke their engagement. Paul soon began dating Linda Eastman.

19. **July 31** The Apple Boutique closed. The Beatles closed the shop by giving away all the remaining merchandise in the store.

20. **August 22** Cynthia Lennon filed for divorce from John. She did so because John was living with Yoko Ono.

21. **August 22** Ringo announced that he was quitting the Beatles and John, Paul, and George recorded several songs without him, including "Back in the U.S.S.R." and "Birthday."

22. **August 26**   The single "Hey Jude"/"Revolution" was released in the United States.

23. **August 30**   The single "Hey Jude"/"Revolution" was released in the United Kingdom.

24. **September 5**   Ringo returned to the Beatles *and* the recording studio. The group continued work on what became known around the world as the *White Album*.

25. **September 14**   The single "Hey Jude" reached number one in the United Kingdom.

26. **October 10**   George Harrison formed another music publishing company for his songs. This one was called Singsong Ltd.

27. **October 18**   John and Yoko were busted for possession of marijuana while staying at Ringo's house and were freed on bail (see November 28, 1967).

28. **November 8**   Cynthia Lennon was granted an uncontested divorce from John Lennon. The divorce settlement gave Cynthia a one-time payment of £100,000 and awarded her full custody of their son Julian. Cynthia remarried three times after John: first to Italian hotelier Roberto Bassanini, then to Liverpool electrical engineer John Twist (both ended in divorce) and, finally, to longtime boyfriend Jim Christie, her spokesman and business partner. During the 1990s, Cynthia appeared regularly at Beatles conventions around the world and in 1995, she made her recording debut with the single, "Those Were the Days," a remake of the Mary Hopkin number.

29. **November 8**   George Harrison did not renew his music publishing contract with Northern Songs Ltd., which expired this day.

30. **November 11**   John and Yoko's album, *Two Virgins*, was released in the United States. The album featured a full frontal nude photo of John and Yoko on the front sleeve, and a naked "bum" shot on the back sleeve. The album was shipped to stores wrapped in plain brown paper.

31. **November 13**   The film *Yellow Submarine* had its U.S. premiere in New York City.

32. **November 22**   *The Beatles,* also known as the *White Album,* was released in the United Kingdom.

33. **November 25**   *The Beatles,* also known as the *White Album,* was released in the United States.

34. **November 28**   John and Yoko appeared before the Marylebone Magistrates Court on charges of marijuana possession. John pleaded guilty in exchange for charges against Yoko being dropped. He was fined £150 plus court costs. John now had a drug conviction on his record, which would haunt him when he attempted to remain permanently in the United States in the seventies.

35. **November 29**   John and Yoko's album, *Two Virgins,* was released in the United Kingdom.

36. **November 30**   The *White Album* reached number one in the United Kingdom.

37. **December 18**   John and Yoko "appeared" in a large white bag at London's Royal Albert Hall, as part of an underground Christmas party called "Alchemical Wedding."

38. **December 28**   The *White Album* reached number one in the United States.

The shocking nude back cover of John and Yoko's *Unfinished Music No. 1—Two Virgins*. (Photofest)

15. 46 "Beginning of the End" Beatles Events 1969

1. **January 2**   Filming of what was eventually released as the film *Let It Be* began at Twickenham Film Studios. Paul envisioned the project—now having the working title of *Get Back*—as concluding with a live concert, an idea which only he liked.
2. **January 10**   George announced that he was quitting the Beatles because he couldn't take Paul's harassment anymore.

    George saw Paul's deliberate attempts to direct the band as arrogant and annoying. What is probably the quintessential example of this friction between Paul and George can be seen in the tense scene in *Let It Be* when Paul tries to tell George how he wants something played. George, clearly resentful of Paul's presumption of authority, tells him, "Look, I'll play whatever you want me to play. Or I won't play at all. Whatever it is that will please you, I'll do it."
3. **January 13**   The LP *Yellow Submarine* was released in the United States.
4. **January 15**   George returned to the Beatles on the condition that Paul's idea for a live concert be scrapped. He agreed to work on a new album but did not want to perform live as the Beatles under any circumstances.

5. **January 17**   The LP *Yellow Submarine* was released in the United Kingdom.

6. **January 18**   John and George came to blows over remarks John made in the magazine *Disc and Music Echo* in which he stated that Apple was poorly managed from the start. Apparently George considered this comment to be the airing of dirty laundry in public and the incident added even more tension to the *Get Back* recording sessions.

7. **January 28**   John hired Allen Klein to handle his business affairs without telling the other Beatles, all of whom were in agreement that they would retain Linda Eastman's father's firm, Eastman and Eastman, to handle the Beatles affairs. Paul ultimately refused to allow Klein to represent him and retained the Eastmans to represent him personally.

8. **January 30**   Although George said he did not want to perform live again, he apparently relented and the Beatles performed a lunch-hour concert on the roof of their Apple building at 3 Saville Row in London. The concert lasted forty-two minutes and they performed several takes of "I've Got a Feeling," "One After 909," "Don't Let Me Down," "I Dig a Pony," and "Get Back." The concert ended when the police stopped their performance because of noise complaints from the Beatles' Saville Row neighbors. This concert ultimately became the final sequence of the *Let It Be* film.

9. **February 2**   Yoko Ono divorced her husband Anthony Cox. Yoko retained custody of their daughter Kyoko.

10. **February 3**   Allen Klein was formally hired by the Beatles—including Paul—as the group's business manager.

11. **February 4**   Eastman and Eastman, the firm owned by Linda Eastman's father, was appointed as general counsel for Apple.

12. **February 12**   Paul formed his own production company called Adagrose Ltd. (see August 21, 1967).

13. **March 12**   Paul McCartney and Linda Eastman were married at Marylebone Register Office in London a month after learning that Linda was pregnant. There was never an official announcement of an engagement. John, George, and Ringo did not attend the ceremony. Paul's brother Mike "McGear" was Paul's best man; Linda's daughter Heather (her daughter with her first husband, Melvin See) was her mother's bridesmaid. Peter Brown and Mal Evans attended the ceremony.

14. **March 12**   George Harrison's house was raided by police when he and his wife were not at home. When they returned, they were both arrested for possession of 570 grams of cannabis.

15. **March 20**   John and Yoko were married "in Gibraltar near Spain."

16. **March 25**   John and Yoko began a one-week honeymoon in the Amsterdam Hilton Hotel. They spent the week in bed and invited the media in to watch them lie there. (See the feature on what posters hung on the wall during the "Bed-in.")

17. **March 31**   George and Pattie Harrison pleaded guilty to possession of marijuana and were each fined £250.

18. **April 11**   The single "Get Back"/"Don't Let Me Down" was released in the United Kingdom.

19. **April 22**   John formally changed his middle name from *Winston* to *Ono*.

Paul and Linda Eastman McCartney during the *McCartney* solo album era. (Photofest)

John and Yoko pose at the Rock of Gibraltar on their wedding day, March 21, 1969. John is holding aloft their wedding certificate. (Photofest)

20. **May 3** The single "Get Back"/"Don't Let Me Down" reached number one in the United Kingdom.

21. **May 5** The single "Get Back"/"Don't Let Me Down" was released in the United States.

22. **May 5** The company ATV (Associated Television) acquired controlling interest in Northern Songs, thus becoming the owners of the Lennon/McCartney song catalog.

23. **May 19** The Beatles received an Ivor Novello Award for "Hey Jude," the largest-selling single in the United Kingdom in 1968.

24. **May 20** Allen Klein, now the Beatles' business manager, implemented mass firings at Apple, stopping the unconscionable and, up to this time, relentless drain of money from the company.

25. **May 30** The single "The Ballad of John and Yoko"/"Old Brown Shoe" was released in the United Kingdom.

26. **June 4** The single "The Ballad of John and Yoko"/"Old Brown Shoe" was released in the United States. "The Ballad of John and Yoko" was banned on many radio stations because of John's use of the name *Christ* in the chorus.

27. **June 21** "The Ballad of John and Yoko"/"Old Brown Shoe" reached number one in the United Kingdom.

28. **July 4** John's Plastic Ono Band single, "Give Peace a Chance" (recorded live during John and Yoko's June 1st "Bed-in" at the Elizabeth Hotel in Montreal and backed with Yoko's "Remember Love") was released in the United Kingdom.

29. **July 7** "Give Peace a Chance"/"Remember Love" was released in the United States.

30. **July 9** Yoko Ono, then pregnant, moved a bed into the Abbey Road recording studios where the Beatles were working on the LP, *Abbey Road*. Yoko lay in bed in the studio for the duration of the recording.

31. **August 8** The Beatles were photographed by Iain MacMillan crossing Abbey Road. The photograph was used for the cover of the *Abbey Road* album.

32. **August 20** This day, all four Beatles were together in the recording studio for the very last time. They finished the recording of John's song, "I Want You (She's So Heavy)" and also worked on an *Abbey Road* master tape.

33. **August 21** Paul changed the name of his production company to McCartney Productions Ltd. (known as MPL).

34. **September 7** *The Beatles,* the ABC-TV animated series about the Fabs, was canceled.

35. **September 26** The LP *Abbey Road* was released in the United Kingdom.

36. **October 1** The LP *Abbey Road* was released in the United States.

37. **October 4** The LP *Abbey Road* reached number one in the United Kingdom.

38. **October 6** The single "Something"/"Come Together" was released in the United States. This record was George's first A-side single.

39. **October 14** A review of *Abbey Road* by Fred LaBour appeared in the University of Michigan's school newspaper, the *Michigan Daily*. In the "review," LaBour alleged that the Beatles have been hiding clues in their records for years to break the news to their fans that Paul McCartney was dead, killed in a 1966 automobile accident. Beatles scholars look to this article as the beginning of the "Paul Is Dead" phenomenon that gripped the world for the last three months of 1969.

40. **October 31**   The single "Something"/"Come Together" was released in the United Kingdom.
41. **November 1**   The LP *Abbey Road* reached number one in the United States.
42. **November 25**   John renounced his MBE. He returned it to the Queen with a note that read, "I am returning this MBE in protest against Britain's involvement in the Nigeria-Biafra thing, against our support of America in Vietnam, and against 'Cold Turkey' slipping down the charts. With Love, John Lennon of Bag."
43. **November 29**   The single "Come Together" reached number one in the United States.
44. **December 1**   The seventy-seventh and final issue of the Beatles fan magazine the *Beatles Book* was published.
45. **December 15**   John and Yoko performed at the Lyceum Ballroom in London in a concert to benefit UNICEF. George Harrison played with the group John formed for this concert, the Plastic Ono Supergroup. (The band also included Eric Clapton, Billy Preston, Keith Moon, and members of the Delaney and Bonnie tour group.) This was the first live appearance of more than one Beatle since their August 29, 1966, farewell concert in San Francisco and their January 30, 1969, Apple rooftop performance for *Let It Be*.
46. **December 30**   *Rolling Stone* magazine named John Lennon its Man of the Year.

16. *20 "The Dream Is Over" Beatles Events 1970*

1. **February 23**   The LP *Hey Jude* (also known as *The Beatles Again*) was released in the United States.
2. **March 1**   The Beatles once again "appeared" on *The Ed Sullivan Show*, this time a film clip of the group performing "Two of Us" and "Let It Be" was shown.

Phil Spector, the renowned record producer who completed the mixing of the *Let It Be* album. (Photofest)

3. **March 6**   The single "Let It Be"/"You Know My Name (Look Up the Number)" was released in the United Kingdom.
4. **March 11**   The single "Let It Be"/"You Know My Name (Look Up the Number)" was released in the United States.
5. **March 23**   Phil Spector began remixing the January 1969 *Get Back* tracks into what would finally be released as the album *Let It Be*.
6. **April 1**   Phil Spector completed the remixing of *Let It Be*. Ringo added new drum tracks to some of the new mixes.
7. **April 10**   Paul McCartney publicly announced the breakup of the Beatles. He did it through a self-interview included in the U.K. version of his new solo album, *McCartney*. (The interview was deleted by Allen Klein for the U.S. release of the album.) McCartney wrote his own questions and many critics saw the self-interview as self-serving and incredibly ill-mannered, considering the history the Fabs had shared over the past ten years or so. Here are a few of Paul's interview questions and his responses:

   > *Q:* Will Paul and Linda become a John and Yoko?
   > *A:* No, they will become a Paul and Linda.

   > *Q:* Do you miss the other Beatles and George Martin? Was there a moment, e.g., when you thought, "Wish Ringo was here for this break?"
   > *A:* No.

   > *Q:* Do you foresee a time when Lennon-McCartney becomes an active songwriting partnership again?
   > *A:* No.

   > *Q:* What do you feel about John's peace effort? The Plastic Ono Band? . . . Yoko?
   > *A:* I love John and respect what he does, but it doesn't give *me* any pleasure.

8. **April 11**   The single "Let It Be" reached number one in the United States.
9. **April 17**   Paul's solo album, *McCartney,* was released in the United Kingdom.
10. **April 20**   *McCartney* was released in the United States.
11. **May 8**   The LP *Let It Be* was released in the United Kingdom in a special boxed limited edition that came with a 160-page book, *Get Back,* detailing the filming of the planned *Get Back* TV special. This is now one of the single most sought-after Beatles collectibles in existence. This limited edition set was also released in Australia, Germany, Canada, Italy, Japan, the Philippines, and Venezuela; but not, surprisingly, in the United States (see May 18, 1970).
12. **May 11**   The single "The Long and Winding Road"/"For You Blue" was released in the United States. (This single will not be released in the United Kingdom.)
13. **May 13**   The film *Let It Be* has its U.S. premiere in New York City.
14. **May 18**   The LP *Let It Be*—packaged in a standard sleeve, without the book *Get Back* that was included in the U.K. edition—was released in the United States.
15. **May 20**   The film *Let It Be* has its U.K. premiere. None of the Beatles attend. Neither do any members of British royalty.
16. **May 23**   Paul's solo album, *McCartney,* reached number one in the United States.

17. **June 6**   The LP *Let It Be* reached number one in the United Kingdom.
18. **June 13**   The single "The Long and Winding Road" reached number one in the United States.
19. **June 13**   The LP *Let It Be* reached number one in the United States.
20. **December 31**   Paul McCartney filed suit in the London High Court seeking to formally dissolve the Beatles. John Lennon, George Harrison, and Ringo Starr opposed Paul's actions.

17. 48 "Post-Beatles" Beatles Events of the Seventies

1. **1971 February 19**   Arguments began in the London High Court in Paul's suit to dissolve The Beatles and Company.
2. **1971 February 26**   Paul McCartney personally testified in his suit to dissolve the Beatles. John, George, and Ringo sent affidavits.
3. **1971 March 12**   The London High Court granted Paul's request that a receivership be created to control the finances of The Beatles and Company.
4. **1971 March 16**   The Beatles received a Grammy Award for Best Original Score Written for a Motion Picture for their LP *Let It Be*.
5. **1971 April 15**   The Beatles received an Academy Award from the Academy of Motion Pictures Arts and Science for Best Film Score for the soundtrack to their film, *Let It Be*.
6. **1971 December 5**   The London High Court appointed a receiver for Maclen Music Ltd.
7. **1972 March 31**   The Beatles Fan Club was officially terminated.
8. **1973 March 31**   Allen Klein's management contract with John, George, and Ringo expired and none of the three renew with Klein.
9. **1973 April 2**   The LPs *The Beatles 1962–1966* (the "red" album) and *The Beatles 1967–1970* (the "blue" album) were released in the United States.
10. **1973 April 19**   The LPs *The Beatles 1962–1966* and *The Beatles 1967–1970* were released in the United Kingdom.
11. **1973 May 19**   The LP *The Beatles 1967–1970* reached number one in the United Kingdom.
12. **1973 May 26**   The LP *The Beatles 1967–1970* reached number one in the United States.
13. **1973 May 27**   The Cavern Club in Liverpool closed permanently. It was demolished and a parking lot was built at its location.
14. **1973 June 9**   The LP *The Beatles 1962–1966* reached number one in the United Kingdom.
15. **1973 November 2**   John, George, and Ringo formally fired Allen Klein. They also sued his company ABKCO for monies they claimed he owed them. Klein countersued for $19 million for fees he claimed were due him and his company. Klein also sued Paul personally for $34 million but this case was thrown out of court. The suits dragged on until January 10, 1977. Klein ended up paying the Beatles $800,000, while the Beatles paid ABKCO between $1 and $5 million. Shortly after the resolution of these suits in London, Klein was convicted in New York of tax crimes, sentenced to two months in prison, and fined $5,000.

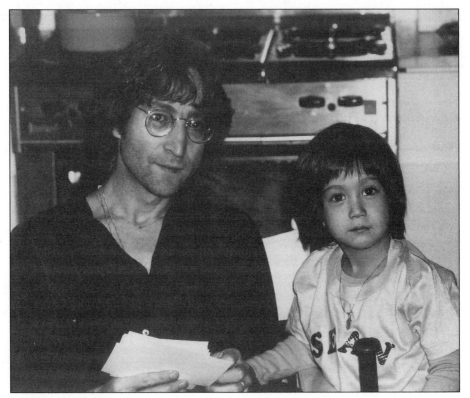

Beautiful Boy: John took a break from the limelight to raise his second child, Sean. Here, they sort through photos in the kitchen of their apartment complex in the Dakota. (Photofest)

16. **1975 January 9**   The Beatles and Company was formally and finally dissolved during a private hearing in the London High Court. This ruling severed any and all remaining legal links among the four Beatles.

17. **1975 May 2**   Apple Records was metaphorically shuttered and the lights turned off for good.

18. **1975 October 9**   Yoko gave birth to John's second son and John and Yoko's only child together on this day, John's thirty-fifth birthday. The baby weighed seven pounds and they named him Sean Ono Taro Lennon.

19. **1976 January 26**   The Beatles' 9-year contract with EMI Records expired.

20. **1976 February 1**   Bill Sargent, an American concert promoter, offered the Beatles $50 million to perform one reunion concert. The Beatles declined his offer.

21. **1976 March 8**   The single "Yesterday"/"I Should Have Known Better" was released in the United Kingdom.

22. **1976 May 31**   The single "Got to Get You Into My Life"/"Helter Skelter" was released in the United States.

23. **1976 June 25**   The single "Back in the U.S.S.R."/"Twist and Shout" was released in the United Kingdom.

24. **1976 July 30**   The LP *The Beatles Tapes* was released in the United Kingdom. George and Ringo tried to block the release of this album but were unsuccessful. (This album was not released in the United States until 1978.)

25. **1976 November 8**   The single "Ob-La-Di, Ob-La-Da"/"Julia" was released in the United States.

26. **1976 November 19**   The LP *Magical Mystery Tour* was released in the United Kingdom.

27. **1977 April 8**   The LP *The Beatles Live! At the Star Club in Hamburg, Germany, 1962* was released in Germany. This album contained recordings that were made by Adrian Barber during the Fabs December 31, 1962, gig at the Star Club. Barber used a handheld microphone and a portable mono Grundig tape recorder and the quality reflected the primitive conditions under which the tapes were made. The Beatles, through Apple, filed an injunction to prevent this double album's release but on April 5, 1977, the courts ruled that the tapes were of historical interest and the Beatles could not stop their release.

28. **1977 May 1**   The LP *The Beatles Live! At the Star Club in Hamburg, Germany, 1962* was released in the United Kingdom. This version did not contain all the songs on the German edition.

29. **1977 May 6**   The LP *The Beatles at the Hollywood Bowl* was released in the United States and the United Kingdom.

30. **1977 May 26**   The Beatles tribute show *Beatlemania* began its run at the Winter Garden Theater in New York City. It opened without an official opening night for critics (see June 4, 1986).

31. **1977 June 13**   The LP *The Beatles Live! At the Star Club in Hamburg, Germany, 1962* was released in the United States. Like the U.K. release, this version did not contain all the songs on the German edition.

32. **1977 June 25**   The LP *The Beatles at the Hollywood Bowl* reached number one in the United Kingdom.

33. **1977 October 11**   At the conclusion of a 4-month stay in Yoko's homeland of Japan, John and Yoko held a press conference at the Okura Hotel in Tokyo. The only Western publication present was *Melody Maker* and they reported that throughout the 45-minute session, Yoko did most of the talking. John did make one statement that was worth noting, however: "We've basically decided to devote our time to be with our baby as much as we can until we feel we can take the time off to indulge ourselves in creating things outside the family." John's self-imposed period of "house-husband" exile lasted until November 1980 when he and Yoko released *Double Fantasy*.

34. **1977 October 19**   The Liverpool City Council rejected a proposal to erect a monument to the Beatles in Liverpool. The vote was 11 to 9 against the monument.

35. **1977 October 21**   The LP *Love Songs* was released in the United States.

36. **1977 November 19**   The LP *Love Songs* was released in the United Kingdom.

37. **1978 February 19**   A TV special about the Beatles called "All You Need Is Love" was aired in the United States.

38. **1978 March 22**   The TV special "All You Need Is Cash," chronicling the history of the legendary group the Rutles, was aired in the United States. This satirical look at the Beatles legend was a creation of former Monty Python members Eric Idle and Neil Innes, as well as Rikki Fatar and John Halsey. The songs of the Rutles sounded so much like the Beatles' songs that one Rutles ballad,

The Rutles

The Rutles were the ultimate Beatles parody—as a concept and a band—and their history and songs provided a scathing and hilarious spin on the entire Beatles mythology.

SELECTIONS FROM THE RUTLES DISCOGRAPHY

The Rutles—Released February 27, 1978, in the United States; March 24, 1978, in the United Kingdom; all songs by Neil Innes.

Side One
"Hold My Hand"
"Number One"
"With a Girl Like You"
"I Must Be in Love"
"Ouch!"
"Living in Hope"
"Love Life"
"Nevertheless"

Side Two
"Good Times Roll"
"Doubleback Alley"
"Cheese and Onions"
"Another Day"
"Piggy in the Middle"
"Let's Be Natural

All You Need Is Cash—Original Television Broadcast, 1978; video released, 1983, as *The Rutles* in the United States; as *The Complete Rutles* in the United Kingdom.

Songs Performed in the Video
"Get Up and Go"

Medley

"Number One"
"Love Life"
"Piggy in the Middle"
"I Must Be in Love"
"Let's Be Natural"

"Living in Hope"
"Ouch!"
"It's Looking Good"
"Another Day"
"Good Times Roll"
"Love Life"

"Goose Step Mama"
"Number One"
"We Were Made for Each Other
   (Between Us)"
"With a Girl Like You"
"Hold My Hand"
"I Must Be in Love"

"Nevertheless"
"Piggy in the Middle"
"Cheese and Onions"
"Let's Be Natural"
"You Need Feet"
"Get Up and Go"
"Doubleback Alley"

Archaeology—Released 1996; all songs by Neil Innes.

"Major Happy's Up and Coming Once Upon a Good Time Band"

"Rendezvous"

"Questionnaire"

"We've Arrived! (And to Prove It We're Here)"

"Lonely-Phobia"

"Unfinished Words"

"Hey Mister!"

"Easy Listening"

"Now She's Left You"

"The Knicker Elastic King"

"I Love You"

"Eine Kleine Middle Klasse Musik"

"Joe Public"

"Shangri-La"

"Don't Know Why"

"Back in '64"

"Lullaby"

"Baby S'il Vous Plaît"

"It's Looking Good"

"My Little Ukelele"

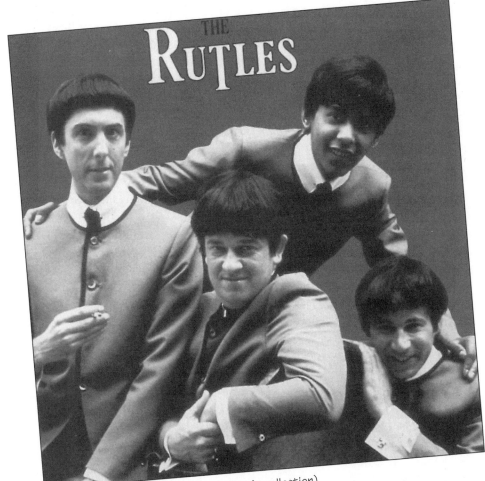

Those other boys from Liverpool (Editor's collection)

"Cheese and Onions," eventually surfaced on a bootleg as a long-lost John Lennon composition.

39. **1978 March 27** "All You Need Is Cash" was aired in the United Kingdom.

40. **1978 August 14** The single "Sgt. Pepper's Lonely Hearts Club Band"—"With a Little Help From My Friends"/"A Day in the Life" was released in the United States.

41. **1978 September 30** The single "Sgt. Pepper's Lonely Hearts Club Band"—"With a Little Help From My Friends"/"A Day in the Life" was released in the United Kingdom.

42. **1978 December 2** The LP *Rarities* was released in the United States.

43. **1979 May 11** The LP *Hey Jude* (also known as *The Beatles Again*) was released in the United Kingdom.

44. **1979 May 19** George, Paul, and Ringo performed together at a party at Eric Clapton's country home at Ewhurst, Surry, about twenty-five miles outside of London. The celebration was to commemorate Eric Clapton and Pattie Boyd's (George's ex-wife) marriage in March. (They wed in Tucson, Arizona.)

    The "band" performed old rock-and-roll standards as well as some Beatles songs. Around 9:00 P.M., Traffic's Jim Capaldi sat down at the drums and accompanied Paul McCartney on bass and a fifteen-year-old wedding guest on guitar. Cream's Ginger Baker took over on the drums while the Moody Blues (and later Wings) Denny Laine and Eric Clapton played guitar. George Harrison and Elton John's percussionist Ray Cooper joined in on keyboards. This configuration played a blues jam which really didn't go anywhere. Paul asked legendary skiffle musician Lonnie Donegan on-stage to do a skiffle number on his guitar. Paul McCartney took charge of the group, and the band—now with Ringo on drums—did some old tunes, including "Lawdy Miss Clawdy" and "High School Confidential." Mick Jagger then jumped on stage and sang lead on the old Eddie Cochran song, "Something Else."

    Several party-goers reported that the band also did several old Beatles tunes, including "Sgt. Pepper's Lonely Hearts Club Band." No recording has ever surfaced of this impromptu Beatles "reunion." (Also, there is supposedly no existing photographic evidence of this historic gathering, something most Beatles watchers find hard to believe, considering that it's a given that almost *everyone* brings at least a *camera* to a wedding party. No tape recorders makes sense, but no cameras?)

    Later, when Paul was asked if it felt strange playing again with George and Ringo, he replied, "No, it didn't feel strange at all. We were having a booze-up and a laugh and suddenly we were playing together again. It felt pretty good to me. . . . Oh, yeah, it'll be great to do one like that again with just the four of us, once Sean is five and John starts playing again."

45. **1979 August 22** A two thousand copy limited edition of George Harrison's autobiography *I Me Mine* was published in the United Kingdom.

46. **1979 October 12** The LP *Rarities* was released in the United Kingdom.

47. **1979 October 24** Paul McCartney was listed in the *Guinness Book of Records* as the most successful composer and recording artist of all time.

48. **1979 November 28** Ringo Starr's house in the Hollywood Hills burned down and many of his irreplaceable Beatles' treasures were lost in the fire.

18. 69 "Death of the Legend" Beatles Events of the Eighties

1. **1980 January 16** Paul McCartney was arrested in Tokyo for possession of marijuana. He arrived in Japan for the beginning of an 11-concert tour which was canceled after his arrest. To this day rumors persist that Yoko Ono deliberately tipped off the Japanese customs police to sabotage Paul's Wings tour in her native country.

2. **1980 January 25** After spending ten days in a Japanese jail, Paul is released and deported to Britain.

3. **1980 March 24** The LP *Rarities* was released in the United States by Capitol Records.

4. **1980 October 13** The LP *The Beatles Ballads—20 Original Tracks* was released in the United Kingdom.

5. **1980 November 3** *The Beatles Box,* a set of eight LPs, was released in the United Kingdom. This set included one hundred twenty-six Beatles recordings and delighted collectors with the inclusion of several rare mixes previously unreleased.

6. **1980 November 28** John Lennon confirmed that he and his fellow Beatles definitely planned to reunite for a concert and film documentary about the Beatles history with the working title *The Long and Winding Road.* John made this statement in a legal deposition taken by attorneys for Apple Corps for the Beatles' lawsuit against the Beatles imitation musical production Beatlemania. *The Long and Winding Road* would eventually be released as *The Beatles Anthology.*

7. **1980 December 8** John Lennon was shot to death at 10:49 P.M. by a sick, twisted individual who actually had the audacity to call himself a Beatles "fan." John was gunned down outside the Dakota building in New York City after he exited his limousine following a recording session at the Hit Factory. Yoko was with him when he was shot. John was transported in a police car to the emergency room at Roosevelt Hospital where the doctors worked desperately to save him, but to no avail. John was pronounced dead at 11:13, at which time it was already December 9 in Great Britain, where his Aunt Mimi had yet to hear the news.

   The afternoon of John's murder, Yoko sent her husband's will to the appropriate New York district court for probate. The will was a 4-page document that had been drafted by David Warmflash and signed by John on November 12, 1979. John's will gave Yoko 50 percent of his entire estate (then estimated to be valued at more than $200 million) and placed the other 50 percent into a private trust. The terms of the trust did not have to be publicly declared, although it is likely that it included provisions for John's children and possibly even Yoko's daughter Kyoko. One odd element of John's will was the appointment of Sam Green—Yoko's friend and business associate—as Sean's guardian in the event of Yoko's death. (Green had not even been consulted about this provision of John's will.)

8. **1980 December 9** Paul McCartney, when asked about John's murder, offhandedly remarked, "It's a drag, isn't it?" This was interpreted by the world as callous

The cover of the December 22, 1980, tribute issue of *People* magazine. It was the bestselling issue in the magazine's history. (Photofest)

and unfeeling but the truth was that Paul was simply unable to immediately absorb and verbalize about such a monumental personal loss. Later in the day, Paul did have more to say about John's murder:

> I have hidden myself in my work today. But it keeps flashing into my mind. I feel shattered, angry, and very, very sad. It's just ridiculous. He was pretty rude about me sometimes, but I secretly admired him for it and I always managed to stay in touch with him. There was no question that we weren't friends—I really loved the guy.
>
> I think that what has happened will in years to come make people realize that John was an international statesman. He often looked like a loony to many people. He made enemies, but he was fantastic. He was a warm man who cared a lot and, with the record "Give Peace a Chance," he helped stop the Vietnam War. He made a lot of sense.

(Paul later issued an "official" statement that read, "He was a great man and will be missed by the whole world and will be remembered for his art, music, and contribution to world peace.")

In November of 1987, Paul spoke at length about his initial controversial comments:

> When John was killed, somebody stuck a microphone [in my face] and said, "What do you think about it?" I said, "It's a drag." But I said, "It's a draaaaaaag," and meant it with every inch of melancholy I could muster. When you put that in print, it says, "McCartney in London today, when asked for a comment on his dead friend, said, 'It's a drag.'" It seemed a very flippant comment to make.

Musical tributes to John from his bandmates eventually included Paul's touching "Here Today" and George's "All Those Years Ago." Other tributes included Elton John's elegiac ballad "Empty Garden." (Elton is Sean's godfather and was very close to John and his family.)

9. **1980 December 10**   John Lennon's body was cremated and his ashes were delivered to his widow in an elaborately gift-wrapped package so as to throw off the hundreds of fans who ceaselessly gathered outside the Dakota since the evening of December 8.

10. **1981 February 20**   The LP *Hear the Beatles Tell All* was released in the United Kingdom.

11. **1981 April 16**   The LPs *Dawn of the Silver Beatles* and *Lightning Strikes Twice* were released in the United States. The fifteen songs on these two albums comprise the Beatles' Decca January 1, 1962, audition tapes.

12. **1981 August 25**   John Lennon's murderer received a 20-years-to-life sentence for his loathsome act of cowardice.

13. **1981 December**   By the end of this year, Paul and Yoko learned that their joint bid to purchase ATV Music, the company that owned the Lennon/McCartney song catalog, had failed. Their bid of £21 million (over $33 million in 1997 dollars) was turned down.

14. **1982 March 7**   BBC Radio aired the 2-hour program *The Beatles at the Beeb* in honor of the twentieth anniversary of the Beatles first BBC Radio appearance.

15. **1982 March 22**   The LP *Reel Music* was released in the United States.

16. **1982 March 22**   The single "The Beatles Movie Medley"/"I'm Happy Just to Dance With You" was released in the United States.

17. **1982 March 29**   The LP *Reel Music* was released in the United Kingdom.

18. **1982 April 20**   An area in New York's Central Park, near the Dakota, was christened "Strawberry Fields" and dedicated to John's memory.

19. **1982 May 24**   The single "The Beatles Movie Medley"/"I'm Happy Just to Dance With You" was released in the United Kingdom.

20. **1982 October 1**   Mobile Fidelity Labs released a 13-album boxed set of original stereo British Beatles LPs. These recordings, which were aimed at the serious audiophile, were pressed on half-speed mastered discs. The set also included a half-speed mastered version of the U.S. edition of the *Magical Mystery Tour* album.

21. **1982 October 1**   The documentary film *The Compleat Beatles* was released worldwide on videotape.

22. **1982 October 15**   The LP *The Beatles—20 Greatest Hits* was released in the United States.

23. **1982 October 18**   The LP *The Beatles—20 Greatest Hits* as released in the United Kingdom.

24. **1982 December 27**   The BBC repeated the two-hour program *The Beatles at the Beeb*, this time including some songs not broadcast in the March program.

25. **1982 December 31**   By the end of this year, Paul McCartney was willing to publicly discuss his friendship and working relationship with John during media interviews. This marked a new period of openness on Paul's part, especially in his willingness to discuss John's death.

26. **1983 May 29**   *The Beatles at the Beeb* was aired for the first time in syndication in the United States. This version of the program included some songs not heard during the original broadcasts.

27. **1983 July 11**   EMI's Abbey Road Studios announced the discovery of four previously unknown early Beatles' recordings. The tapes were of the songs, "How Do You Do It?," "That Means a Lot," "If You've Got Trouble," and "Leave My Kitten Alone." All of them appeared more than a decade later in *The Beatles Anthology*.

28. **1983 July 18**   EMI opened Abbey Road Studios to the general public. EMI offered a multimedia tour program called "The Beatles at Abbey Road" that covered the Beatles' career and included the playing of unreleased Beatles tracks from the Abbey Road archives.

29. **1983 August 22**   The film *The Beatles at Shea Stadium* was aired on several U.S. Public TV stations.

30. **1983 December 1**   Paul, George, Ringo, and Yoko met at the Dorchester Hotel in London to discuss and finalize all Apple business.

31. **1983 December 3**   Paul revealed that he burned Peter Brown's newly-published book *The Love You Make*. Brown was roundly criticized when the book came out for divulging confidences and revealing secrets he came to know during his many years as an aide to the Beatles.

32. **1983 December 26**   BBC Radio 2 aired a one-hour special called *The Beatles at Christmas.*

33. **1984 January 1**   A 45-minute documentary by Granada TV called *The Early Beatles: 1962–1965* aired on British television.

34. **1984 April 3**   A statue of the Beatles—Liverpool's first—was unveiled on Mathew Street. The sculpture by David Hughes, a graduate of John's alma mater the Liverpool College of Art, was installed above the doorway of the Beatles Shop on Mathew Street.

35. **1984 April 26**   Another statue of the Beatles was unveiled on Mathew Street in Liverpool near the site of the long-gone Cavern Club. Paul's brother Mike McCartney (McGear) dedicated the statue, which was to be the centerpiece of a proposed $12.6 million shopping district.

36. **1984 May 2**   The Beatle Maze at the Liverpool International Garden Festival was officially opened by Queen Elizabeth II. As part of the festivities, a life-sized yellow submarine was docked near the festival and the queen thrilled Beatles fans by actually going aboard the sub. "We all live on a yellow submarine" indeed!

37. **1984 July 6**   The film *A Hard Day's Night* was released in the United States on videocassette and laser disc.

38. **1984 October 1**   John's estate and Paul McCartney were paid approximately £2 million and the royalty rates on Beatles recordings were increased in a secret deal with ATV. (All parties involved agreed to strict "no publicity" terms for this new deal.)

39. **1984 December 3**   The documentary *Ivan,* part of the *Horizon* series, aired on BBC2 TV. This film told the story of 43-year-old Ivan Vaughan's struggle with Parkinson's disease. Ivan was the Quarry Man who introduced John Lennon to Paul McCartney in July 1957. Paul gave the *Ivan* filmmakers the right to use "Blackbird" at the beginning and end of the film at no charge. Paul, who was very close to Ivan until his death in 1994, had Ivan stay with him at his home in Sussex for Christmas 1984. Reportedly, Paul began writing poetry for the first time since his childhood years following Ivan's death. Of the documentary, Ivan said, "I decided to make my illness my hobby. Not as something useful. Not to help thousands. Just selfishly, to find out all I could about it and its implications. I wanted to explore it, to play with it, and even to laugh about it." Ivan's autobiography, *Ivan: Living With Parkinson's Disease,* was published in 1986.

40. **1984 December 13**   The London High Court resolved the 1979 lawsuit involving EMI and Apple Corps. Each ex-Beatle and Yoko Ono were added to the suit as plaintiffs with Apple and released from any legal ties to Capitol. Capitol immediately countersued the Beatles for $1.5 million, claiming that they failed to deliver two albums they were required to produce by contract.

41. **1985 February 25**   George, Ringo, and Yoko reportedly sued Paul McCartney for $8.6 million for breach of contract. The suit alleged that Paul received more royalties for Beatles recordings than the others did.

42. **1985 February 28**   This month, the first licenses for the use of Beatles songs in TV commercials were issued. Cover versions of "Help!" were used by Lincoln-Mercury; "We Can Work It Out" was used by Hewlett-Packard in the United

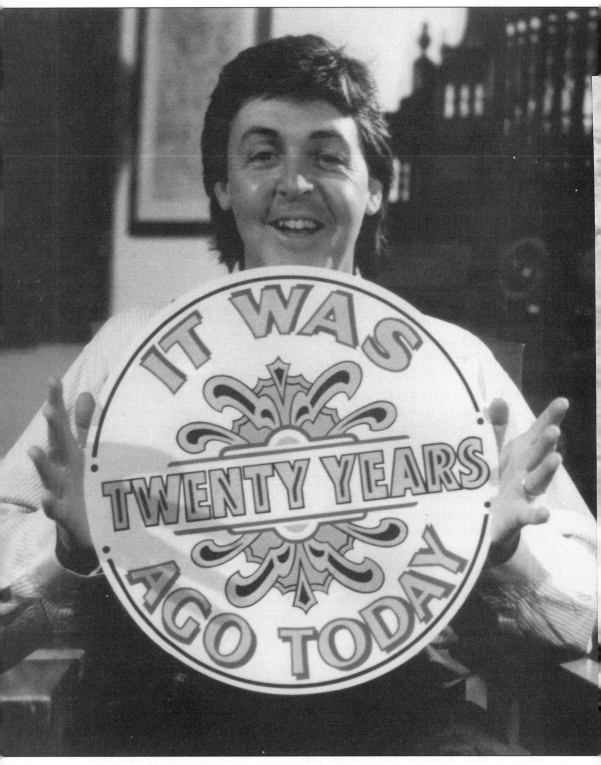

Paul promotes the cable premiere on the Discovery Channel of the documentary *It Was Twenty Years Ago Today*, which profiled the year 1967—one of sweeping change which many say was driven by the release of *Sgt. Pepper*. (Photofest)

Kingdom; and "She Loves You" was used by Schweppes on Spanish TV. The actual Beatles' version of "Revolution" was later used by Nike on American TV.

43. **1985 August 10**   Michael Jackson purchased ATV Music, thus becoming the owner of the Lennon/McCartney song catalog. Jackson ended up owning everything John and Paul wrote except for "Love Me Do," "P.S. I Love You" (owned by Paul's publishing company MPL), and "Please Please Me," "Don't Bother Me," and "Ask Me Why" (owned by Dick James).

44. **1985 September 20**   Posthumous copyrights for twenty-eight songs by John Lennon were registered. Included were "Girls and Boys," a song which was eventually released in 1996 as "Real Love" on *The Beatles Anthology;* and "Free as a Bird," which was expanded and rerecorded by the surviving Beatles and released as a "new" Beatles single in 1995 and also was included on *The Beatles Anthology.*

45. **1985 December 31**   By the end of this month, Paul withdrew from the legal battle between Apple and EMI/Capitol over Beatles royalties. (Paul recently signed a new recording contract with Capitol.) George, Ringo, and Yoko continued their legal war against the record company, however, seeking $30 million in compensatory damages, $50 million in punitive damages, and joint custody of all Beatles master tapes.

46. **1986 March 26**   EMI paid £2,832,264 (around $4.5 million in 1997 dollars) in back royalties to the Beatles as a result of a 1984 High Court ruling.

47. **1986 March 29**   The first legitimate release of Beatles recordings in the former Soviet Union was marked by the release of the LP *A Hard Day's Night* and the compilation LP *A Taste of Honey.* Black market and bootleg Beatles recordings were available in the Soviet Union for years.

48. **1986 June 4**   The producers of *Beatlemania* were ordered to pay Apple Corps $10.5 million for commercially exploiting the Beatles with their stage show.

49. **1986 October 9**   John Lennon's third book, *Skywriting by Word of Mouth,* was posthumously published.

50. **1987 February 26**   The Beatles albums *Please Please Me, With the Beatles, A Hard Day's Night,* and *Beatles for Sale* were released worldwide on compact disc. Unbelievably, these CDs were released in mono only, a blunder which caused Beatles fans around the globe to scream their bloody heads off.

51. **1987 April 30**   The British versions of the Beatles albums *Help!, Revolver,* and *Rubber Soul* were released on stereo CD.

52. **1987 June 1**   On its twentieth anniversary, the Beatles album *Sgt. Pepper's Lonely Hearts Club Band* was released worldwide on stereo CD.

53. **1987 August 24**   The Beatles albums *The Beatles* (also known as the *White Album*) and *Yellow Submarine* were released worldwide on stereo CD.

54. **1987 August 28**   The film *Yellow Submarine* was released on videocassette in the United Kingdom. The "Hey Bulldog" number was omitted from the videocassette.

55. **1987 September 21**   The Beatles album *Magical Mystery Tour* was released worldwide on stereo CD.

56. **1987 October 19**   The Beatles albums *Abbey Road* and *Let It Be* were released worldwide on stereo CD.

57. **1987 October 20**   The film *Yellow Submarine* was released on videocassette in the United States. The "Hey Bulldog" number was omitted from the videocassette.

58. **1988 January 20**   The Beatles were inducted into the Rock and Roll Hall of Fame during ceremonies at the Waldorf-Astoria Hotel in New York City. George Harrison, Ringo Starr, Yoko Ono, Sean Lennon, and Julian Lennon attended. Paul sent a statement in which he matter-of-factly told the world that the business differences that still existed among them all made him decide not to attend. In July of 1989, Paul said the following about his decision:

> I keep saying to everyone, "We've got to sort out our problems. We can't move forward in harmony while you're suing me." So I wanted that to be the reunion night, and I said, "If you can drop this lawsuit guy, or just nearly drop it, show me something that says you love me, give me a sign, a wink." And it just went and went, I kept ringing. George was in Hawaii. I got a message back from him, "Sit tight, don't rock the boat, don't worry." But that wasn't good enough. So I had to ring him up and say I couldn't go to the Rock and Roll Hall of Fame, no way was I standing up on stage going, "Yo! United!" when I know they're suing me. I just couldn't do it.

59. **1988 February 15**   George published his second book, *Songs by George Harrison,* again in a limited edition. Each copy was signed by George and the book was only available by mail order. Buyers chose either a 7-inch EP or a CD containing four George Harrison songs, three of which were previously unreleased.

60. **1988 March 5**   George and Ringo appeared together on the U.K. TV show *Aspel and Company*. This was the first ever joint TV interview by two or more Beatles since the breakup.

61. **1988 March 8**   The CDs, *Past Masters Vol. 1* and *Past Masters Vol. 2* were released worldwide. (The two CDs were also released as a double LP.) These two CDs contained all of the Beatles' songs not originally released on their U.K. albums. The releases of these two CDs completed the CD release of everything the Beatles ever recorded. In 1995 and 1996, the release of *The Beatles Anthology* would mine the Abbey Road archives and delight fans with works-in-progress, unreleased tracks, and other Beatles historical memorabilia.

62. **1988 March 21**   The four videotapes *The Beatles at Shea Stadium, The Beatles in Tokyo, The Beatles in Washington, D.C.,* and *The Beatles in Magical Mystery Tour* were illegally released by a variety of distributors. Apple sued.

63. **1988 September 12**   *The Lost Lennon Tapes* began airing on the Westwood Radio Network. This popular series ultimately comprised twenty-nine volumes of John Lennon interviews, outtakes, and rare performances.

64. **1988 October 1**   The BBC began a 14-week series of 30-minute shows called *The Beeb's Lost Beatles Tapes.*

65. **1988 October 26**   The film *Magical Mystery Tour* was released on videocassette in the United States.

66. **1988 November 28**   EMI began releasing all of the original Beatles singles on a 3-inch CD.

67. **1989 November 8**   After twenty years, the legal battle between the Beatles and EMI/Capitol concluded with a settlement. The Beatles reportedly received £100

million (over $150 million in 1997 dollars) in back royalties. Perhaps even more important, the Beatles also regained complete control over their entire body of work, including recordings and cover art.

68. **1989 November 27**   Paul said publicly that the Beatles might perform together again. He also stated that he had never composed songs with George and would someday like to do so.

69. **1989 November 28**   George Harrison released a statement in which he said that there would never be a Beatles reunion "so long as John Lennon remains dead."

19. 35 "The Beatles Live On" Beatles Events From 1990 to the Present

1. **1990 February 21**   Paul McCartney received the Lifetime Achievement Award at the annual Grammy Awards at Radio City Music Hall in New York City.

2. **1990 May 26**   The October 1988, 14-part BBC radio series *The Beeb's Lost Beatles Tapes* was syndicated in the United States during the Memorial Day weekend. The original seven hours of material was edited down to a 6-hour special and retitled *The BBC's Beatles Tapes: The Original Masters*.

3. **1990 June 28**   For the first time, Paul performed what became known as his "Lennon Medley" at a concert at King's Dock in Liverpool. This was the first time Paul publicly performed John Lennon compositions and the medley consisted of "Strawberry Fields Forever," "Help!" and "Give Peace a Chance."

4. **1990 October 8**   The single "Birthday"/"Good Day Sunshine" by Paul McCartney was released in the United Kingdom, marking a milestone event: This was the first single containing Beatles songs recorded by a member of the group after the breakup.

5. **1990 October 16**   Paul's single "Birthday"/"Good Day Sunshine" was released in the United States as a cassette single only.

6. **1990 December 3**   A second edition of Paul's CD single "All My Trials"/"C Moon" was released with the original bonus tracks "Mull of Kintyre" and "Put It There" replaced with his "Lennon Medley." In all likelihood, Paul rereleased songs that had been originally credited to John and himself as songs now credited only to John.

7. **1990 December 31**   *Amusement Business* magazine announced that Paul McCartney's solo tour this year included the top-grossing booking of the year, the first time an ex-Beatle had achieved such a commercial milestone as a solo act.

8. **1991 February 20**   John Lennon posthumously received the Lifetime Achievement Award at the annual Grammy Awards at Radio City Music Hall in New York City. The award was presented by Aerosmith, who then did a kick-ass live rendition of "Come Together."

9. **1991 June 14**   Paul's promotional video for the song "Birthday" was released in Japan by EMI as the first video single CD.

10. **1991 November 13**   *The Beatles: The First U.S. Visit* was released in the United States on videocassette and laser disc. This film included footage of the Beatles'

February 1964 *Ed Sullivan Show* appearance and their Washington, D.C., concert.

11. **1991 December 6** John's Aunt Mimi died at the age of eighty-eight in Poole, England.

12. **1992 May 31** Apple announced that the three surviving Beatles will work together on a massive film project chronicling the history of the Beatles. The project, having the title *The Long and Winding Road,* would be a multipart TV series and the Beatles would participate with interviews, private film footage, and new music. This was the first public confirmation of the project that would eventually become *The Beatles Anthology.*

13. **1992 June 14** The TV special *The Making of Sgt. Pepper* was aired in the United Kingdom on the ITV network. The special boasted new interviews with Paul, George, Ringo, and George Martin.

14. **1992 June 15** The EP set *The Beatles EP Set* was released in the United Kingdom. The set consisted of a boxed set of original British Beatles EPs on 5-inch CDs.

15. **1992 June 15** The EP set *The Beatles EP Set* was released in the United States.

16. **1992 September 27** The TV special *The Making of Sgt. Pepper* was aired in the United States on the Disney Channel.

17. **1992 October 8** Paul, George, and Ringo were seen leaving Paul's MPL office in London, reportedly on their way to a meeting with Yoko.

18. **1992 November 2** The boxed set *The Beatles Singles Collection* was released in the United Kingdom. The set consisted of the original 22 British Beatles singles on 5-inch CDs.

19. **1992 November 17** The boxed set *The Beatles Singles Collection* was released in the United States.

20. **1992 December 11** Paul commented publicly for the first time on *The Long and Winding Road.* Speaking at a press conference in the United States, he said, "We've talked for years and years about doing this thing . . . it's bringing us together. And there's a chance we might write a little bit of music for it."

21. **1992 December 31** By now, the title of the planned Beatles documentary was changed to *The Beatles Anthology.*

22. **1993 February 28** Paul again spoke publicly about *The Beatles Anthology,* this time in an interview for Italian TV. He said, "A documentary is being prepared in England, in ten parts. George, Ringo, and I have been asked to record an instrumental piece for the soundtrack of the film. I think we're going to do it this year. But we aren't planning to get back together for a tour or anything like that. Just for this soundtrack." Paul made no mention of the two new Beatles songs ultimately released with *The Beatles Anthology,* "Free as a Bird" and "Real Love."

23. **1993 March 31** By the end of this month, George Martin also spoke publicly about the proposed *Beatles Anthology,* only his comments were surprising for their negative appraisal of the "quality" of the Abbey Road Beatles archives: "I've listened to all the tapes. There are one or two interesting variations, but otherwise it's all junk. Couldn't possibly release it."

24. **1993 September 20**   Digitally remastered CD editions of *The Beatles 1962–1966* (the "blue" album) and *The Beatles 1967–70* (the "red" album) were released in the United Kingdom.

25. **1993 October 5**   Digitally remastered CD editions of *The Beatles 1962–1966* ("blue") and *The Beatles 1967–70* ("red") were released in the United States.

26. **1993 November 30**   By the end of this month, George Martin announced that he would compile material from the Abbey Road Beatles archives for accompanying CDs to be released with the video documentary *The Beatles Anthology*. In March, Martin called the archives "junk," but now obviously has changed his opinion about the material. "We're going to put in everything that I consider to be valid from every source, including the Beatles' own private collections, demos that they made, outtakes, and alternative versions of songs. For example, there's Take 1 of 'Strawberry Fields Forever' which is well worth . . . hearing now. And I don't think the famous 'How Do You Do It?' has ever been properly released, so that'll come out." (Take 1 of "Strawberry Fields Forever" appears on Disc 2 of *The Beatles Anthology 2*; "How Do You Do It?" appears on Disc 1 of *The Beatles Anthology 1*.)

27. **1994 January 19**   John Lennon was inducted into the Rock and Roll Hall of Fame. Paul made the induction speech and Yoko accepted on behalf of her late husband. (See the chapter "The Letter Paul McCartney Wrote to the Late John Lennon on the Occasion of John's Induction into the Rock and Roll Hall of Fame on January 19, 1994.") In 1995, when asked how he felt about John being in the Hall of Fame and he himself not being inducted, Paul told *Newsweek* magazine, "We are in it as the Beatles, of course, and that's kind of enough, isn't it? I mean, a million times in my life I've like, not passed an exam or someone beat me in something. . . . [Y]ou can't sit around saying . . . 'I wish they'd put me in the Rock and Roll Hall of Fame.' I'm not that fussed, you know? I'm in my hall of fame. You've got to deal with yourself. Funnily enough, in his early days, John was very much wondering how he would be remembered. And I said, 'You're crazy, man. What are you talking about? Number one, you'll be remembered as something fantastic. Number two, you won't give a shit. You'll be in the cosmos somewhere. And I have a feeling that other things will be of more consequence at that point.' "

28. **1994 February 22**   Digitally remastered colored vinyl LP editions of *The Beatles 1962–1966* (the "blue" album) and *The Beatles 1967–70* (the "red" album) were released in both the United Kingdom and the United States.

29. **1994 February 28**   By the end of this month, Paul, George, and Ringo had completed work on the "new" Beatles single, "Free as a Bird," working from a demo tape given to them by Yoko Ono.

30. **1994 December**   By the end of this year, the mining of the Beatles archives began in earnest with the release of *Live at the BBC*. The release of recordings heretofore available only on bootlegs continued with the release of the six *Beatles Anthology* CDs in 1995 and 1996.

31. **1995 November 20**   *The Beatles Anthology* juggernaut began with the release of Volume 1 of the 3-volume CD set of *The Beatles Anthology*. It sold two million copies in a week. Also this month, a 6-hour version of *The Beatles Anthology* aired as a miniseries on ABC.

20. The 10 Pieces of a Classic Ringo Starr Drum Kit

Everyone else knows exactly what the drummer should play, and if anything goes wrong on stage, the front line automatically looks at the drummer. I actually found it helpful that John, Paul, and George would say, "Do this, do that, what about that?" But the classic one was when John brought some Motown records in and said, "I want you to play like this." And I said, "Well, there are two drummers on that." "Yeah, but just play like that." So I did the best I could and that's how we got a lot of the beats we did.

—Ringo Starr, in the July 1997 issue
of *Modern Drummer* magazine

Ringo himself has been embarrassingly self-effacing and modest about his contributions to the art of rock drumming but there is no doubt that he changed the way rock drummers play. Today, Ringo Starr is one of the most respected drummers in the history of rock. In the July 1997 issue of *Modern Drummer* magazine, session drummer and music producer John Bryant listed thirteen reasons why Ringo deserved respect in the field of rock drumming. For some, this list will surprise; for musicians, it simply states the obvious.

Some of Bryant's reasons included the fact that Ringo changed the way drumsticks were held (he used a powerful "hammer" grip that Bryant says emphasized that rock music needed *power* drumming); he pioneered a clearer, more "upfront" sound for drumming; and he deftly proved that rock drumming could accommodate varying time signatures with ease, such as Ringo's "makes it look easy" playing in the 11/8, 4/4, 7/8 passage in the chorus of George's "Here Comes the Sun."

This feature looks at the ten pieces of equipment in a classic Ringo Starr drum kit and proves that Ringo has probably been the best thing to ever happen to the Ludwig company since the company's inception.

1. Ludwig *Vintage Super Classic* 5 × 14 *Black Beauty* snare
2. Ludwig *Vintage Super Classic* 9 × 13 tom
3. Ludwig *Vintage Super Classic* 16 × 16 floor tom
4. Ludwig *Vintage Super Classic* 16 × 22 bass drum
5. Zildjian 14″ *New Beat* hi-hat cymbal
6. Zildjian 18″ *A* crash cymbal (from the '60s)
7. Zildjian 13″ *K/Z* mounted hi-hat cymbal
8. Zildjian 20″ *A* crash-ride cymbal (from the '60s)
9. Zildjian 16″ *A* medium-thin crash cymbal
10. Pro-Mark *5AL* drumsticks with wood tips

(Photofest)

32. **1996 February**   Volume 2 of the 3-volume CD set of *The Beatles Anthology* was released.

33. **1996 November**   The 10-hour, 8-tape version of *The Beatles Anthology* was released on video. Also this month, the third volume of the *Anthology* CD series was released.

34. **1997 January 13**   Paul McCartney was knighted by the Queen of England. "It's a fantastic honor," Paul said, "and I'm gratefully receiving it on behalf of the people of Liverpool and the other Beatles, without whom it wouldn't have been possible."

35. **1997 May**   Paul released his solo CD, *Flaming Pie,* named in honor of John Lennon's July 1961 quote in which he said that the name of the Beatles was given to him by a man on a flaming pie.

21. The 4 Slogans Used to Describe Each of the Beatles in Revell's Official 1964 Plastic Model Kits of the Group

1. **Paul McCartney:**   "The Great McCartney!"
2. **John Lennon:**   "Kookiest of Them All!"
3. **George Harrison:**   "Lead Guitar—Loud and Strong!"
4. **Ringo Starr:**   "Wildest Skins in Town!"

I'll Often Stop and Think About Them . . .

22. 78 Important People from All Across the Beatles Universe

Here is a look at 78 of the fascinating people who were—or still are—part of the lives of John, Paul, George, and Ringo.

1. **Jane Asher**   Paul McCartney's former fiancée and one of his first loves. Paul met Jane when she was seventeen and she was a writer covering a 1963 Beatles concert at the Royal Albert Hall for *Radio Times*. They hit it off (even though George also seemed to be interested in Jane) and began dating. Paul ultimately moved into the Asher family home in London after he missed a train back to Liverpool and her parents asked him to spend the night. They generously offered him an upstairs room and he accepted.

   Jane inspired several of Paul's best songs, including "She Loves You" (which was written in the Asher home), "And I Love Her," "Every Little Thing," "We Can Work It Out," "You Won't See Me," "I'm Looking Through You," and the song that John considered his favorite of Paul's, "Here, There, and Everywhere."

   Despite troubles revolving around the nature of their relationship (Paul wanted a supportive stay-at-home Liverpool wife; Jane was career-minded), the two bought a house and a farm together and were engaged briefly in 1968. They split up because of Paul's dalliances with other women and Jane eventually married, wrote books, and started her own magazine, appropriately named *Jane Asher's Magazine*.

   Jane Asher's importance in the history of the Beatles is profound: Not only did she inspire some of Paul's greatest songs, once during a spring cleaning session she threw away a notebook filled with lyrics to early Lennon/McCartney songs!

2. **Neil Aspinall**   The managing director of Apple and one of the Beatles' closest friends and confidants. Neil started out as the Beatles' driver and eventually became an intimate friend of everyone in the band and a critical player in the group's artistic and financial dealings. Neil was one of the only three "non-Beatles" (the others were George Martin and Derek Taylor) who were interviewed on camera for *The Beatles Anthology*.

A little-seen photo taken at Ringo and Barbara Bach's wedding reception. (*Left to right*) George and Olivia, Ringo and Barbara, Paul and Linda, and a selection of Beatle offspring. (Photofest)

3. **Richard Avedon** The fashion photographer who took some of the most famous photographs of the lads. Avedon, known for putting a subject's face half in shadow, inspired Robert Freeman's famous black-and-white *With the Beatles* cover, as well as some of Astrid Kirchherr's pix of the Fabs during their Hamburg years. Avedon is also the photographer who took the famous color psychedelic pictures of the Beatles that showed George with an eye in the palm of his hand; Ringo holding a white dove on his finger; John with "kaleidoscope" eyes; and Paul holding a sprig of flowers. Avedon photographed the Bea-

tles for the cover of the January 9, 1968, issue of *Look* magazine and for a color folio section inside the magazine. This cover photo was used later as the basis for the cover of the Beatles' *Love Songs* compilation album.

4. **Barbara Bach**   Ringo Starr's second wife. Ringo met Barbara in 1980 while they were filming his movie *Caveman*. They were married on April 27, 1981, in London and George and Olivia Harrison and Paul and Linda McCartney attended the ceremony. Ringo, with Barbara, was the only one of the former Beatles to travel to New York to be with Yoko following John Lennon's assassination.

    In 1983, Ringo and Barbara were almost killed in a car accident and for years, Ringo wore a piece of their demolished car in a lapel pin he had made to remind him of how close they had come to death. Barbara has not done much film work following *Caveman* and her marriage to Ringo. Her most visible acting roles since then were her appearances in the miniseries *Princess Daisy* and in Paul McCartney's musical, *Give My Regards to Broad Street*. In 1997, Barbara and Ringo celebrated their sixteenth wedding anniversary. They have not had any children together.

5. **Chuck Berry**   A major influence on the Beatles and, ironically, the musician John Lennon was accused of plagiarizing. Chuck Berry's songs "Roll Over Beethoven," "Johnny B. Goode," and "Rock and Roll Music" were standards for the Fabs when they were still performing live. Berry's "Roll Over Beethoven" was on their *With the Beatles* album and his "Rock and Roll Music" was on *Beatles for Sale*. Berry's blend of raunchy rock and roll and black-roots rhythm and blues greatly appealed to the Beatles in their early years and Berry's influence can be heard in many of their original songs.

    In 1969, John Lennon used the melody and lyrics of Berry's song "You Can't Catch Me" as a jumping off point for the draft of a song that would eventually become "Come Together." Today this kind of "borrowing" is considered a tribute and known as "sampling" and many artists do it and don't pay for rights to borrow riffs, melody lines, etc. (Once again, John Lennon was a visionary!) John was sued and the case was settled out of court when John agreed to perform two Chuck Berry songs on his *Rock 'N' Roll Music* album.

6. **Mona Best**   Pete Best's mother. In addition to giving birth to a Beatles drummer, Mona was the owner of the Casbah Coffee Club in Liverpool, a club that she opened in the basement of a Victorian house she and her husband John bought after World War II. The "house band" at the Casbah was the Quarry Men and some Beatles historians consider this to be an even more important venue than the Cavern Club.

    Mona Best was a staunch supporter of the boys in their earliest incarnation, obviously due to the fact that her son was in the group. All that changed when Brian Epstein entered the picture and Pete was sacked. Mona was livid but there was nothing she could do about it. John, Paul, and George had moved on and her Pete was not making the trip. Mona died of a heart attack in 1988.

7. **Pete Best**   The Beatles' "pre-Ringo" drummer. Pete was unceremoniously dumped and replaced with Ringo when George Martin decided he wasn't good enough for the group. Pete published his autobiography, *Beatle! The Pete Best Story*, in 1985. In it, Pete related the moment when Brian Epstein told him he was finished as a Beatle:

"The boys want you out and Ringo in . . ."

I was stunned and found words difficult. Only one echoed through my mind. Why, why, why?

"They don't think you're a good enough drummer, Pete," Brian went on. "And George Martin doesn't think you're a good enough drummer."

"I consider myself as good, if not better, than Ringo," I could hear myself saying. Then I asked, "Does Ringo know about this yet?"

"He's joining on Saturday," Eppy said.

Today, Pete Best is back in the music business and tours Britain regularly with his group, the Pete Best Band. He recently received some good fortune when Beatles cuts on which he played drums were included in *The Beatles Anthology.*

8. **Pattie Boyd**   George Harrison's first wife. George met Pattie during filming of *A Hard Day's Night* (she was hired as an extra) and they were married in January 1966. They divorced in June 1977. Pattie married George's friend Eric Clapton in 1979 and, seven years later, that marriage also ended in divorce.

9. **Peter Brown**   An "ex-friend" of the Beatles. (See the "Peter Brown" entry in the chapter "68 People Mentioned by Name in the Beatles' Songs" for more details on just what Brown did to alienate the Fabs and actually incite book-burning.)

10. **William Campbell**   Paul's alleged "replacement" during the "Paul Is Dead" period. There *is* no Beatle replacement named William Campbell. *Really.*

11. **Eric Clapton**   Legendary British guitarist and close friend of the Beatles. Eric plays on the *White Album* (on "While My Guitar Gently Weeps") and he married George Harrison's ex-wife Pattie Boyd.

12. **Sid Coleman**   The Beatles' first music publisher and the man who introduced Brian Epstein to George Martin.

13. **Michael Cooper**   The photographer of the *Sgt. Pepper's Lonely Hearts Club Band* album cover. Cooper committed suicide in 1970.

14. **Kyoko Cox**   Yoko Ono's daughter with Tony Cox. For a time, John and Yoko fought for custody of Kyoko but she and her father vanished and she remained with Tony Cox.

15. **Hunter Davies**   The author of the first authorized Beatles biography. Following a successful interview with Paul in 1966, Davies, a *Sunday Times* journalist, was granted permission to write the official bio of the band in January 1968. He spent 18 months with them and eventually turned in a 150,000-word manuscript which, from all reports, was heavily vetted and edited by the Beatles and their people to eliminate anything embarrassing or negative.

Following the publication of *The Beatles: The Authorized Biography,* Davies was granted another Beatles-related privilege: the London *Sunday Times* officially commissioned him to write John, Paul, George, and Ringo's obituaries when each member of the Beatles died. (Assuming, of course, that Davies survived all four.) So far, he's only had to fulfill *this* obligation once.

16. **Lonnie Donegan**   Scottish musician who was known as the "King of Skiffle" and who was an influence on the early Beatles. In 1979 Donegan performed

with Paul, George, and Ringo at a party commemorating Eric Clapton's marriage to Pattie Boyd.

17. **Bob Dylan** Legendary singer/songwriter who was a major influence on the Beatles' during their *Rubber Soul* period.

18. **Geoff Emerick** Recording engineer who was George Martin's assistant during production of some of the Beatles' most important work, including *Sgt. Pepper* and *Abbey Road*. Emerick won a Grammy for his engineering work on Paul's solo album *Band on the Run* and worked with George Martin on the remastering of the unreleased Beatles tapes ultimately released on *The Beatles Anthology* CD set.

19. **Brian Epstein** The Beatles' first manager and the man who guided them to stardom. Brian died of a drug overdose in 1967.

20. **Mal Evans** The Beatles' second road manager. He was hired by Brian Epstein to help Neil Aspinall when the Beatles were still on the road. Mal was fired when Allen Klein appeared on the Beatles' scene and he moved to Los Angeles. In January 1976 Mal was shot to death by two policemen who had been called by the woman he was living with when he began acting crazy. When the police arrived at his house, they found Mal in a manic state, waving a pistol in the air. Mal's autobiography, *Living the Beatles Legend,* remains unpublished.

21. **Marianne Faithfull** Folk singer involved with the Beatles throughout their career. Faithfull sang in the *Our World* "All You Need Is Love" video and she accompanied the Beatles and their entourage to India to visit the Maharishi.

22. **Mia Farrow** Highly regarded actress who accompanied the Beatles to India in 1968. Nearly thirty years later, Mia admitted she had a crush on John at the time.

23. **Prudence Farrow** Mia Farrow's sister and John's inspiration for his song "Dear Prudence." (She locked herself in her room to practice meditation and when John wrote the line "Won't you come out to play?" he wasn't kidding.)

24. **Peter Fonda** Actor (brother of Jane Fonda) who kept telling John Lennon at a party, "I know what it's like to be dead." This was John's inspiration for the first line of his song, "She Said She Said."

25. **Dick Fontaine** The first TV director to film the Beatles. His film of the Fabs performing "Some Other Guy" at the Cavern Club survives and has been seen in several Beatles' documentaries, including in the *Anthology* series.

26. **Russ Gibbs and Fred Labour** The two Michigan guys who started the "Paul Is Dead" rumor. (See the chapter on the "Paul Is Dead" debacle.)

27. **Richard Hamilton** The artist who came up with the idea for the stark white cover of *The Beatles,* the album which became known as the *White Album.*

28. **Bill Harry** The editor of the Liverpool music publication *Mersey Beat* and a renowned Beatles authority. Bill Harry was the first person to publish John Lennon's writings and he has written several books about the Beatles, his most recent being *The Encyclopedia of Beatles People* (London: Blandford, 1997).

29. **Dhani Harrison** George and Olivia Harrison's son. He was born in 1978 and played guitar on stage with his father at the Royal Albert Hall in 1992. His early education utilized the Montessori Method, a teaching method based on a child's natural development and growing awareness of the world as perceived through the senses. Today, in his early twenties, he is currently studying design

technology. Dhani influences his father musically and turned George on to the Black Crowes.

30. **Louise Harrison**   George Harrison's sister. Louise is beloved by Beatles fans and often appears at Beatles conventions.

31. **Olivia Harrison**   George Harrison's second wife. George met Olivia in 1974 when she was working as a secretary in the offices of his company, Dark Horse Records. They were married in September 1978, a month after the birth of their son Dhani.

32. **Buddy Holly**   Early rock guitar legend who was a big influence on the Quarry Men. The first song John Lennon ever learned to play was Holly's "That'll Be the Day." Holly's band the Crickets inspired Stu Sutcliffe to suggest another insect name and that's how they came up with "Beetles" (John later changed the *e* to an *a*). In the mid-seventies, Paul McCartney bought the Buddy Holly song catalog.

33. **Dick James**   The music publisher who initially acquired the publishing rights to almost all of the Beatles' songs through his company Northern Songs, a division of Dick James Music.

34. **Astrid Kirchherr**   The blond German photographer who, in 1960, gave boyfriend Stu Sutcliffe a "mushroom" haircut that was soon adopted by the other Beatles and ultimately became known as the Beatles "moptop." George was the first one to allow Astrid to cut his hair in this style, then Paul, and, finally, John.

35. **Allen Klein**   The business manager retained by all the Beatles except Paul to straighten out the mess their finances had become by the late sixties. Klein was good at his job and thanks to new contracts he negotiated with the Beatles' record companies, the Fabs finally started to *really* see some of the big money their records had been making for others for so many years.

36. **Cynthia Lennon**   John Lennon's first wife. John met Cynthia in school in 1957 and they were married in August 1963. At the time of their marriage, Cynthia had already given birth to their son, John Charles Julian, in June 1963. John and Cynthia were divorced in 1969 after Cynthia learned of John's ongoing affair with Yoko Ono. In 1978, Cynthia published a book about her life with John called *A Twist of Lennon.* She periodically attends Beatles conventions and is respected and admired by Beatles fans around the world.

37. **Julia Lennon**   John Lennon's mother and the inspiration for his song "Julia."

38. **Julian Lennon**   John and Cynthia Lennon's son. Julian is a singer/songwriter like his father and made his debut with an album called *Valotte* on which he sounds (and looks) *uncannily* like his dad.

39. **Sean Lennon**   John Lennon and Yoko Ono's son and John's inspiration for his post-Beatles song, "Beautiful Boy." Sean has a band and has recently been playing and recording with his mother.

40. **Richard Lester**   The legendary director of *A Hard Day's Night* and *Help!*

41. **Mark Lewisohn**   The Beatles expert and author of what Paul McCartney refers to as "The Bible," *The Beatles Recording Sessions.*

42. **Maharishi Mahesh Yogi**   The Indian guru who seduced the Beatles in the late sixties with his talk of transcendental meditation and world peace. The Fabs became disillusioned with the Maharishi after a brief infatuation and severed

John's first wife, Cynthia, shares memories in the 1988 film, *Imagine: John Lennon*. (Photofest)

Julian Lennon, son of John and Cynthia, is also depicted in the film, *Imagine: John Lennon*. (Photofest)

ties with him. The Maharishi inspired John's scathing diatribe "Sexy Sadie," which he wrote with the working title of "Maharishi."

43. **Charles Manson**   The insane mass murderer who believed that the Beatles' *White Album* was a musical message to him, instructing him to fulfill Biblical prophecies that required him and his followers to go on killing sprees. When asked about Manson's delusions, John said, "Well, he's barmy. He's like any other Beatles fan who reads mysticism into it. I don't know what 'Helter Skelter' had to do with knifing somebody." Manson believed that "Blackbird" meant that blacks were going to destroy the white race and that the "bang bang shoot shoot" chorus in "Happiness is a Warm Gun" was an instruction manual.

44. **George Martin**   The Beatles' longtime recording manager and producer and one of the major contributors to capturing their genius on tape. George Martin's work on early Beatles albums and singles was good basic producing and engineering. Martin's gift for eliciting the absolute best from the Beatles came during what he calls "the studio years," that period from the mid-sixties until their breakup when they had stopped performing live and did all their work in the studio.

George's engineering masterpiece is unquestionably *Sgt. Pepper's Lonely Hearts Club Band*. He worked with Paul on many of his solo projects. His autobiography, *All You Need Is Ears,* was published in 1979.

George worked on *The Beatles Anthology* but Paul, George, and Ringo chose Electric Light Orchestra's Jeff Lynne to produce their new singles "Free as a Bird" and "Real Love" because George Harrison was reportedly concerned about George Martin's seventy-year-old hearing. George Martin retired in January 1996.

45. **Heather McCartney**   Linda Eastman McCartney's daughter from her marriage to Melvin See. Heather was born on New Year's Eve, 1963, in Colorado. When Paul and Linda were wed in 1969, Paul officially adopted six-year-old Heather as his daughter.

     After an eclectic range of jobs, the artistic genes from her mother and the creative vibe given off by her stepfather kicked in and today, Heather is a respected potter. In spring 1997, she had two big exhibitions of her work in London and New York. In June 1997, Paul McCartney spoke proudly of Heather and her work during a Town Hall meeting on MTV to promote his new CD, *Flaming Pie*.

46. **James McCartney**   Paul and Linda's only son. In 1997, at the age of twenty, he played guitar on his father's CD *Flaming Pie*. He is currently attending college.

47. **Linda Eastman McCartney**   Paul McCartney's wife. Paul met Linda in 1967 and they were married in 1969. Paul taught Linda to play keyboards and he made her a member of his band Wings. Linda is a respected photographer and has authored a bestselling book of vegetarian recipes. She also created a successful line of vegetarian frozen dinners. Her most recent involvement in a "Paul-related" project was her appearance in the 1997 video for Paul's *Flaming Pie* song "The World Tonight." In 1996 Linda was diagnosed with breast cancer and died from it on April 17, 1998.

48. **Mary McCartney**   Paul McCartney's mother and the inspiration for his song, "Let It Be." Mary died when Paul was a teen.

49. **Mary McCartney**   Paul and Linda's first daughter. Mary works for her father's music publishing company MPL.

50. **Mike McCartney**   Paul McCartney's brother, known in the music industry as "Mike McGear." Mike and his brother first worked together in 1968 when Paul produced Mike's album, *McGough and McGear*. Paul later produced Mike's album, *McGear*. Mike also writes children's books and is a professional photographer. One of his photo books, *Thank U Very Much: Mike McCartney's Family Album*, tells the story of Paul's family in pictures.

51. **Stella McCartney**   Paul and Linda's second daughter. Stella is a highly regarded fashion designer with Ralph Lauren.

52. **Murray the K**   The American disk jockey who became known as the Fifth Beatle due to his unabashed enthusiasm and wholehearted support for the Beatles during their early forays into the United States.

53. **Jimmy Nicol**   The unknown British drummer who was once in the Beatles. When Ringo was in the hospital having his tonsils removed in 1964, Jimmy Nicol was hired to fill in for him during Beatles performances in Copenhagen, Holland, Hong Kong, and their first four shows in Australia. Ringo rejoined the boys in Melbourne on June 14, 1964. Jimmy slipped back into obscurity.

     At first, George was adamant about not performing without Ringo, even to the point of telling Brian Epstein that he would need to get *two* replacements if they used Nicol. George eventually relented and Nicol not only played with the Beatles for several concerts, he also appeared at all the press conferences the group did. As might be imagined, many questions were directed at Jimmy and revolved around what it was like to suddenly be a member of the most popular and successful band in history. Nicol was appropriately self-effacing and humble and the temporary reshuffling of Beatle personnel did not impact one whit the group's worldwide popularity. (Although Beatles fans certainly knew what was going on: At many of Nicol's appearances, fans held up signs that expressed get well wishes for Ringo.)

54. **Yoko Ono**   John Lennon's second wife. Yoko took a bad rap in the late sixties when the Beatles were each beginning to go his own way. She was accused of splitting up the group when, in reality, Paul's release of his solo album *McCartney* and his December 1970 lawsuit seeking to dissolve The Beatles and Company were the catalysts that severed all ties among the Fab Four.

Yoko was unquestionably John Lennon's soulmate. They were virtually inseparable until his death in 1980. Whatever personal creative transformations John worked his way through following the breakup of the Beatles, it must be acknowledged that Yoko was instrumental in serving as his muse during this period.

In an October 23, 1995, interview with *Newsweek,* Yoko addressed the charges that her presence in the studio was what alienated Paul, George, and Ringo and ultimately split up the group: "I was just trying to sit there very quietly without disturbing them," she said. "You know, John always wanted me there and if I was not there, John might not have gone to those sessions. So think of that side of it. If he didn't go to those sessions, maybe *Abbey Road* and the *White Album*—maybe all those albums wouldn't have been made." She's got a point, wouldn't you agree?

Artistically, Yoko's output has been a mixed bag of pleasant-enough standards-like tunes and screeching, yodeling, experimental sound collages. Her work influenced later groups, including the B-52s, whose eighties hit "Rock Lobster" could easily be mistaken for a Yoko Ono song. In the mid-nineties Yoko wrote and produced the original musical *New York Rock* and has lately been working with her son Sean on a range of musical projects.

After John's death, Yoko's respect for his legend and her willingness to work with the surviving Beatles has endeared her to Beatles fans and erased much of the rancor many held for her when John was alive. Yoko is the keeper of the flame and she clearly understands precisely what being John Lennon's widow means.

Yoko willingly participated in *The Beatles Anthology*—but only behind the scenes—and thanks to her, we now have the "new" Beatles recordings "Free as a Bird" and "Real Love." As to why she refused to appear in the documentary, she said, "It was much more important that John get the right amount of space." Right answer.

55. **Alun Owen**   The British screenwriter who penned the Beatles first feature film, *A Hard Day's Night.* Paul McCartney was the one who suggested that Owen write the screenplay for their first film. Interestingly, one scene that was cut from the film included the following dialogue intended for Paul: "I know your sort—two Cokes and a packet of cheese and onion crisps suddenly it's love and we're stopping in an empty street doorway."

The Beatles parody group the Rutles performed a song on their first album called "Cheese and Onions" (actually written by Neil Innes) which sounded so much like a John Lennon song that it was actually included on a bootleg recording as a Lennon original.

After *A Hard Day's Night,* Alun Owen completed *Maggie May,* a musical based on a Liverpool folk song. Owen died in 1994 at the age of 69.

56. **May Pang**   John and Yoko's secretary. May accompanied John to California in the early seventies during the eighteen months' "lost weekend" he was separated from Yoko. They became lovers during that period and in 1983, May published a book about their affair called *Loving John—The Untold Story.*

57. **Elvis Presley**   The King.

58. **Billy Preston**   Respected session keyboardist who worked with the Beatles during *Let It Be.* Preston first met the Beatles in Hamburg when he was touring with Little Richard. Initially he became friends with George and eventually the Beatles bought out his Vee Jay contract and signed him to Apple. Billy Preston enjoys the honor of being the first musician to ever share label credit with the Beatles. The Beatles' "Get Back" single was released as "The Beatles with Billy Preston."

59. **Dick Rowe**   Somewhat shortsighted Decca record executive. How would you like to be known in the music industry as the record executive who turned down the Beatles? (This is akin to being the editor who rejected the young Stephen King as unpublishable.) Dick Rowe was the Decca bigwig who listened to Mike Smith's New Year's Day 1962 audition tapes of the Beatles and rejected the band as Decca recording artists, telling Brian Epstein that guitar groups were on their way out—although Rowe eventually signed another guitar group that did rather well, the Rolling Stones. As related in *A Cellarful of Noise,* Rowe said, "Not to mince words, Mr. Epstein, we don't like your boys' sound." Some Beatles scholars think that Mike Smith made the final decision, but Epstein claims it was Rowe. Rowe died from complications of diabetes in 1986.

60. **Tom Schultheiss**   Michigan publisher known for his definitive Beatles reference books. Schultheiss, also the author of *The Beatles: A Day in the Life,* is responsible for such comprehensive and groundbreaking Beatles discographies as *All Together Now, The Beatles Again,* and *The End of the Beatles?*

61. **Ravi Shankar**   Indian sitarist who was a major musical influence on George Harrison and who continues to have a close personal and professional relationship with the ex-Beatle.

62. **Helen Shapiro**   The headliner of the Beatles very first concert tour. (See the entry "George's Embarrassment" in the chapter "78 'Toppermost of the Poppermost' Moments from *The Beatles Anthology*" for details on the Shapiro tour.)

63. **Tony Sheridan**   Popular sixties singer for whom the early Beatles played backup and with whom they recorded the much sought-after single "My Bonnie."

64. **Pete Shotton**   John Lennon's childhood friend and author of *John Lennon in My Life.*

65. **Mike Smith**   The Decca executive who auditioned and recorded the Beatles on New Year's Day 1962.

66. **Phil Spector**   The "Wall of Sound" record producer who completed the mixing of the *Let It Be* album. Some of his artistic choices were not met with glee by the Beatles (for instance, the oh-so-lush strings on "The Long and Winding Road") but by the time the record was recorded no one really seemed to have

any interest in completing it. Spector was brought in to essentially "salvage" the album.

67. **Victor Spinetti**   The only actor to appear in all three live-action Beatles films, *A Hard Day's Night, Help!,* and *Magical Mystery Tour.*

68. **Jason Starkey**   Ringo and Maureen Starkey's son, born in 1967. Jason did not like the notoriety that came with being "Ringo's son" and for a time rebelled against his famous name by getting involved with stealing and drugs. In 1995, nearing the age of thirty, he was known to be playing drums in a pub band.

69. **Maureen Cox Starkey**   Ringo Starr's first wife and the mother of his three children, Jason, Lee, and Zak. Ringo began dating Maureen during the Beatles' Cavern Club days and they were married February 11, 1965. They divorced on July 17, 1975. Maureen died of leukemia in December 1994. (In a promotional interview for his 1997 CD, *Flaming Pie,* Paul revealed that he wrote the *Flaming Pie* song "Little Willow" after hearing of Maureen's death.)

70. **Zak Starkey**   Ringo and Maureen Starkey's son. (See the chapter "6 Famous Musicians and Bands with which Ringo's Son Zak Starkey Has Played Drums" for details on Zak's career.)

71. **Rory Storm**   Leader of Rory Storm and the Hurricanes, the band in which Ringo played before joining the Beatles.

72. **Ed Sullivan**   The host of *The Ed Sullivan Show* and a big promoter of the Beatles during their early years in America. The Beatles appeared on Ed's show four times during their career (twice in performance and twice in videos) and Sullivan was the one who introduced the Fabs at their record-breaking August 1965 Shea Stadium concert.

    On February 4, 1964, Ed Sullivan introduced the Beatles for their first appearance on his show with the following:

> Now, yesterday and today, our theater's been jammed with newspapermen and hundreds of photographers from all over the nation, and these veterans agree with me that the city never has witnessed the excitement stirred by these youngsters from Liverpool who call themselves the Beatles.

73. **Stuart Sutcliffe**   Painter who became a musician to join the Quarry Men. (See the chapter on the several early incarnations of the Beatles for more details on Stu.)

74. **Derek Taylor**   The Beatles' press officer, confidant, and friend. A *major* player in the Beatles universe. Derek died in 1997 after a long battle with cancer.

75. **James Taylor**   Singer/songwriter known for his sensitive and intelligent ballads. James was one of the first artists signed to the Beatles' Apple label.

76. **Ivan Vaughan**   The Liverpudlian who introduced John Lennon to Paul McCartney on July 6, 1957. Ivan was an original Quarry Man and later on became very close friends with Paul McCartney. Ivan died of Parkinson's disease in 1994.

77. **Klaus Voorman**   The artist who designed the groundbreaking *Revolver* cover.

78. **Andy White**   The session drummer who played on the Beatles' first single, "Love Me Do." (At the time, George Martin didn't think that Ringo was up to the task.) This single (the one in which no tambourine—played by Ringo—can be heard) still exists and is sought after by Beatles collectors.

23. 15 Occupations of the Fathers of the Beatles

ALFRED LENNON
Father of John Lennon

Relationship with John   Good and bad. Even though Freddie was at sea when John was born and had little to do with his boy until he was twenty, father and son reestablished contact when John was a Beatle and from that point on, John sent his father money every month. Later, though, when John was in his thirties, he rejected his father (apparently after recalling his father's less-than-stellar parenting skills) and, according to biographer Albert Goldman, even threatened his life at one point. After six years of estrangement, however, John called his father as he lay dying of cancer in a nursing home. They apparently reconciled their differences (as well as they could over the phone) before Freddie died in April 1976.

1. Clerk
2. Merchant seaman
3. Porter in a London hotel

JAMES McCARTNEY
Father of Paul McCartney

Relationship with Paul   Excellent. After he became famous, Paul bought his father a house and arranged for him to have a steady income. (Paul's mother, Mary, had died when Paul was just a teen.) Since James was also a musician, he and Paul shared much in common and even collaborated creatively when Paul put words to his father's instrumental tune "Eloise" and released it in 1974 as the song, "Walking in the Park With Eloise." (The song was performed by Wings with Floyd Cramer and Chet Atkins and released as a single by the Country Hams.) Jim McCartney died in March 1976.

4. Cotton Exchange worker
5. Professional pianist with the Masked Melody Makers

HAROLD HARRISON
Father of George Harrison

Relationship with George   Close. In 1965, George gave his father five times what he was making as a bus driver to persuade him to retire early. George later bought his parents a house on three acres of land in Cheshire, England. Harold kept in very close and frequent contact with his famous son and even traveled with him when he toured. (Harold was with George on his successful 1974 *Dark Horse* tour.) Harold died of emphysema in May 1978.

6. Delivery boy
7. First class steward on a cruise ship
8. Bus conductor

9. Bus driver
10. Union official
11. Master of ceremonies at the Speke Depot Social Club
12. Ballroom dancing instructor

RICHARD STARKEY
Father of Ringo Starr

Relationship with Ringo Essentially nonexistent. Richard left the family when Ringo was only three and apparently had almost no contact with Ringo from that point on except for casual encounters. (He did, however, continue to send thirty shillings a week back home to help support his wife and son.) After Ringo became famous, a reporter for the London *Daily Express* tracked the elder Starkey down in the northern English town where he was living and working. "He's done well, the lad, and good luck to him," he said. "But he owes me nothing." Starkey Sr. did admit, however, to owning an autographed photo of the Beatles. It was the one and only piece of Beatles memorabilia in his possession.

13. Liverpool dockworker
14. Baker
15. Window cleaner

A little-seen still of Paul at the piano in 1964, possibly composing one of the 52 Beatles songs he alone penned. (Photofest)

The Singer's Gonna Sing a Song . . .

24. A Song-by-Song Breakdown of Who Wrote the 205 Beatles Songs

From the very beginning, John Lennon and Paul McCartney agreed that any Beatles song they recorded would be published as a "Lennon/McCartney" composition.

So when the Beatles were the Beatles, the world believed that the brilliant songs they kept coming up with were the result of a rare, artistically flawless collaboration between John Lennon and Paul McCartney.

We soon knew better.

After the breakup, both Paul and John began speaking openly about who wrote what, and it was learned that just over 50 of the songs recorded by the Beatles were actually written by John and Paul together. In many cases, Paul or John would only contribute a line or two to a song that was essentially written by the other.

This feature looks at who wrote what. There are many interviews with John and Paul in which they discuss their songwriting credits, and many books about the Beatles that analyze individual songs.

If John and Paul had *anything at all* to do with one another's songs, I have credited the song as a Lennon/McCartney collaboration.

For example, "Norwegian Wood (This Bird Has Flown)" was always believed to have been written solely by John Lennon. In fact, in a 1980 interview with *Playboy,* John said, " 'Norwegian Wood' is my song completely." Yet, in 1972, John told *Hit Parader* magazine that he wrote the song, "but Paul helped me on the lyric." "Norwegian Wood," then, is credited as a Lennon/McCartney song.

Likewise, "Blackbird" was always thought of as a Paul McCartney song—and it is. John admitted in his 1980 *Playboy* interview "I gave him a line on that one," thus "Blackbird" must also be considered a Lennon/McCartney tune.

Since it is our belief that any creative contribution by a Beatle can not—and should not—be ignored or dismissed, we have elected to be meticulous (obsessive?) in acknowledging any and all creative collaborations in the creation of the Beatles' songs.

A NOTE TO THE PURISTS:
A WORD ABOUT CRITERIA

Any song officially released on a recording by the Beatles through Apple or Capitol with the full cooperation of the Beatles is included on this list.

This includes several Beatle-penned cuts from *The Beatles Anthology* and the BBC releases that were previously available only on bootlegs or on solo recordings by one of the Fabs. Thus, songs that are universally considered solo hits—George's "All Things Must Pass," Paul's "Junk," and even Badfinger's "Come and Get It"—got their starts before the band broke up and are included here because versions of these songs were released on *The Beatles Anthology*. As nitpicky as this might appear to be, if we're going to be complete, these songs *must* be considered Beatles recordings.

Also, we deliberately did *not* include Beatles cover songs, such as "Twist and Shout," "Till There Was You," and other songs not written by one of the boys—no matter how successful the Beatles were with these recordings. These cuts may be Beatles *recordings,* and the Beatles were often a great cover band, but these cover tunes sure as heck aren't Beatles *songs.*

The songs on this list are from the U.S. and U.K. Beatles albums and CDs, the complete *Anthology* series, and the *Live at the BBC* album.

A

1. "Across the Universe" (John Lennon)
2. "All I've Got to Do" (John Lennon)
3. "All My Loving" (Paul McCartney)
4. "All Things Must Pass" (George Harrison)
5. "All Together Now" (Paul McCartney)
6. "All You Need Is Love" (John Lennon)
7. "And I Love Her" (John Lennon/Paul McCartney)
8. "And Your Bird Can Sing" (John Lennon)
9. "Another Girl" (Paul McCartney)
10. "Any Time at All" (John Lennon)
11. "Ask Me Why" (John Lennon)

B

12. "Baby, You're a Rich Man" (John Lennon/Paul McCartney)
13. "Baby's in Black" (John Lennon/Paul McCartney)
14. "Back in the U.S.S.R." (Paul McCartney)
15. "The Ballad of John and Yoko" (John Lennon)
16. "Because" (John Lennon)
17. "Being for the Benefit of Mr. Kite!" (John Lennon)
18. "Birthday" (John Lennon/Paul McCartney)
19. "Blackbird" (John Lennon/Paul McCartney)

C

20. "Can't Buy Me Love" (John Lennon/Paul McCartney)
21. "Carry That Weight" (Paul McCartney)
22. "Cayenne" (Paul McCartney)
23. "Christmas Time (Is Here Again)" (John Lennon/Paul McCartney/George Harrison/Ringo Starr)
24. "Come and Get It" (Paul McCartney)
25. "Come Together" (John Lennon)
26. "The Continuing Story of Bungalow Bill" (John Lennon)

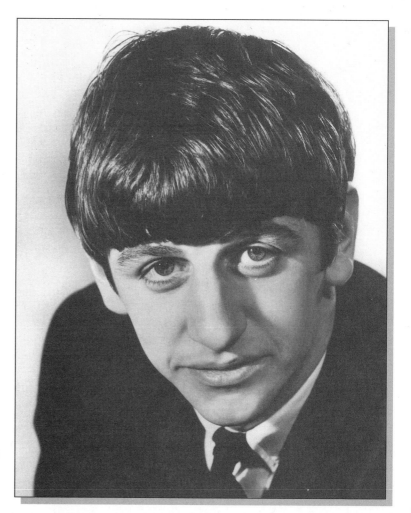

Ringo, composer of two
Beatles tunes. (Photofest)

E

39. "Eight Days a Week" (John Lennon/Paul McCartney)
40. "Eleanor Rigby" (John Lennon/Paul McCartney)
41. "The End" (Paul McCartney)
42. "Everybody's Got Something to Hide Except Me and My Monkey" (John Lennon)
43. "Every Little Thing" (John Lennon/Paul McCartney)

F

44. "Fixing a Hole" (Paul McCartney)
45. "Flying" (John Lennon/Paul McCartney/George Harrison/Ringo Starr)
46. "The Fool on the Hill" (Paul McCartney)
47. "For No One" (Paul McCartney)
48. "Free as a Bird" (John Lennon/Paul McCartney/George Harrison/ Ringo Starr)
49. "From Me to You" (John Lennon/Paul McCartney)

G

50. "Get Back" (Paul McCartney)
51. "Getting Better" (John Lennon/Paul McCartney)
52. "Girl" (John Lennon)
53. "Glass Onion" (John Lennon)
54. "Golden Slumbers" (Paul McCartney)
55. "Good Day Sunshine" (Paul McCartney)
56. "Good Morning, Good Morning" (John Lennon)
57. "Good Night" (John Lennon)
58. "Got to Get You Into My Life" (Paul McCartney)

H

59. "Happiness is a Warm Gun" (John Lennon)
60. "A Hard Day's Night" (John Lennon)
61. "Hello Goodbye" (Paul McCartney)
62. "Hello Little Girl" (John Lennon)
63. "Help!" (John Lennon/Paul McCartney)
64. "Helter Skelter" (Paul McCartney)
65. "Her Majesty" (Paul McCartney)
66. "Here Comes the Sun" (George Harrison)
67. "Here, There and Everywhere" (Paul McCartney)
68. "Hey Bulldog" (John Lennon/Paul McCartney)
69. "Hey Jude" (Paul McCartney)
70. "Hold Me Tight" (John Lennon/Paul McCartney)
71. "Honey Pie" (Paul McCartney)

I

72. "I Am the Walrus" (John Lennon)
73. "I Call Your Name" (John Lennon)
74. "I Dig a Pony" (a.k.a. "Dig a Pony") (John Lennon)

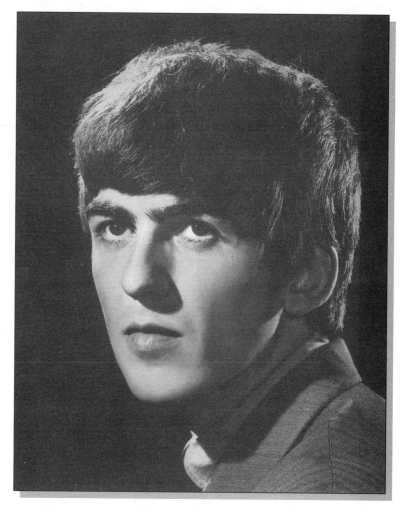

George checks in with 22 Beatles songs. (Photofest)

75. "I Don't Want to Spoil the Party" (John Lennon)
76. "I Feel Fine" (John Lennon)
77. "I Me Mine" (George Harrison)
78. "I Need You" (George Harrison)
79. "I Saw Her Standing There" (John Lennon/Paul McCartney)
80. "I Should Have Known Better" (John Lennon)
81. "I Wanna Be Your Man" (John Lennon/Paul McCartney)
82. "I Want to Hold Your Hand" (John Lennon/Paul McCartney)
83. "I Want to Tell You" (George Harrison)
84. "I Want You (She's So Heavy)" (John Lennon)
85. "I Will" (Paul McCartney)
86. "If I Fell" (John Lennon)
87. "If I Needed Someone" (George Harrison)
88. "If You've Got Trouble" (John Lennon/Paul McCartney)
89. "I'll Be Back" (John Lennon)
90. "I'll Be on My Way" (John Lennon/Paul McCartney)
91. "I'll Cry Instead" (John Lennon)
92. "I'll Follow the Sun" (Paul McCartney)

93. "I'll Get You" (John Lennon/Paul McCartney)
94. "I'm a Loser" (John Lennon)
95. "I'm Down" (John Lennon/Paul McCartney)
96. "I'm Happy Just to Dance With You" (John Lennon)
97. "I'm Looking Through You" (Paul McCartney)
98. "I'm Only Sleeping" (John Lennon)
99. "I'm So Tired" (John Lennon)
100. "In My Life" (John Lennon/Paul McCartney)
101. "In Spite of All the Danger" (Paul McCartney/George Harrison)
102. "It Won't Be Long" (John Lennon)
103. "It's All Too Much" (George Harrison)
104. "It's Only Love" (John Lennon)
105. "I've Got a Feeling" (John Lennon/Paul McCartney)
106. "I've Just Seen a Face" (Paul McCartney)

J

107. "Julia" (John Lennon)
108. "Junk" (Paul McCartney)

L

109. "Lady Madonna" (Paul McCartney)
110. "Let It Be" (Paul McCartney)
111. "Like Dreamers Do" (Paul McCartney)
112. "Little Child" (John Lennon/Paul McCartney)
113. "The Long and Winding Road" (Paul McCartney)
114. "Long, Long, Long" (George Harrison)
115. "Los Paranoias" (John Lennon/Paul McCartney/George Harrison/
     Ringo Starr)
116. "Love of the Loved" (John Lennon/Paul McCartney)
117. "Love Me Do" (John Lennon/Paul McCartney)
118. "Love You To" (George Harrison)
119. "Lovely Rita" (Paul McCartney)
120. "Lucy in the Sky With Diamonds" (John Lennon/Paul McCartney)

M

121. "Magical Mystery Tour" (John Lennon/Paul McCartney)
122. "Martha My Dear" (Paul McCartney)
123. "Maxwell's Silver Hammer" (Paul McCartney)
124. "Mean Mr. Mustard" (John Lennon)
125. "Michelle" (John Lennon/Paul McCartney)
126. "Misery" (John Lennon/Paul McCartney)
127. "Mother Nature's Son" (Paul McCartney)

N

128. "The Night Before" (Paul McCartney)
129. "No Reply" (John Lennon)
130. "Norwegian Wood (This Bird Has Flown)" (John Lennon/
     Paul McCartney)

131. "Not a Second Time" (John Lennon)
132. "Not Guilty" (George Harrison)
133. "Nowhere Man" (John Lennon)

O

134. "Ob-La-Di, Ob-La-Da" (Paul McCartney)
135. "Octopus's Garden" (Ringo Starr)
136. "Oh! Darling" (Paul McCartney)
137. "Old Brown Shoe" (George Harrison)
138. "One After 909" (John Lennon)
139. "Only a Northern Song" (George Harrison)

P

140. "Paperback Writer" (John Lennon/Paul McCartney)
141. "Penny Lane" (John Lennon/Paul McCartney)
142. "Piggies" (George Harrison)
143. "Please Please Me" (John Lennon)
144. "Polythene Pam" (John Lennon)
145. "P. S. I Love You" (John Lennon/Paul McCartney)

R

146. "Rain" (John Lennon)
147. "Real Love" (John Lennon)
148. "Revolution" (John Lennon)
149. "Revolution 1" (John Lennon)
150. "Revolution 9" (John Lennon)
151. "Rocky Raccoon" (Paul McCartney)
152. "Run for Your Life" (John Lennon)

S

153. "Savoy Truffle" (George Harrison)
154. "Sexy Sadie" (John Lennon)
155. "Sgt. Pepper's Lonely Hearts Club Band" (Paul McCartney)
156. "She Came in Through the Bathroom Window" (Paul McCartney)
157. "She Loves You" (John Lennon/Paul McCartney)
158. "She Said She Said" (John Lennon)
159. "She's a Woman" (John Lennon/Paul McCartney)
160. "She's Leaving Home" (John Lennon/Paul McCartney)
161. "Something" (George Harrison)
162. "Step Inside Love" (Paul McCartney)
163. "Strawberry Fields Forever" (John Lennon)
164. "Sun King" (John Lennon)

T

165. "Taxman" (George Harrison)
166. "Teddy Boy" (Paul McCartney)
167. "Tell Me What You See" (Paul McCartney)
168. "Tell Me Why" (John Lennon)

John was undoubtedly proud of his 70 Beatles ditties. (Photofest)

169. "Thank You Girl" (John Lennon/Paul McCartney)
170. "That Means a Lot" (Paul McCartney)
171. "There's a Place" (John Lennon)
172. "Things We Said Today" (Paul McCartney)
173. "Think For Yourself" (George Harrison)
174. "This Boy" (John Lennon)
175. "Ticket to Ride" (John Lennon)
176. "Tomorrow Never Knows" (John Lennon)
177. "12-Bar Original" (John Lennon/Paul McCartney/
     George Harrison/Ringo Starr)
178. "Two of Us" (Paul McCartney)

W

179. "Wait" (John Lennon/Paul McCartney)
180. "We Can Work It Out" (John Lennon/Paul McCartney)
181. "What Goes On" (John Lennon/Paul McCartney)
182. "What You're Doing" (John Lennon/Paul McCartney)
183. "What's the New Mary Jane" (John Lennon)

184. "When I Get Home" (John Lennon)
185. "When I'm Sixty-Four" (John Lennon/Paul McCartney)
186. "While My Guitar Gently Weeps" (George Harrison)
187. "Why Don't We Do It in the Road?" (Paul McCartney)
188. "Wild Honey Pie" (Paul McCartney)
189. "With a Little Help From My Friends" (John Lennon/Paul McCartney)
190. "Within You Without You" (George Harrison)
191. "The Word" (John Lennon/Paul McCartney)

Y

192. "Yellow Submarine" (John Lennon/Paul McCartney)
193. "Yer Blues" (John Lennon)
194. "Yes It Is" (John Lennon)
195. "Yesterday" (Paul McCartney)
196. "You Can't Do That" (John Lennon)
197. "You Know My Name (Look Up the Number)" (John Lennon)
198. "You Know What to Do" (George Harrison)
199. "You Like Me Too Much" (George Harrison)
200. "You Never Give Me Your Money" (Paul McCartney)
201. "You Won't See Me" (Paul McCartney)
202. "You'll Be Mine" (Paul McCartney/John Lennon)
203. "Your Mother Should Know" (Paul McCartney)
204. "You're Gonna Lose That Girl" (John Lennon)
205. "You've Got to Hide Your Love Away" (John Lennon)

205 Songs Total
70 Songs written by John Lennon
52 Songs written by Paul McCartney
22 Songs written by George Harrison
 2 Songs written by Ringo Starr
52 Songs cowritten by John and Paul
 1 Song cowritten by John and George
 1 Song cowritten by Paul and George
 5 Songs cowritten by John, Paul, George, and Ringo

25. 30 Geographic Locations Mentioned in Beatles Songs

I remember an old college professor of mine who used to drill into our heads the writing rule, "Be specific!" His point was that "Colonial Drive was blanketed in fog" is stronger than "The street was blanketed in fog." He was right. When you consider the specificity with which the Beatles composed their lyrics, it seems as though the Fabs learned that lesson early on. The Beatles were always fond of using geographical place names in their songs and here is a listing of thirty of them.

Amsterdam (in "The Ballad of John and Yoko") ▪ Arizona (in "Get Back") ▪
The Atlantic (in "Honey Pie") ▪ Blackburn, Lancashire (in "A Day in the Life") ▪
The Black Hills (in "Rocky Raccoon") ▪ Blue Jay Way, Los Angeles (in "Blue Jay
Way") ▪ California (in "Get Back") ▪ Dakota (in "Rocky Raccoon") ▪ England
(in "Honey Pie") ▪ France (in "The Ballad of John And Yoko") ▪ Georgia (in
"Back in the U.S.S.R.") ▪ Gibraltar (in "The Ballad of John and Yoko") ▪
Holland (in "The Ballad of John and Yoko") ▪ Hollywood (in "Honey Pie") ▪
The Isle of Wight (in "When I'm Sixty-Four") ▪ Kircaldy (in "Cry Baby Cry") ▪
L.A. (in "Blue Jay Way") ▪ Lime Street (in "Maggie Mae") ▪ London (in "The
Ballad of John and Yoko") ▪ Miami Beach (in "Back in the U.S.S.R.") ▪ Moscow
(in "Back in the U.S.S.R.") ▪ Paris (in "The Ballad of John and Yoko") ▪ Penny
Lane (in "Penny Lane") ▪ The Seine (in "The Ballad of John and Yoko") ▪
Southampton (in "The Ballad of John and Yoko") ▪ Spain (in "The Ballad
of John and Yoko") ▪ Tucson, Arizona (in "Get Back") ▪ The Ukraine
(in "Back in the U.S.S.R.") ▪ The U.S.S.R. (in "Back in the U.S.S.R.") ▪
The United States (in "Honey Pie")

26. The 2 Beatles Songs in Which the Boys Are "On Bended Knees"

"Tell Me Why" This John Lennon composition first appeared in and on *A Hard Day's Night* and includes the line, "Well, I beg you on my bended knees." It was recorded on Thursday, February 27, 1964, and included John on rhythm guitar and lead vocal, Paul on bass and harmony vocal, George on lead guitar, and Ringo on drums.

"One After 909" This was one of the first songs John Lennon ever wrote and it includes the lyric, "I begged her not to go and I begged her on my bended knee." It was recorded on Thursday, January 30, 1969, and included John on lead guitar and lead vocal, Paul on bass and lead vocal, George on rhythm guitar, Ringo on drums, and Billy Preston on organ.

Note: The Ringo-crooned song "Act Naturally" (the B-side of the "Yesterday" single) also includes a "bended knee" reference but since it is not a Beatles composition, it is mentioned here only for completeness.

27. 39 Working Titles of Beatles Songs

As is common practice with all creative artists, the Beatles often assigned working titles to their compositions in progress.

Sometimes, as in the case of "Thank You Girl," a song whose original title was "Thank You Little Girl," they would ultimately truncate the working title to something catchier. This makes sense and is understandable as part of the creative process.

There are inexplicable working titles, such as "Laxton's Superb," which ultimately became "I Want to Tell You," or "This Is Some Friendly," which ended up on the *White Album* as Ringo's relentlessly bouncy "Don't Pass Me By."

This feature looks at thirty-nine ways the Fab Four kept track of what songs they were working on and recording . . . before even they knew what the final name of the tune would be!

This Classic Beatle Song . . .	*Started Out As . . .*
1. "Cry for a Shadow" (The only known George Harrison/ John Lennon composition)	"Beatle Bop"
2. "I Saw Her Standing There"	"Seventeen"
3. "Thank You Girl"	"Thank You Little Girl"
4. "I'll Get You"	"Get You in the End"
5. "It's Only Love"	"That's a Nice Hat-Cap"
6. "I've Just Seen a Face"	"Auntie Gin's Theme"
7. "Yesterday"	"Scrambled Eggs"
8. "Norwegian Wood (This Bird Has Flown)"	"This Bird Has Flown"
9. "Think for Yourself"	"Won't Be There With You"
10. "Eleanor Rigby"	"Daisy Hawkins"
11. "Love You To"	"Granny Smith"
12. "She Said She Said"	Untitled
13. "Good Day Sunshine"	"A Good Day's Sunshine"
14. "I Want to Tell You"	"Laxton's Superb," then "I Don't Know"
15. "Tomorrow Never Knows"	"The Void," then "Mark I"
16. "Penny Lane"	Untitled
17. "With a Little Help From My Friends"	"Bad Finger Boogie"
18. "Within You Without You"	Untitled
19. "A Day in the Life"	"In the Life of . . ."
20. "Hello Goodbye"	"Hello Hello"
21. "Flying"	"Aerial Tour Instrumental"
22. "The Inner Light"	Untitled
23. "Only a Northern Song"	"Not Known"
24. "It's All Too Much"	"Too Much"
25. "Happiness Is a Warm Gun"	"Happiness Is a Warm Gun in Your Hand"
26. "Don't Pass Me By"	Ringo's Tune (untitled); then "This Is Some Friendly"
27. "Revolution 1"	"Revolution"
28. "Everybody's Got Something to Hide Except Me and My Monkey"	Untitled
29. "Long Long Long"	"It's Been a Long Long Long Time"
30. "Good Night"	Untitled

This Classic Beatle Song . . .	*Started Out As . . .*
31. "Two of Us"	"On Our Way Home"
32. "Dig a Pony"	"All I Want Is You"
33. "For You Blue"	"George's Blues (Because You're Sweet and Lovely)"
34. "The Ballad of John and Yoko"	"The Ballad of John and Yoko (They're Gonna Crucify Me)"
35. "Oh! Darling"	"Oh! Darling (I'll Never Do You Harm)"
36. "I Want You (She's So Heavy)"	"I Want You"
37. "Sun King"	"Here Comes the Sun-King"
38. "She Came in Through the Bathroom Window"	"Bathroom Window"
39. "The End"	"Ending"

28. The 3 Beatles Songs With "Diamonds" in Their Lyrics

"Can't Buy Me Love"   "I'll buy you a diamond ring my friend" and other mentions.

"I Feel Fine"   "He buys her diamond rings you know, she said so."

"Lucy in the Sky With Diamonds"   The title and the chorus.

Rocking Horse People . . .

29. 68 People Mentioned by Name in the Beatles Songs

The following sixty-eight people culled from dozens of the Beatles' songs are some of the denizens who live in the fabulous world the Beatles sang about and which we have all been lucky enough to be able to visit.

1. **Billy**   Billy is none other than "the one and only Billy Shears" from the song "Sgt. Pepper's Lonely Hearts Club Band" on the album of the same name. After Paul "introduces" Billy, Ringo then sings "With a Little Help From My Friends," leading us, logically, to believe that "Billy Shears" is an alias for Ringo. When Paul was supposed to be dead, some of the hidden clues supposedly hinted that "Billy Shears"—a name which sounded like the words "Billy's here" to some— was the pseudonym of William Campbell, the guy who replaced Paul after his terrible and fatal 1966 car accident.

2. **Peter Brown**   Peter Brown was a close associate of Brian Epstein's when Brian was managing the Beatles. Brown was also close to the individual Beatles and served as John's best man at his marriage to Yoko Ono. John mentions Brown by name in the single, "The Ballad of John and Yoko."

   Peter Brown destroyed any relationships he had with the Beatles or their associates in 1983 when he published a book called *The Love You Make: An Insider's Story of the Beatles,* which he had originally said was about the sixties in general to secure participation from the Beatles and their intimates.

   In *The Love You Make,* Brown suggested that Yoko broke up the Beatles; that Yoko turned John into a heroin addict; and he went public with Brian Epstein's homosexuality, ultimately causing Brian's mother to have a nervous breakdown and be hospitalized.

3. **Bungalow Bill**   The story of this white hunter is told in "The Continuing Story of Bungalow Bill" and the song regales us with his exploits, mainly consisting of tiger hunting and being scolded by his mum, a stern woman whom he always took along on expeditions "in case of accidents."

4. **Matt Busby**   Matt Busby is one of the people John mentions in "Dig It" as he sings his litany of oddly juxtaposed people and institutions, including the CIA, BBC, and Doris Day.

5. **Christ**   John shouts out an entreaty to Jesus in "The Ballad of John and Yoko" when he sings "Christ! You know it ain't easy! They're gonna crucify me!" This was probably in response to his early misquoted remarks about Christianity.

6. **Chuck**   Chuck is one of the three grandchildren Paul sings about in "When I'm Sixty-Four." (Vera and Dave are the other two "on your knee.")

7. **Dan**   Dan, also known as Danny and Daniel, is the guy who stole Rocky Raccoon's girl and ultimately shot Rocky when the cuckolded Black Mountain boy confronted him in the hotel room. Paul McCartney calls him Daniel when he tells us that "Daniel was hot" and that he drew his gun first and shot Rocky. Rocky called him Danny when he burst in the hotel room and told him that this was "a showdown."

8. **Dave**   This is one of Paul's imagined grandchildren from "When I'm Sixty-Four." The others are Vera and Chuck.

9. **Doc**   This is the unnamed doctor who treated Rocky Raccoon's bullet wound in "Rocky Raccoon." Rocky insisted to the doc that it was "only a scratch."

10. **Doris**   There are two ladies named Doris in the Beatles' songs and they both appear on the *Let It Be* album. The first is none other than the famous actress Doris Day, who is mentioned in "Dig It." The other Doris is the one who "gets her oats" in "Two of Us."

11. **Doris Day**   The famous actress is mentioned in "Dig It."

12. **Dylan**   This "Dylan" is the one-and-only Bob Dylan and he is mentioned by John in "Yer Blues" in the line "Just like Dylan's Mr. Jones."

13. **Maxwell Edison**   This is the murderous guy who asked Joan out for a date in "Maxwell's Silver Hammer" and then killed her with a hammer when he showed up for their date. Max was majoring in medicine and called Joan to ask her out to the movies. In a killing spree, Maxwell also killed his teacher and the judge assigned to try his case.

14. **Pablo Fanques**   Pablo is presumably the founder and director of the delightful carnival/fair that John sings about in "Being for the Benefit of Mr. Kite!"

15. **Moretta Fart**   Moretta is apparently an alias of Sweet Loretta Martin in "Get Back."

16. **Gideon**   This was the previous occupant of Rocky Raccoon's hotel room. He checked out and left a Bible with his name on it "to help with good Rocky's revival."

17. **Charles Hawtrey**   Charles Hawtrey on the Deaf Aids was the artist John mentions in "Two of Us." According to John, Mr. Hawtrey was responsible for the song "I Dig a Pygmy."

18. **Heath**   This is former British Prime Minister Edward Heath. George unapologetically bashes him (and former Prime Minister Wilson as well) in "Taxman."

19. **The Hendersons**   This performing family dances and sings as Henry the Horse dances the waltz in "Being for the Benefit of Mr. Kite!"

20. **Elmore James**   In "For You Blue," George scats that "Elmore James got nothing on this," as John plays an especially tasty slide guitar riff. George is referring to the legendary blues guitarist who influenced everybody from B. B. King to the Rolling Stones and Jimi Hendrix.

21. **Jo**   This is Jojo from "Get Back." At one point in the song, Paul sings "Get back Jo."

22. **Joan**   This was Maxwell Edison's first victim in "Maxwell's Silver Hammer." Max crushed Joan's head with his silver hammer when he arrived at her door to pick her up for a date.

23. **John**   This is a reference to John Lennon. Paul sings to him to "hurry up" in "I'm Down."

24. **Johnny**   This is also John Lennon. George sings to him in "For You Blue" to "Go Johnny go."

25. **Jojo**   Paul tells the story of Jojo in "Get Back." It seems that Jojo thought of himself as a loner and so decided to move from Tucson, Arizona, to California. Apparently the move didn't work out and so Paul recommended that Jojo get back to where he once belonged.

26. **Desmond Jones**   This guy has a "barrow in the marketplace" and his story is told in "Ob-La-Di, Ob-La-Da." He sees Molly, tells her, "I like your face" and then takes a trolley to the jewelers. They end up having a couple of kids.

27. **Molly Jones**   Desmond's wife from "Ob-La-Di, Ob-La-Da." She is a singer in the band and likes to do "her pretty face."

28. **Mr. Jones**   This is a character from a Bob Dylan song that John refers to in "Yer Blues."

29. **Jude**   Jude is the title character of the classic McCartney ballad "Hey Jude," the song that John Lennon once said was Paul's best song ever. The genesis of the song came when John and his first wife Cynthia were splitting up and Paul wanted to write something to cheer up their son Julian. On his way to visit the Lennons, Paul began singing "Hey Jules," but then decided that "Hey Jude" was better. In December 1996, Julian Lennon paid $39,030 at a London auction for Paul McCartney's recording notes for "Hey Jude." Julian Lennon's manager, John Cousins, told the *London Times* that Julian was "collecting for personal reasons. These are family heirlooms if you like."

30. **Judy**   This is a nickname Paul uses for the character of "Jude" in "Hey Jude" at the end of the song when he sings, "Jude, Jude, ah, Judy, Judy, Judy, Judy."

31. **Julia**   Julia is the title character of John Lennon's haunting ballad, "Julia." Julia Lennon was John's mother, although he said that the Julia in the song was a combination of his mother and Yoko Ono. ("Yoko" means "ocean child" in Japanese.)

32. **Mr. Kite**   This is the acrobat who was the main attraction at the circus show chronicled in "Being for the Benefit of Mr. Kite!"

33. **Krishna**   The eighth and principle avatar (incarnation) of the God Vishnu. In Hinduism, Vishnu is the second member of the holy trinity; the other two are Brahma and Shiva. In "I Am the Walrus," John sings about an "elementary penguin singing Hare Krishna." "Hare Krishna" translates as "praise Krishna" and is used as an invocation to the God by Hinduism's devotees.

34. **Lil**   In "Rocky Raccoon," we learn that Lil is the nickname used by the object of Rocky's affection, Magill, although everyone knew her as Nancy. Daniel stole Lil away from Rocky.

35. **Lucy**   This woman might be the most famous character in a Beatles song (although "Jude" is certainly in close contention). Lucy is the girl with kaleidoscope eyes whom John sees "in the sky with diamonds" in "Lucy in the Sky With Diamonds." There was tremendous controversy surrounding this song when the *Sgt. Pepper* album was first released because of the "LSD" acronym supposedly hidden in the song's title.

Because of this alleged drug reference, the song was actually banned for a time by the BBC, but the truth is that the title came from a drawing by John's then four-year-old son Julian. In 1970, John said that he had not even been aware of the acronym until somebody pointed it out to him. In 1980 he told *Playboy,* "My son Julian came in one day with a picture he painted about a school friend of his named Lucy. He had sketched in some stars in the sky and called it 'Lucy in the Sky with Diamonds.' Simple."

In *John Lennon in My Life,* John's childhood friend Pete Shotton talked about being there the day Julian came home with the drawing, confirming that the title had, indeed, come from the little Lennon's artwork. Shotton did remark, however, "Though John was certainly ingesting inordinate amounts of acid around the time he wrote 'Lucy in the Sky With Diamonds,' the pun was indeed sheer coincidence."

36. **Father McKenzie**   This clergyman presided at the burial of Eleanor Rigby. He also may have participated in actually digging Eleanor's grave since Paul tells us in the song that the good Father wiped the dirt from his hands as he walked from her grave (or he could have been the only one to throw dirt on her casket). It seems that Father McKenzie ministers to a completely apathetic parish and that he writes sermons "no one will hear." (The back of Father McKenzie is briefly glimpsed in the "Free as a Bird" video.)

37. **Lady Madonna**   In "Lady Madonna," we learn that this poor woman—obviously a single mother—is struggling to make ends meet with a baby at her breast and children at her feet. Sometimes she just lies on the bed and listens to music, but this is but a brief respite from stockings that need mending and a rent that needs to be paid.

38. **Magill**   This is the woman everyone knew as Nancy in "Rocky Raccoon." Magill was her given name, but she called herself Lil. Daniel stole Magill away from Rocky.

39. **Chairman Mao**   Mao Tse-tung, the founder of the Chinese Communist Party and one of the world's leading Marxist theoreticians, is mentioned twice in a Beatles song. The first is in "Revolution"; the second in "Revolution 1." Both times John tells us that if you go carrying pictures of Chairman Mao, you probably won't make it with anyone (anyhow).

40. **Martha**   Martha, the title character of "Martha My Dear" is actually Paul McCartney's sheepdog Martha, although the lyrics of the song could apply to a woman of human persuasion ("you have always been my inspiration"; "please be good to me, Martha my love"; "Don't forget me"; etc.).

41. **Loretta Martin**   Is Loretta Martin a man or a woman? If Loretta *is* a man, is he a transvestite? The lyrics of "Get Back," one of the Beatles' last songs, plead for personal interpretation, and so, we'll leave it there, with the question of Loretta's sexuality yours to decide.

42. **Captain Marvel**   This legendary hero of comic book fame zaps Bungalow Bill right between the eyes in "The Continuing Story of Bungalow Bill," and never appears again in a Beatles song.

43. **Mary**   The character of Mary appears in the hymn-like McCartney ballad "Let It Be" as "Mother Mary" and some Beatles fans have seen this as a reference to Mary, the Blessed Mother. The truth is that Paul is singing about his mother, Mary McCartney, who died of breast cancer when he was in his teens.

Much like "Yesterday," Paul's classic "Let It Be" was inspired by a dream. "I had a dream one night about my mother," he told *Musician* magazine in 1986.

"She died when I was fourteen so I hadn't really heard from her in quite a while, and it was very good. It gave me some strength 'in my darkest hour, Mother Mary comes to me.' "

It seems as though Paul recognized from the very start that he had written a magnificent song. On *The Beatles Anthology 3*, we hear a tape of Paul performing "Let It Be" for his bandmates before he had even completed writing the lyrics. He sat at a piano in a basement studio at Apple and introduced the song by telling them, "This is gonna knock you out." At the conclusion of Paul's performance, we hear John say, "I think that was rather grand. *I'd* take one home with me." Indeed.

44. **Michelle** This young lady is Paul's "belle" in the song "Michelle" and she is notable for being the first woman any Beatle ever sang about in a foreign language. In the song, Paul cannot find enough ways to tell Michelle he loves her. She was never heard of again.

45. **Mr. Mustard** This guy is one mean old man. He's cheap, dirty, and generally unpleasant to be around. His sister Pam, on the other hand, seems to be a responsible, hardworking young woman. Too bad her sense of enterprise and manners didn't rub off on her brother, eh?

46. **Nancy** This is Magill from "Rocky Raccoon." It seems as though Magill called herself Lil, but for some unexplained reason, everyone knew her as Nancy.

47. **Dennis O'Bell** This guy is mentioned several times in "You Know My Name (Look up the Number)" and is apparently some kind of performer.

48. **Yoko Ono** John's wife and soulmate is mentioned twice in the songs of the Beatles. The first time is in "Come Together" when John tells us that the guy he's singing about wears an "Ono sideboard." The second mention of Yoko is in the title of the autobiographical song, "The Ballad of John and Yoko."

49. **Pam** This is Mean Mr. Mustard's hardworking sister and she is mentioned in her brother's song on *Abbey Road* (and in a different take on *The Beatles Anthology 3*). (It should be noted that *this* Pam is probably not *Polythene* Pam. On a bootleg of the *Let It Be* sessions, a rehearsal of "Mean Mr. Mustard" is heard with essentially the same lyrics, except that, at this time, Mr. Mustard's sister was named Shirley, not Pam.)

50. **Paul** The walrus was Paul . . . but you knew that already, didn't you?

51. **Sgt. Pepper** This is the gentleman responsible for forming and conducting the orchestra that the Beatles so unforgettably memorialized in their 1967 album *Sgt. Pepper's Lonely Hearts Club Band*. The good sergeant is the one who taught the band to play. In 1967 when the album came out, they had been together for twenty years, since 1947. Even though they had apparently been going in and out of style, Paul assured us that they were still guaranteed to raise a smile. He was right.

52. **Edgar Allan Poe** The famous author of "The Raven," "The Pit and the Pendulum," and "The Masque of the Red Death" is mentioned by name in "I Am the Walrus." In the song, it seems as though the elementary penguins who were singing Hare Krishna were kicking Poe, although it really isn't clear as to *why* they were assaulting him.

53. **Polythene Pam** Is this woman Mean Mr. Mustard's sister Pam who works in a shop? Probably not, since John is on record as saying in *Playboy* that "Polythene Pam" is about a girl a poet had once introduced to him who liked "perverted sex in a polythene bag."

97

54. **Prudence**   This is actually Prudence Farrow, Mia Farrow's sister. Prudence accompanied her sister and the Beatles to India in 1968 to study meditation with the Maharishi Mahesh Yogi and she immediately went off the deep end. She took to locking herself in her room and practicing deep meditation for so long that everyone—including the Maharishi himself—began to worry about her. John wrote "Dear Prudence" to try and lure her out and also to make some sense out of her obsessive behavior. John's plea for Prudence "to come out and play" was mainly rhetorical, however, since she never even heard the song until the *White Album* was released. On an unreleased demo of "Dear Prudence," John can be heard saying, "All the people around were very worried about [Prudence] because she was going insane."

55. **Rocky Raccoon**   Poor Rocky. This young man lived in the Black Mountain hills of Dakota and was in love with Magill. One day, Magill (she called herself Lil) hit Rocky in the eye and ran off with Daniel. Rocky decided to defend his honor and get Lil back. We all know the rest of the story and when "Rocky Raccoon" ends, Rocky is recovering from gunshot wounds inflicted upon him by the thief of his beloved's affection, the man who called himself Dan. Understand?

56. **Sir Walter Raleigh**   Sir Raleigh is mentioned in "I'm So Tired" when John curses him for introducing tobacco to England.

57. **Eleanor Rigby**   Paul tells the sad story of Ms. Rigby in the song "Eleanor Rigby," which first appeared on the *Revolver* album. We don't know very much about Paul's Eleanor except that she spent a lot of time at Father McKenzie's church. It's a reasonable guess that she worked for the parish cleaning the church since Paul has her picking up the rice after a wedding and he also tells us that she died in the church. She was apparently terribly lonely and did not have any friends since no one attended her funeral.

58. **Ringo**   Our beloved Mr. Starr is mentioned by name twice in "You Know My Name (Look Up the Number)." Ringo shares a bill with Dennis O'Bell at Slaggers and John introduces him to the crowd.

59. **Rita**   "Lovely Rita" is a meter maid whom Paul courts in the song of the same name on the *Sgt. Pepper* album. Obviously an independent working woman (and a civil servant to boot), Rita paid the bill when Paul took her out to dinner and when the song ends, it seems if Rita was becoming quite enamored of our singer since he "nearly made it" with her on her sofa after their dinner date.

60. **Dr. Robert**   In "Doctor Robert," we learn the story of a physician who will "pick you up" with his wonderful potions and cups.

In Pete Shotton's book, *John Lennon in My Life,* Shotton writes that John was paying "sardonic tribute to an actual New York doctor—his real name was Charles Roberts, with an *s*—whose unorthodox prescriptions made him a great favorite of Andy Warhol's entourage, and the Beatles themselves, whenever they passed through town."

However, in John's 1980 *Playboy* interview, he said that "['Doctor Robert'] was about myself. I was the one who carried all the pills on the tour and always [dispensed] them . . . in the early days. Later on, the roadies did it."

61. **Rose**   Rose and Valerie were two friends of Maxwell Edison. The two of them screamed from the gallery that Maxwell should go free rather than be put to death for his crimes.

62. **Rosetta**   Rosetta is mentioned only on the LP version of "Get Back" and she

might very well be another alter ego for Sweet Loretta Martin or Sweet Moretta Fart in the same song.

63. **Sexy Sadie**   Sadie was an alias for the Indian guru, the Maharishi Mahesh Yogi. John's original lyric used *Maharishi* instead of *Sexy Sadie* but he decided to be more circumspect on the final version of the song. The lyrics of the song express John's feelings at the time for the guru with the feet of clay. "Sexy Sadie" is one of Julian Lennon's favorite songs by his father.

64. **Mother Superior**   According to John, Yoko Ono is the Mother Superior who jumps the gun in "Happiness Is a Warm Gun" on the *White Album*. Other than that, the lyrics of the song (one of John's personal favorites) are open to interpretation. John said he got the title of the song from a magazine article in an American gun magazine, but the rest of the surrealistic lyric imagery is pure Lennon.

65. **Valerie**   As discussed previously, Rose and Valerie were two friends of Maxwell Edison. These two generous souls screamed from the gallery that Mr. Edison should be set free rather than be put to death.

66. **Vera**   This is one of Paul's imagined grandchildren from "When I'm Sixty-Four." The others are Dave and Chuck.

67. **Wilson**   This is former British Prime Minister Harold Wilson. George bashes him (and former Prime Minister Heath as well) in "Taxman."

68. **Georgie Wood**   According to John, Georgie Wood is the *real* composer of the song he refers to as "Can You Dig It?," which was released as "Dig It" on the *Let It Be* album.

30. 5 Beatles Songs in Which an Individual Beatle Is Mentioned by Name

This feature looks at Beatles songs written by the Beatles in which any of the Fabs are mentioned by name. Yes, we know that Ringo mentions himself by name in "Matchbox," and that other Beatles are mentioned in various other cover recordings of songs by others, but if the Fabs didn't write it, we didn't include it.

John

"I'm Down"   In this rocker, Paul sings to his bandmate, "Hurry up, John!"

"The Ballad of John and Yoko"   John isn't actually mentioned by name in the lyrics to this song, but since the whole song is about Yoko and him and his name is part of the title, it is included here.

"For You Blue"   In this George Harrison song, George sings to Mr. Lennon, "Go Johnny go!"

Paul

"Glass Onion"   This might be the most famous lyrical mention of a Beatle in their entire song catalog. "Glass Onion," of course, is the *White Album* song in which John sings, "The walrus was Paul."

Ringo

"You Know My Name (Look Up the Number)"   In this odd Beatles concoction, Ringo is mentioned as being part of the bill (along with Dennis O'Bell) at the nightclub known as Slaggers.

31. 3 Songs Written by George Harrison After an LSD Trip

"It's All Too Much" In his autobiography *I Me Mine,* George wrote, " 'It's All Too Much' was written in a childlike manner from realizations that appeared during and after some LSD experiences and which were later confirmed in meditation."

"See Yourself" (solo) George has also written of this song as being composed following one of his mental "journeys."

"Here Comes the Moon" (solo) This one as well.

George has admitted receiving inspiration for his songwriting from some "unusual" places. (Photofest)

32. The 2 People John Lennon Referred to in His Songs as "Mother Superior"

Yoko Ono   Yoko is the "Mother Superior" who "jumped the gun" in John's *White Album* song, "Happiness Is a Warm Gun."

May Pang   Yoko's secretary and John's one-time lover May Pang was credited on John's *Rock 'N' Roll* album as "Production Coordinator and Mother Superior." (May Pang also received "Production Coordinator" credit on John's *Walls and Bridges* album.)

(Photofest)

33. 2 Different Men Named Stephen King Who Had Some Connection With the Beatles

Stephen King, accountant   On January 30, 1969, Stephen King, the accountant in a nearby office, took steps to stop the Beatles' impromptu concert that was taking place on the roof of the Abbey Road studio.

Stephen King, writer   Stephen King the writer used two lines from the Beatles song "Drive My Car" as the epigraph to the chapter "LeBay Passes" in his 1983 novel *Christine*. King's novel *The Shining* was originally called *The Shine*, inspired by John Lennon's song, "Instant Karma." King changed the title when he learned that the term "the shine" was derogatory to blacks.

Look What You're Doing . . .

34. *576 "Interesting" Cover Versions of 120 Beatles Songs*

I don't know about you, but I don't cotton too well to Beatles cover versions.

The original Beatles version of a Beatles song is, well, let's face it, *perfect,* and so hearing someone else do a Beatles song brings with it an odd sense of displacement, a kind of groundless feeling. We keep waiting for that certain thrill we know so well that comes with hearing one of John's trademark vocal inflections, or one of George's perfect guitar licks. We're thrown off when they're not there. Cover versions almost always fall flat.

Frankly, there aren't too many cover versions of Beatle tunes that make the grade in *this* Beatles fans' opinion. Oh sure, there are some that work: Jimi Hendrix's cover of "Sgt. Pepper's Lonely Hearts Club Band" kicks ass; as does Billy Joel's "Back in the U.S.S.R." and Aerosmith's "Come Together." But Peter Sellers doing "Help!"? Chevy Chase doing "Let It Be"? Kiri Ti Kanawa doing "The Long and Winding Road"? Eddie Murphy doing "Good Day Sunshine"? (EDDIE MURPHY?) Of course, the classic example of the "What Was I Thinking?" School of Musicology, William Shatner doing "Lucy in the Sky With Diamonds"?

Puh-leeeeeeeze.

Some of these covers, though, do seem like unions made in musical heaven. I'll bet John Denver would have given his granny glasses and his driver's license to have written "Mother Nature's Son." He didn't, so he covered it. Can you even begin to imagine a more perfect song for Johnny Mathis than "Something"? Like I said, some of these homages do work.

Some of these renditions speak volumes and are more than the sum of their musical parts, so to speak. Don't you find it the quintessential definition of irony that "I Saw Her Standing There" and "Love Me Do" were covered by the *Pete Best Band*? I thought so. Doesn't it also say something that the Beach Boys, one of the Beatles' artistic rivals of the sixties—remember *Pet Sounds?*—covered no less than five Beatles' songs during their career? How many *Beach Boys* songs did the *Beatles* cover? I rest my case.

I have heard many of the covers on this list, some I can only dream about what they sound like. I have included this wide-ranging selection of Beatles covers for its undeniable entertainment value but also to make the point that the Beatles are unquestionably "universal" artists. Their appeal crosses all lines of age, ethnicity, and musical styles. This is both a good and a bad thing. It's *good* because musicians the world over have an enormous library of brilliant pop songs to choose from, and sometimes their renditions of Beatles songs are quite enjoyable.

On the other hand, it's a *bad* thing because musicians the world over have an enormous library of brilliant pop songs to choose from and thus, we are "blessed" with the Carpenters' astonishingly watered-down and insipid version of "Ticket to Ride" as well as Sonny and Cher's painful rendition of "Hey Jude."

If reading over this list moves you to actually seek out some of these recordings, don't say I didn't warn you. Some of these songs are still in print and available (on albums or as singles); many are not. Our suggestion would be to start with the Master Catalog of artists and recordings available at any good record store and look up the artist first. A listing of all his, her, or their in-print titles—complete with the songs included on the listed albums—will be provided and you can start from there.

Special thanks, as always, to Tom Schultheiss for his ongoing mission to compile and chronicle absolutely *everything* possible to know about the Beatles no matter how obscure, eclectic, specialized, esoteric, or cryptic. Tom, 'ol boy: We are not worthy.

"A Day in the Life"
Wes Montgomery
Lighthouse
Eric Burdon and War
Sting
Shirley Bassey

"A Hard Day's Night"
Peter Sellers
The Ramsey Lewis Trio
Otis Redding
Billy Joel
Chet Atkins
Count Basie
The Boston Pops
Ella Fitzgerald
Quincy Jones
John Mayall
Billy Preston
Dionne Warwick

"Across the Universe"
David Bowie
10CC

"All My Loving"
Hollyridge Strings

Herb Alpert and the
   Tijuana Brass
Count Basie
Duke Ellington
Matt Monro
Frank Sinatra

"All Together Now"
The Muppets

"All You Need Is Love"
Echo and the Bunnymen
Tom Jones
The Fifth Dimension
Anita Kerr

"And I Love Her"
Jose Feliciano
Julio Eglesias
Bob Marley and the Wailers
Chet Atkins
The Count Basie Orchestra
The Boston Pops
Xavier Cugat
Connie Francis
Lena Horne
Jack Jones
Ramsey Lewis

Peter Nero
Smokey Robinson and the
   Miracle
Nancy Wilson
Bobby Womack

"And Your Bird Can Sing"
The Flamin' Groovies

"Another Girl"
The Kingsmen

"Any Time at All"
Nils Lofgren
Dweezil Zappa
Frank Sinatra

"Baby, You're a Rich Man"
Fat Boys

"Back in the U.S.S.R.
Chubby Checker
Billy Joel
The Beach Boys

"Because"
Stanley Jordan
Percy Faith

"Blackbird"
Billy Preston
Kenny Rankin
Crosby, Stills, and Nash
Bobby McFerrin
Mickey Dolenz
The Chieftains

"Can't Buy Me Love"
Ella Fitzgerald
Peter Sellers
Dick James
Brenda Lee
Henry Mancini
Johnny Rivers

"Come Together"
Diana Ross
Ike and Tina Turner
Aerosmith
Soundgarden
The Neville Brothers
Blues Traveler
Howard Jones
Michael Jackson
Butthole Surfers
Charlie Byrd
Dionne Warwick
Barbara Feldon

"Cry Baby Cry"
Del Shannon
Throwing Muses

"Day Tripper"
Ramsey Lewis
Otis Redding
Nancy Sinatra
Sergio Mendes and Brazil
    '66
Electric Light Orchestra
Anne Murray
James Taylor
Whitesnake
Cheap Trick
Julian Lennon (live
    performance only)

Jimi Hendrix
10CC
Lulu
Mae West

"Dear Prudence"
Siouxie and the Banshees
The Jerry Garcia Band
The Jackson 5

*"Do You Want to Know
    a Secret?"*
Billy J. Kramer and the
    Dakotas
Count Basie
Ray Charles Singers

"Don't Let Me Down"
Ben E. King
The Hollies
Phoebe Snow
Annie Lennox

"Drive My Car"
Bobby McFerrin
The Breakfast Club

"Eight Days a Week"
Procol Harum
Lorrie Morgan

"Eleanor Rigby"
Joan Baez
Richie Havens
Vanilla Fudge
Wes Montgomery
Diana Ross and the
    Supremes
Blonde on Blonde
Aretha Franklin
Ray Charles
Rare Earth
Oscar Peterson
Stanley Jordan
Booker T and the MGs
Rick Wakeman
Tony Bennett

John Denver
The Boston Pops
The Four Tops
Johnny Mathis
Paul Mauriat
Frankie Valli

"Every Little Thing"
Yes
The Spencer Davis Group

*"Everybody's Got Something
    to Hide Except Me
    and My Monkey"*
Fats Domino

"The Fool on the Hill"
Sergio Mendes and Brazil
    '66
Mickey Dolenz
Ray Stevens
Stone the Crows
Lena Horne
Andre Kostelanetz
Petula Clark
Shirley Bassey
The Boston Pops
Lana Cantrell
Bobby Gentry

"For No One"
Cilla Black
Emmylou Harris
Maureen McGovern

"From Me to You"
Del Shannon
Debby Boone
Bobby McFerrin
Dick James
Mae West

"Get Back"
Paul Mauriat
Elton John
Al Green
Ike and Tina Turner

Elvis Presley
Veruca Salt
Mongo Santamaria

"Girl"
Charlie Byrd

"Golden Slumbers/Carry That Weight"
Jackson Browne
Mary Hart
Billy Joel

"Good Day Sunshine"
Claudine Longet
Eddie Murphy

"Good Night"
Mickey Dolenz
Manhattan Transfer
The Flirtations

"Got to Get You Into My Life"
The Four Tops
Sonny and Cher
Blood, Sweat and Tears
Dino, Desi and Billy
Ella Fitzgerald

"Happiness Is a Warm Gun"
U2

"Help!"
Peter Sellers
Deep Purple
The Carpenters
Tina Turner
Bananarama
Ray Stevens
Andre Kostelanetz
Peter Nero
Dolly Parton
Jose Feliciano
Count Basie
Buddy Greco

"Helter Skelter"
Siouxsie and the Banshees
Pat Benatar
U2
Aerosmith
Mötley Crüe
Husker Dü

"Here Comes the Sun"
Richie Havens
Hugo Montenegro
Nina Simone

"Here, There, and Everwhere"
Jose Feliciano
Emmylou Harris
Perry Como
Kenny Loggins
George Benson
Liberace
Johnny Mathis
Petula Clark
Jackie Gleason
Jay and the Americans
Claudine Longet
Hugh Masekela
Matt Munro
Dick Smothers

"Hey Jude"
Wilson Pickett
Smokey Robinson and the Miracles
Petula Clark
Jose Feliciano
Stan Kenton
Ray Stevens
The Temptations
Jr. Walker and the All Stars
Maynard Ferguson
Sonny and Cher
Elvis Presley
Bing Crosby
The Ray Charles Singers
Tom Jones
Peter Nero

The New Christy Minstrels
Lawrence Welk
Petula Clark
Charlie Byrd
The Ray Coniff Singers
The Lettermen
Frank Sinatra

"Hold Me Tight"
Johnny Cash

"Honey Pie"
Barbra Streisand

"I Am the Walrus"
Oasis
Frank Zappa
Men Without Hats

"I Call Your Name"
Billy J. Kramer and the Dakotas
The Buckinghams
The Mamas and the Papas

"I Don't Want to Spoil the Party"
Rosanne Cash

"I Feel Fine"
Vanilla Fudge

"I Saw Her Standing There"
Little Richard
Elton John
The Jerry Garcia Band
Tiffany
The Pete Best Band
The Tubes
Hank Williams, Jr.

"I Should Have Known Better"
The Beach Boys
Jan and Dean
Phil Ochs
Johnny Rivers

"I Wanna Be Your Man"
The Rolling Stones
Count Basie
Suzi Quatro

"I Want to Hold Your Hand"
The Boston Pops
    Orchestra
Al Green
The New Christy
    Minstrels
Pat Boone
Petula Clark
The Crickets
Duke Ellington
Nelson Riddle
Vanilla Fudge

"I Want to Tell You"
Ted Nugent

"I Want You (She's So Heavy)"
Alvin Lee

"I Will"
Tim Curry
Maureen McGovern
Alison Krauss
Ben Taylor

"If I Fell"
Peter and Gordon
Lou Christie
Gerry Mulligan

"If I Needed Someone"
The Hollies
Hugh Masekela

"I'll Be Back"
The Buckinghams
Charlie Byrd

"I'll Cry Instead"
Joe Cocker

Billy Joel
Johnny Rivers

"I'll Follow the Sun"
Floyd Cramer

"I'm a Loser"
Marianne Faithfull

"I'm Down"
Heart
Aerosmith
Beastie Boys
Yes

"I'm Happy Just to Dance With You"
The Cyrkle
Anne Murray
Maureen McGovern

"I'm Only Sleeping"
Rosanne Cash

"I've Got a Feeling"
Pearl Jam

"I've Just Seen a Face"
The Dillards
Arlo Guthrie
Leon Russell

"In My Life"
Judy Collins
Jose Feliciano
Keith Moon
Rod Stewart
Stephen Stills
Bette Midler
Crosby, Stills, and Nash
Lena Horne
Joel Grey

"It Won't Be Long"
Alison Moyet
Lester Flatt

"It's Only Love"
Gary U.S. Bonds
Eddy Arnold
Ella Fitzgerald
Tommy James and the
    Shondells

"Julia"
Charlie Byrd

"Lady Madonna"
Fats Domino
Ramsey Lewis
Jose Feliciano
Booker T. and the MGs
Elvis Presley
The Four Freshmen
Richie Havens
Union Gap

"Let It Be"
Aretha Franklin
Dion
Joan Baez
John Denver
The Persuasions
Joe Cocker
Chevy Chase
The Ray Conniff Singers
John Davidson
The Everly Brothers
Tennesse Ernie Ford
Gladys Knight and the
    Pips
Wes Montgomery

"Love Me Do"
Badfinger
The Pete Best Band
Fats Domino

"Lucy in the Sky With Diamonds"
Elton John
Hugo Montenegro
The Hooters
Bela Fleck and the
    Flecktones

Bill Murray
Natalie Cole
William Shatner

"Magical Mystery Tour"
Cheap Trick

"Michelle"
The Four Tops
The Lettermen
Booker T and the MGs
Perry Como
Bela Fleck and the
    Flecktones
Ed Ames
Bobby Goldsboro
Andre Kostelanetz
Bobby Vinton
Count Basie
The Boston Pops
Charlie Byrd
John Davidson
The Four Freshmen
Jan and Dean
Jack Jones
Sammy Kaye
Stan Kenton
Johnny Mathis
David McCallum
Peter Nero
Wayne Newton
Andre Previn
George Shearing
Rudy Vallee
Sarah Vaughan
Andy Williams

"Mother Nature's Son"
John Denver
Ramsey Lewis

"No Reply"
John Mayall

"Norwegian Wood"
Jan and Dean

The Kingston Trio
The Buddy Rich Big Band
Sergio Mendes and Brazil
    '66
Vicki Carr
Charlie Byrd

"Not a Second Time"
Robert Palmer

"Nowhere Man"
Vikki Carr
Dino, Desi and Billy
Placido Domingo

"Ob-La-Di, Ob-La-Da"
Floyd Kramer
John Davidson
The Anita Kerr Singers
Peter Nero
Herb Alpert and the
    Tijuana Brass
The Boston Pops
Johnny Mathis

"Octopus's Garden"
Raffi

"Oh! Darling"
Bela Fleck and the
    Flecktones

"One After 909"
The Smithereens

"Paperback Writer"
The Cowsills
Bee Gees
10CC

"Please Please Me"
David Cassidy
Petula Clark

"Rain"
Petula Clark
Todd Rundgren

Gregg Allman
Dan Fogelberg

"Revolution"
Mike and the Mechanics

"Rocky Raccoon"
Richie Havens
Benny Goodman
Lena Horne

"Run for Your Life"
Gary Lewis and the
    Playboys
Nancy Sinatra
Al Hirt
Johnny Rivers

"Savoy Truffle"
Ella Fitzgerald

*"Sgt. Pepper's Lonely Hearts
    Club Band"*
Jimi Hendrix
Bill Cosby

*"She Came in Through the
    Bathroom Window"*
Joe Cocker
Ray Stevens
Ike and Tina Turner

"She Loves You"
Peter Sellers
Count Basie
Neil Sedaka
Vanilla Fudge

"She's a Woman"
Jose Feliciano
Jeff Beck

"She's Leaving Home"
Nilsson
Al Jarreau
Richie Havens

"Something"
Booker T. and the MGs
Joe Cocker
Sonny and Cher
Frank Sinatra
Elvis Presley
James Brown
Ferrante and Teicher
Jack Jones
Bert Kaempfert
Liberace
Johnny Mathis
Telly Savalas
Bobby Vinton
Dionne Warwick
Andy Williams
Perry Como
Shirley Bassey
Tony Bennett
John Davidson
Percy Faith
Lena Horne
Englebert Humperdinck
Peggy Lee
The Lettermen
Jim Nabors
Martha Reeves and the
    Vandellas
Ray Stevens
Sarah Vaughan
Jr. Walker and the All Stars
Hugo Montenegro
Peter Nero

"Strawberry Fields Forever"
The Ventures
Richie Havens
Todd Rundgren
Debbie Harry

"Taxman"
Black Oak Arkansas
Stevie Ray Vaughan

"Tell Me Why"
The Beach Boys

"Thank You Girl"
John Hiatt

**"The Ballad of John
    and Yoko"**
Hootie and the Blowfish

**"The Long and Winding
    Road"**
Diana Ross
Cher
Kiri Te Kanawa
Olivia Newton-John
Melba Moore
Aretha Franklin
Andre Kostelanetz

"Things We Said Today"
Jackie DeShannon
Maureen McGovern

"Ticket to Ride"
The Carpenters
The Bee Gees
Husker Dü
The Fifth Dimension
Vanilla Fudge

"Tomorrow Never Knows"
Phil Collins
Jimi Hendrix

"Wait"
Roy Orbison

"We Can Work It Out"
Stevie Wonder
The Dillards
Chaka Khan
Tesla
Franki Valli and the Four
    Seasons
Petula Clark
Deep Purple
Leslie Uggams
Dionne Warwick

"When I Get Home"
Billy Joel and the Hassles
The Searchers

"When I'm Sixty-Four"
Claudine Longet
John Denver
Archie and Edith Bunker

**"While My Guitar Gently
    Weeps"**
The Jeff Healey Band
Charlie Byrd

**"With a Little Help From
    My Friends"**
Sergio Mendes and Brazil
    '66
Joe Cocker
Santana
Richie Havens
Ike and Tina Turner
Barbra Streisand
Herb Alpert and the
    Tijuana Brass
The Beach Boys

"Yellow Submarine"
Ferrante and Teicher

"Yer Blues"
The Jeff Healey Band

"Yes It Is"
Peter Sellers

"Yesterday"
Cilla Black
Marianne Faithfull
The Supremes
Perry Como
Ray Charles
Smokey Robinson and the
    Miracles
Elvis Presley

Bob Dylan
Dr. John
Benny Goodman
En Vogue
Michael Bolton
Boyz II Men
The Ray Conniff Singers
Percy Faith
Ferrante and Teicher
Sergio Franchi
Bobby Goldsboro
Don Ho
Tom Jones
Andre Kostelanetz
Herbie Mann
Al Martino
Peter Nero
Nelson Riddle
Dionne Warwick
Andy Williams
Tammy Wynette
Wes Montgomery
Ed Ames

Anita Bryant
Charlie Byrd
The Dillards
Dino, Desi, and Billy
Placido Domingo
Patty Duke
Tennessee Ernie Ford
Marvin Gaye
Burl Ives
Jan and Dean
Jack Jones
Gladys Knight and the
   Pips
Brenda Lee
The Lettermen
Liberace
Johnny Mathis
Willie Nelson
Ray Price
Lou Rawls
The Seekers
Frank Sinatra
Kate Smith

The Smothers Brothers
Enzo Stuarti
The Temptations
Sarah Vaughan
Nancy Wilson

"You Won't See Me"
The Bee Gees
Bryan Ferry
Anne Murray
REO Speedwagon

*"You've Got to Hide Your
   Love Away"*
The Beach Boys
Gary Lewis and the
   Playboys
Joe Cocker
Elvis Costello
Dino, Desi and Billy
Percy Faith
Jan and Dean

35. 17 Songs Written by Bob Dylan and Recorded by the Beatles But Never Released

"Abandoned Love" ▪ "Like a Rolling Stone"
"All Along the Watchtower" ▪ "Mama You Been on My Mind"
"Blowing in the Wind" ▪ "Mister Tambourine Man"
"Born in Time" ▪ "One Too Many Mornings"
"Don't Think Twice, It's All Right" ▪ "Please Mrs. Henry"
"Every Grain of Sand" ▪ "Rainy Day Women #12 & 35"
"I Shall Be Released" ▪ "Song to Woody"
"I Threw It All Away" ▪ "Watching the River Flow"
"It Ain't Me Babe"

George (left) on stage with Bob Dylan (right) during the star-studded 1992 concert tribute to the legendary singer/songwriter at Madison Square Garden. (Photofest)

The Life That We Once Knew . . .

36. Beatles Videos

When we did Sgt. Pepper, *we pretended we were other people. It sometimes helps to get a little bit of a scenario going in your mind. So we pretended that John had just rung us up and said, "I'm going on holiday in Spain. There's this little song that I like. Finish it up for me. I trust you." Those were kind of the crucial words: "I trust you."*

—Paul, in the October 23, 1995, issue of *Newsweek,*
talking about completing "Free as a Bird" from
John's cassette demo

It sounds like the bloody Beatles!

—Ringo, after first hearing the completed version
of "Free as a Bird"

112 "BEATLES" AND BEATLES SONG REFERENCES IN THE VIDEO "FREE AS A BIRD"

Since November 1995 when the "Free as a Bird" video first aired at the conclusion of part one of the ABC-TV airing of *The Beatles Anthology*, Beatles fans have been having a splendid time finding all the Beatles references in the video.

This feature is going to list absolutely every Beatles and post-Beatles reference I could come up with in the "Free as a Bird" video.

Some of these will seem obscure, but the Fab Four took great delight in embedding all kinds of arcane and odd references and images in their songs, so that is the spirit with which this list was compiled. Also, it is a certainty that many of the following song references were most assuredly *not* intentionally planted in the video, but the correlations between certain visual moments and Beatles lyrics is uncanny and so I've included everything and anything we could come up with for this compilation. (Special thanks to Tom Schultheiss of Popular Culture, Ink. for his invaluable Beatles lyric concordance *Things We Said Today: The Complete Lyrics and a Concordance to the Beatles' Songs, 1962–1970.*)

It is our belief that this is the most comprehensive compilation of "Free as a Bird" references to date. However, the author and publisher welcome hearing from readers who think they have found something we left out.

I do not provide the times for the individual appearances of visual cues because the video is only a few minutes long and since this list is in running order, it shouldn't be too difficult to find a specific reference.

Of course, let's not take all this too seriously, luvs, okay? We don't want to start any rumors about secret messages hidden in the video. The last time a Beatles rumor got started, Paul had to prove to the world that he wasn't dead, and so, we'll have none of that, okay? (Just for conversation, though, do you think it's a coincidence that I found precisely *112* individual images worth analyzing and that the Beatles songs alluded to came out to a list of *exactly* 112 tunes? Just wondering.)

By the way, I think that some allusions have previously been overlooked, specifically the references to *individual* Beatles works. Whether or not these additional references were actually intended is not known (no one's talking), but there are unquestionably some "post-Beatles" references that jump out at the knowledgeable fan.

For example, in the "Paperback Writer" scene (around two and a half minutes into the video), there's a shot of John sitting in a chair watching the writer.

Is it too much of a stretch to read this as a reference to "Watching the Wheels" from John and Yoko's *Double Fantasy* album, specifically the lyric, "I'm just sitting here watching the wheels go round and round"? After all, we've all heard the expression in which the term "the wheels are turning" is used to metaphorically describe the thought process. So couldn't John be sitting there watching the wheels go round and round in the writer's head?

Sure he could. So, for fun, there are a couple of instances in this feature where I refer to some solo Beatles' songs.

So put your finger on that "Pause" button and ready, steady, let's go flying!

(Note: The "Free as a Bird" video was directed by Joe Pytka, the single was produced by Jeff Lynne.)

1. **Flapping wings/flying** "Free as a Bird" opens with the sound of a flying bird's flapping wings, an auditory reference that can refer to several Beatles songs, including "Flying," "And Your Bird Can Sing," "Blue Jay Way," "Blackbird" ("take these broken wings and learn to fly"), "Back in the U.S.S.R." ("flew in from Miami Beach"), "Mother Nature's Son" ("listen to the pretty sound of music as she flies"), "I Am the Walrus" ("See how they fly"), "Everybody's Got Something to Hide Except Me and My Monkey" ("the deeper you go, the higher you fly"), "Norwegian Wood" ("this bird had flown"), "Cry Baby Cry" ("the local bird and bee"), "Dear Prudence" ("the birds will sing"), and, in the spirit of inclusiveness, the name of Paul's first post-Beatles band, Wings. The wings sound itself imitates the beginning of the original version of "Across the Universe." Of course, the name of this new Beatles song is "Free as a *Bird*."

2. **Photographs** The camera (from the bird's perspective) flies around the room and we see several photographs—of a variety of unrecognized people and scenic shots—on the walls. This can refer to "A Day in the Life" ("I saw the photograph"), and "Penny Lane" ("a barber showing photographs"). Also, the

image of photographs refers to "In My Life" ("people and things that went before"), and "You've Got to Hide Your Love Away" ("everywhere people stare"). Post-Beatles, Ringo had a hit with a song called "Photograph."

3. **The kite in the corner**   This is probably a reference to "Being for the Benefit of Mr. Kite!" but there's a more blatant "Mr. Kite" visual later in the video (see number 57).

4. **The Beatles as children**   On the mantel there are framed photos of the Beatles as youngsters. (Left to right, Paul, John, Ringo, and George.) This image could refer to "Little Child," "Help!" ("when I was younger, so much younger than today"), "Hey Bulldog" ("childlike, no one understands"), "You Never Give Me Your Money" ("all good children go to heaven"). See the previous "photograph" reference.

5. **The coffee mug**   Among the pictures of the Beatles is a coffee mug with a woman's face on it. Some fans have speculated that the woman on the mug is John's mother Julia, but there is no concrete evidence of this. I tend to lean towards the line in "A Day in the Life" in which Paul tells us that he found his way downstairs "and drank a cup," although the "Julia" speculation would fit with the idea of the video as a tribute to John.

6. **The sailor statue and the model ship**   Next to the coffee mug on the mantel stands a figurine of a sailor, and a little way over is the model of a ship. These could be a reference to John's father, Freddie, a merchant seaman. Pertinent Beatles' song references to these artifacts include "Honey Pie" ("sail across the Atlantic" and "kindly send her sailing back to me"), "All Together Now" ("sail the ship"), "It's All Too Much" ("sail me on a silver sun"), and "Yellow Submarine" ("lived a man who sailed to sea" and "so we sailed on to the sun"). In Paul's Wings song "Band on the Run," there's a line about "Sailor Sam."

7. **The mother bunny and baby bunny**   On the mantel are two bunny figurines, a larger one, followed by a little one. Since there are no blatant "rabbit" or "bunny" references in any of the Beatles' songs, and since it is highly unlikely they were *not* placed there intentionally, the only interpretation I can come up with is that these two *hares* are a visual play on the Mop Tops' scandalous *hair* in their early years. A stretch? Maybe, but I'm sure these two figurines don't appear in the video accidentally.

8. **The clock on the mantel**   In front of the model of the sailing ship is a clock that could be a part of the ship. For the few seconds the clock can be seen, it looks as if its hands are reading 7:40, a time with no significance in any of the Beatles' songs. If you play the scene in slow motion and advance the tape one frame at a time as the camera pans across the clock, there are a few frames where it looks as though the hands are actually reading 11:13. On December 8, 1980, John Lennon was shot at 10:49 P.M. and officially pronounced dead at 11:13 P.M. The hands could be shadows, or they could have been intentionally inserted by the Beatles and the director. If they *were* inserted, it makes sense, since "Free as a Bird" *is* a John Lennon composition and this would have been a nice way to pay tribute to John's soul becoming "free as a bird." If it's just an optical illusion, then it once again illustrates the kind of myriad and profound impact the whole Beatles gestalt can have on fans.

Another interesting visual fluke seen at the moment the clock appears to read 11:13 is that the hands seen earlier seem to blend into one curved shape that looks like a body. The "new" hour and minute hands (the 11:13 hands) appear to be arms extending out from the body—just like the Christ seen on a crucifix. When you consider John's early "the Beatles are more popular than Jesus" remark and take into account the allegation by some of his biographers that he had a Messiah complex, then the mystery deepens, doesn't it!

To *really* add fuel to the fire, there is precisely one line in all of John's work as a Beatle that may confirm this leitmotiv once and for all. (I'm sure serious Beatle maniacs have already made the connection.) The line is from "The Ballad of John and Yoko," specifically, "they're gonna *crucify* me."

9. **The butterfly on the wall**   This could be a reference to the line "when you sigh, my inside just flies, butterfly" from "It's Only Love."

10. **The silver beetle on the mantel**   The Beatles were known as the Silver Beatles in their early days (after the break up, re-forming, and renaming of the Quarry Men).

11. **The kitty on the chair**   This could refer to the initially unreleased Lennon/McCartney song "Leave My Kitten Alone."

12. **The two vases of flowers and the picture frame on the table**   In addition to being the first of several "three" references (as in *three* surviving Beatles) these vases can refer to a couple of songs in the Beatles canon. References to "Lucy in the Sky With Diamonds" are obvious ("cellophane flowers of yellow and green," and "as you drift past the flowers, that grow so incredibly high"—the bird/camera drifts past the vases). There's a line about "picking flowers for a friend who came to play" in "Cry Baby Cry."

13. **Aerial shots of Liverpool**   Very briefly, the masts of a ship are seen as the bird swoops down to the docks. A clock in the tower of a Gothic-style building is briefly seen. The time on it is 7:55, which does not have any meaning in the Beatles lyrics. However, this is one of several clock faces that appear throughout the video, all of which display different times, which could be a reference to the song, "Any Time at All."

14. **Liverpool docks**   There are several allusions in the scene in which the Beatles walk with the dockworkers. First is the demeanor and bearing of the exiting workers. They are the quintessential manifestation of the people Paul described in "Eleanor Rigby" as "all the lonely people." Another is that the Liverpool docks are where the ships arrived with rock and roll, blues, and Elvis forty-fives and albums from the United States back in the fifties, recordings that had enormous influence on the Beatles. (Following their 1964 Australia tour, John said, "That's all we ever played, American records.") Also in this scene, we see the dock workers leaving work in the "Rain" for "A Hard Day's Night" after they have obviously "been working like a dog."

15. **The Cavern Club**   This is obvious: Liverpool's Cavern Club is where the Beatles performed in their early years. There are several visual allusions (Numbers 16–21) within this scene worth noting.

16. **The people in line**   The crowd is eager with anticipation, but they are being forced to "Wait." The sentiment of the band inside the club could be expressed by the line from "Sgt. Pepper's Lonely Hearts Club Band" in which they tell

the crowd "we hope you will enjoy the show." Also, in "Good Morning, Good Morning" is the line, "go to a show you hope she goes."

17. **The woman with the ticket**   One woman in line is offering a clearly visible ticket, which could be interpreted as a reference to "Ticket to Ride."

18. **The woman in red**   One woman in the line is wearing a red coat (shades of *Schindler's List!*). The lines "if you wear red tonight," and "red is the color that my baby wore" are in "Yes It Is."

19. **The bouncer**   The guy guarding the door has a no-nonsense "flat-top" haircut, as in "here come old flat top" from "Come Together."

20. **The see-through guy**   Inside the Cavern Club, the Beatles are performing the song "Some Other Guy" (which is not heard) and in the audience is a skeletal figure with a halo of translucent hair. Several lyrical allusions come to mind regarding this guy, most notably the song "I'm Looking Through You." The line "I know what it's like to be dead" (something this guy would seem to know, too!) is in "She Said, She Said." Because of this guy's "bony" bod, we might also cite the line "the worm he licks my bone" from "Yer Blues" as a possible allusion here.

21. **The too-eager fans**   After we see a snippet of the Beatles performing, the bird swoops out of the Cavern Club where a couple of fans are being forced back into line, probably being told to "Get Back."

22. **Strawberry Field**   The bird flies over the Strawberry Field (no final *s*) Salvation Army orphanage, a well-known Liverpool landmark and the inspiration for the title of one of John's most famous songs, "Strawberry Fields Forever." (John composed "Strawberry Fields" during the six weeks he spent on location in Spain filming *How I Won the War*. He was bored and came up with a classic.) If we draw from John's solo work, then the use of the orphanage may be an allusion to one of his most tormented songs, "Mother," specifically the "orphaned" lines, "Mother, you left me" and "Mama don't go."

23. **The walker**   Ringo is briefly seen walking a country lane near the orphanage, carrying a walking stick. He is clearly a "Mother Nature's Son" and his solitude brings to mind the sadness of "This Boy." In the song, "What Goes On" (sung by Ringo, remember) is the line, "the other day I saw you as I walked along the road." "I think I'll take a walk and look for her" is found in "I Don't Want to Spoil the Party." In "When I Get Home," John sings, "'till I walk out that door again." In "Good Day Sunshine" is the line, "we take a walk, the sun is shining down." Most significantly, in "Good Morning, Good Morning" is the lyric, "then you decide to take a walk by the old school."

24. **The trees**   In the "Strawberry Fields" scene, the camera/bird swoops up and down from tree tops to a tree trunk, visually illustrating John's line from "Strawberry Fields Forever" in which he sings, "no one I think is in my tree, I mean it must be high or low."

25. **The marketplace**   The next segment of the video takes place on a busy Liverpool street lined with shops and jammed with people passing by. The "happy ever after in the marketplace" line from "Ob-La-Di, Ob-La-Da" comes immediately to mind.

26. **The "Silver" sign**   On the building above the eggman's truck is the "Silver Hammer Hardware" sign, a reference to the *Abbey Road* song, "Maxwell's Silver Hammer."

27. **The "Dylan" sign**   A shop called Dylans is next to the hardware store, a nod to the line "Just like Dylan's Mr. Jones" from "Yer Blues."

28. **The eggman**   The Liverpool Egg Co. delivery man is holding a tray of eggs, referring to the line in "I Am the Walrus" in which John sings, "I am the eggman."

29. **The running children**   Five children are running towards us. We (and the bird) "see how they run" (from "Lady Madonna"). This scene brings to mind the song "Little Child," which includes the line, "don't you run and hide, just come on, come on." In "Ob-La-Di Ob-La-Da" is the line, "with a couple of kids running in the yard of Desmond and Molly Jones." The line, "you'll come running home." is found in "All I've Gotta Do."

30. **Holding hands**   Three of the running children are holding hands, which is another "three" reference, as well as an allusion to the song, "I Want to Hold Your Hand." The song "If I Fell" has the line, "I found that love was more than just holding hands."

31. **Paul, Ringo, and George come together**   Briefly, the Beatles minus John ("one and one and one is three") are seen crossing the street, providing another "Come Together" allusion.

32. **The covered truck**   The three Beatles pass by a truck covered in a tarpaulin. A word or words impossible to completely identify are written on the tarp. The text could read *O sister, Dexter,* or *Oyster.* If it's *O sister,* the reference could be to one of Yoko Ono's songs, the feminist rallying cry, "Sisters, O Sisters." There are no mentions of the words *Dexter* or *Oyster* in the Beatles lyrics. One strong possibility is that the word could be *Disaster,* which could be a painful acknowledgment of John's assassination. The tarp is, after all, seen with only Paul, George, and Ringo visible in the same shot. After the three lads pass out of camera range, they reappear on the opposite side of the street, but this time John is with them (he's last in the procession), smirking at us with his tongue firmly planted in his cheek.

33. **The fire engine fans**   Two men across the street from the Beatles are admiring a fire engine, reminding us of the line "he likes to keep his fire engine clean" from "Penny Lane." (Paul has admitted that when he used the term "fire engine," he was referring to a somewhat more personal type of "equipment," possessed solely by the male of the species.)

34. **The taxmen**   Two "veddy proper" elderly gentlemen—British Prime Ministers Edward Heath and Harold Wilson—pass by the Beatles, bringing to mind the lines "ha ha Mr. Wilson, ha ha Mr. Heath" from George's song, "Taxman."

35. **Happy Beatles**   After the Taxmen pass by them, the four Beatles are seen laughing and smiling, alluding to the line "Everybody's laughing, everybody's happy" from "Sun King."

36. **The poppy lady**   Next we see "a pretty nurse is selling poppies from a tray" (a direct line from "Penny Lane"). As the bird (camera) flies by her, the nurse stares directly at it, again alluding to "I'm Looking Through You." A couple of other images from this brief scene are worth noting, specifically the advertising message written on the nurse's poppy tray, "Wear Your Poppy With Pride." There are several relevant "pride" references in the Beatles canon, including "pride can hurt you too" from "She Loves You," and "true pride

comes before a fall" from "I'm a Loser." The nurse's customer may be lighting his pipe as the bird flies past him, which would be the first nod to the "choking smoker" lyric from "I Am the Walrus," or "had a smoke" from "A Day in the Life."

37. **The barber shop**   The barber shop displays the sign in its window with the French word *coiffeur,* which might be an allusion to "Michelle," the only Beatles song with French lyrics. There are photographs of the four Beatles in the barber shop's window, which is an illustration of the "Penny Lane" line, "there is a barber showing photographs of every head he's had the pleasure to know." These pictures could also visually allude to the hare/hair image from the opening mantel scene. (After all, the only reason a barber shop would have photographs in the window, would be to show passersby the haircuts of the people in the pictures.) A gentleman (who could be a banker) carrying a briefcase exits the barber shop as the bird flies by, probably alluding to the line "I see the banker sitting waiting for a trim," also from "Penny Lane." (We obviously see him *after* his haircut.) The barber greets a new customer, bringing to mind the song "Hello Goodbye."

38. **The cigarettes sign**   The second "choking smoker" allusion.

39. **Help**   On the building is a handlettered sign (probably a help wanted sign) on which only the word *Help* is discernable.

40. **Does she want to know a secret?**   A little boy cups his mouth to whisper something to a little girl, as in "let me whisper in your ear" from "Do You Want to Know a Secret?"

41. **The two women**   Two women exit the confectioner's shop next door to the barber. One is dressed in an all-black shiny coat, alluding to the songs "Baby's in Black" and "Polythene Pam." The other woman is gorgeous and also seems to be wearing some kind of raincoat. Could this woman be Sexy Sadie? This is probably a stretch because John wrote "Sexy Sadie" with the Maharishi Mahesh Yogi in mind. The more likely reference is to the line "two of us wearing raincoats" from the song "Two of Us." An interesting visual element in this scene is the car parked in the street in front of the shop. As the camera/bird passes by the shop, the top of the car very briefly looks like the cover of a closed coffin, yet another "death" reference.

42. **Ringo**   As the bird flies by the "Penny Lane" bakery ("Penny" is lettered on the window), Ringo steps out of a doorway onto the sidewalk. In the song "When I Get Home" is the line "'till I walk out that door again." A (weak) case could also be made for this image illustrating the line "in an octopus's garden in the shade." (It's worth considering if only because "Octopus's Garden" was written by Ringo.) Some fans have seen an "If I Fell" allusion here because Ringo is "falling" out of the shadows. Perhaps he's a "Day Tripper"? We digress.

43. **The striped door**   Very briefly, the camera pans over a closed door with a striped pattern on the window. This could be a reference to the line "when I came to your door" from "No Reply," as well as the phrase "my old front door" from "Don't Pass Me By."

44. **The soda rack**   In front of the bakery is a two-level rack on which soda is displayed for sale, which could be viewed as a generic reference to the "he shoot Coca-Cola" line from "Come Together."

45. **The couple in the beetle**   Inside what looks like a parked Volkswagen (known around the world as a "beetle") are a couple in an amorous embrace, visually illustrating the song "Why Don't We Do It in the Road?" The camera looks *through* the car window, again alluding to "I'm Looking Through You."

46. **The record store window**   This window has several visible Beatles album covers, posters, and photographs. The identifiable graphic art includes *Abbey Road, Let It Be, Meet the Beatles, With the Beatles!,* a poster from the Shea Stadium concert, *Help!, The Beatles* (the *White Album*), *The Beatles Anthology, The Beatles Second Album,* and the "I Want to Hold Your Hand" single sleeve-photo.

47. **The birthday cake**   In the bakery window is a cake with "Happy Birthday" written on it. This refers to the song "Birthday," as well as the lines "birthday greetings" from "When I'm Sixty-Four" and "all the world is birthday cake" from the song "It's All Too Much."

48. **The frosting 64**   The number 64 is written on the cake, again referring to the song, "When I'm Sixty-Four."

49. **The wedding cake**   We see a wedding cake in the bakery as well, a nod to the song "Eleanor Rigby," specifically the line "where a wedding has been." In "The Ballad of John and Yoko" is the line "you can get married in Gibraltar near Spain."

50. **Driver George**   The bird flies across the street where George is locking his car and pocketing his keys. The most obvious allusion here is to the song "Drive My Car." A vague connection can also be made to the line "on the corner is a banker with a motorcar" from "Penny Lane."

51. **The doctor's office**   George enters 3 Saville Row (the black 3 on the right of the door is another "three" reference in the video), the actual late-sixties location of Apple headquarters, but for the purpose of this video, the offices of Dr. Robert. We learn this when the bird flies by a sign on the side of the building that says "Dr. Robert."

52. **The runners**   People are running along the sidewalk toward the scene of a car crash, the next segment of the video. This is another "see how they run" allusion from "Lady Madonna" as well as a reference to the song title "Run for Your Life." We also find allusions here to the lines "silly people they run around" from "Fixing a Hole"; "see how they run like pigs from a gun" from "I Am the Walrus"; "you got me running" from "What You're Doing"; "running everywhere at such a speed" from "I'm Only Sleeping"; and "people running round it's five o'clock" from "Good Morning, Good Morning."

53. **The accident**   A crowd gathers around an automobile accident, alluding to the line, "a crowd of people stood and stared" from "A Day in the Life." There are several other Beatles lyrics and songs referred to here, the most obvious being "you were in a car crash" from "Don't Pass Me By" and "he blew his mind out in a car" from "A Day in the Life" (which, of course, is a reference to the crash that "killed" Paul). Several children run up to a pregnant woman watching the accident, alluding to "Lady Madonna" (the "children at your feet" line).

54. **The girl in shock**   A young girl sits in the open side door of an ambulance, obviously in shock from the accident. It's quite possible that she could be saying, "I nearly died," a line from "No Reply."

55. **Policemen in a row**   The bird flies by four "pretty little policemen in a row," a visual reference to that line from "I Am the Walrus."

56. **The helter skelter**   The bird flies up and past a spiral-slide lighthouse tower with minaret-type windows and a pennant on top. This structure is known as a helter skelter in England.

57. **The kite**   The second kite in the video—and the second reference to "Being for the Benefit of Mr. Kite!"—is seen, this one flying in the sky.

58. **The ladder**   "She Came in Through the Bathroom Window" is alluded to by the sight of a foot disappearing through a small window from a ladder placed against the side of a tract house.

59. **The sunflower**   A giant sunflower is next to the house with the ladder, alluding to "I'll Follow the Sun" (that's what sunflowers do), as well as referring to the flowers "that grow so incredibly high" from "Lucy in the Sky With Diamonds."

60. **The piggies**   We see a big piggy followed by a group of little piggies running down an alley. This scene refers to the complete lyrics of George's *White Album* song, "Piggies." (The Beatles themselves are seen behind the piggies.)

61. **The lizard**   The bird/camera flies through an open window and very briefly, for only a few frames, the small, dark outline of "a lizard on a window-pane" is seen on the window glass, a reference to "Happiness Is a Warm Gun."

62. **The paperback writer's apartment**   There are several Beatles references in this brief scene, the first to the resident of the apartment himself: a man sitting at a typewriter surrounded by books and papers. He is a "paperback writer."

63. **The book**   The bird flies over a paperback book that some fans claim is by Edgar Allan Poe. I could not read the author's name although it does appear to be a three word name. If the tome *is* by Poe, then it is an obvious allusion to the line "man you should have seen them kicking Edgar Allan Poe" from "I Am the Walrus."

64. **The clock**   The clock in the writer's apartment reads approximately 10:10. A dubious link can be made here to the song "One After 909." If you add one to each digit of 9:09, you get 10:10, right?

65. **The queen**   A picture of Queen Elizabeth appears next. This refers most blatantly to the song "Her Majesty" as well as to the lyric, "in his pocket is a portrait of the queen" from "Penny Lane." Other "queen" references in the Beatles lyrics are the lines "cooking breakfast for the queen," "the queen was in the parlor," "the queen was in the playroom," and "look at the queen," all from "Cry Baby Cry."

66. **The newspaper**   The paper is the *Daily Mail*, referring to the line "his son is working for the *Daily Mail*" from "Paperback Writer."

67. **The headline**   The *Daily Mail* has a headline about "four thousand holes in Blackburn, Lancashire," a direct nod to the line from "A Day in the Life."

68. **The ashtray**   A cigarette is burning in an ashtray, another reference to the "choking smoker" from "I Am the Walrus."

69. **The glass onion**   On top of the cabinet behind the writer's desk is a large, round, glass object that looks very much like a glass onion. If it is, it is a direct allusion to the song "Glass Onion" from the *White Album*.

70. **The candy box**   A box on the table has "Savoy Truffle" printed on it, a nod to George's *White Album* song of the same name.

71. **The apples**   A bunch of green apples is in a basket, a reference to the Beatles' company Apple.

72. **Chairman Mao**   A photograph of Chairman Mao is in the window of the apartment. This probably refers to the line "carrying pictures of Chairman Mao" from "Revolution" but there is a more blatant nod to this image later (see number 81).

73. **The Beatles on TV**   A clip from one of the Beatles' performances on *The Ed Sullivan Show* is on the TV in the writer's apartment.

74. **John**   John is sitting in a chair watching the writer. As mentioned in the introduction to this feature, this could be a nod to John and Yoko's *Double Fantasy* song, "Watching the Wheels." John is tapping his foot in the air, which could be an allusion to "Old Brown Shoe."

    Another interpretation of this scene is that it is a reference to "Come Together," specifically the line that is most often cited as "hold you in his armchair you can feel his disease." Some Beatles chroniclers have reported this "Come Together" line as "hold you in his arms *till you* can feel his disease," but most lyric compilations and concordances use *armchair*. Perhaps settling the question once and for all, on Disc 2 of *The Beatles Anthology 3*, John clearly sings "armchair."

75. **The roof**   The bird flies out of the writer's apartment over a roof with scaffolding on it because someone is "fixing a hole where the rain gets in," illustrating the song "Fixing a Hole" from *Sgt. Pepper*. (This roof scene could also be a nod to the Beatles rooftop performance in *Let It Be*.)

76. **The Blue Meanie**   A nasty Blue Meanie pops his head up out of a hole in the roof, referring to the villains in the Beatles animated *Yellow Submarine* movie.

77. **The bulldog**   A man is walking a bulldog, an allusion to the *Yellow Submarine* song, "Hey Bulldog."

78. **The taxi**   Swooping down over a residential side street, we see a "newspaper taxi" (from "Lucy in the Sky With Diamonds") pull up in front of a row house. A woman exits the building and gets into the taxi. Many fans have seen this as a reference to "She's Leaving Home," but since there's a more obvious reference to this song later (number 100) when a young woman sadly walks a road alone, this city scene is more likely an allusion to the lyric "I was alone, I took a ride" from "Got to Get You Into My Life." The line "the girl that's driving me mad is going away" from "Ticket to Ride" also works here. The line "Sunday mornings go for a ride" from "When I'm Sixty-Four" might work if we accept that all the Liverpool shops are open for business on Sundays. Adding weight to this would be the pertinent line "you and me Sunday driving" from "Two of Us." (After all, someone else could be waiting in the cab for her, right?)

79. **John and Yoko**   We briefly see John and Yoko, in a scene from the film *Let It Be*, waltzing in the street. This is a nod to "I'm Happy Just to Dance With You." The lyrics "how could I dance with another?" and "we danced through the night" from "I Saw Her Standing There" applies to this scene, as does "won't you dance with me?" from "Little Child." The line "let's all get up and dance to

a song" from "Your Mother Should Know" resonates here, as well as "I would like you to dance" from "Birthday" and "we would sing and dance around" from "Octopus's Garden."

80. **Another Blue Meanie**   This one *must* be named "Mean Mr. Mustard" because he "sleeps in a hole in the road." This could be another allusion to the "four thousand holes in Blackburn, Lancashire" line in "A Day in the Life."

81. **Chairman Mao**   Two people are carrying a large picture of Chairman Mao a block down from where the taxi stops. This is another "Revolution" reference, more blatant than number 72.

82. **The bus**   Very briefly, off in the distance a brightly painted, multicolored bus is passing by the street. Some fans have suggested that this is a visual allusion to the Beatles' bus from "Magical Mystery Tour."

83. **Bungalow Bill**   The bird glides into a gathering of many characters from the Beatles' recordings. The first is Bungalow Bill, followed by his mother and leading a procession of guides and an elephant. This is an enactment of the lines "he went out tiger hunting with his elephant and gun/in case of accidents he always took his mom" from "The Continuing Story of Bungalow Bill."

84. **Ringo**   The procession passes Ringo sitting alone at a table. He takes a picture of the group, which could be another nod to his solo hit, "Photograph." In "It Won't Be Long" is the line, "Here I am sitting all on my own." "But you left me sitting on my own" appears in "Tell Me Why."

85. **The beefeaters**   Leading Bungalow Bill's procession are what looks like two beefeater guards of the English army in full dress uniform. This could be a visual allusion to the line "the English Army had just won the war" from "A Day in the Life."

86. **Sean (?)**   A guide is at the end of Bungalow Bill's procession who looks exactly like John and Yoko's son, Sean Lennon. It might actually be Sean making a cameo appearance, but it's more likely a hired actor who looks like Sean— John's "Beautiful Boy"—a tribute to his father. (Interestingly, the Sean look- alike is the only one in the parade wearing modern eyeglasses.)

87. **The elephant**   The huge animal following Bill and his mum could be an allu- sion to "She's So Heavy" as well as "Carry That Weight."

88. **The girl in the blue dress**   The bird flies by a dark-haired girl with a wine glass in her hand, standing by a column talking to two men. There are shapes on her dress that some fans have interpreted as diamonds, which would make this woman "Lucy in the Sky With Diamonds." The only problems are that the patterns are most definitely not diamond-shaped and she is not in the sky. I do think, however, that "Lucy" *is* being referenced here. For a couple of seconds, sunlight can be seen bathing the top of the girl's hair. It isn't too much of a stretch to imagine that she also has the sun in her face, leading us to the line "look for the girl with the sun in her eyes" from "Lucy." (The room where the cocktail party is held has an open skylight through which the sun pours and through which the bird ultimately exits.) Another allusion in this scene might be found in the girl's wine glass, referencing the line "drinking her wine" from "Norwegian Wood." The woman and the two men she's talking to are yet another "three" image.

89. **Ravi Shankar** The bird flies by Indian musician Ravi Shankar sitting cross-legged playing the sitar. The legendary sitarist was a tremendous influence on George Harrison and inspired George to include Indian instruments like the tabla, swordmandel, dilruba, and tamboura in "Within You Without You" on *Sgt. Pepper's Lonely Hearts Club Band* and in many of his solo pieces.

90. **Brian Epstein** The Beatles' manager Brian Epstein is wrapping a scarf around his neck. Epstein died in 1967 of an overdose of the drug Carbitral and this scene could be alluding to the line, "some day you'll find that I have gone" from "I'll Follow the Sun."

91. **The Sgt. Pepper scene** This scene briefly recreates part of the cover photo of the *Sgt. Pepper* album. Notable figures from the photo seen here are H. G. Wells, Lawrence of Arabia, Edgar Allan Poe, Marilyn Monroe, and a life-size photo of James Dean with Quarry Men bass player Stu Sutcliffe's head attached. (I also see a guy dressed in white who reminds me of Mark Twain but since Twain does not appear on the *Sgt. Pepper* cover, it may not be he.)

92. **The Maharishi** Standing on the dais next to the James Dean/Stu Sutcliffe composite is the Maharishi Mahesh Yogi, the guru who inspired John to write "Sexy Sadie."

93. **The sun** The bird flies up into the blinding sunlight through an open, multi-paneled glass dome that is apparently known in England as a "Glass Onion." This would be the second "Glass Onion" allusion if the one spotted in the paperback writer's apartment is also correct. The flight into the bright sun alludes to several Beatles tunes, most notably "I'll Follow the Sun," "Here Comes the Sun," "Sun King," "Rain" ("when the sun shines"), "Good Day Sunshine" ("the sun is shining down"), "I Am the Walrus" ("waiting for the sun"), "Dear Prudence" ("the sun is up"), "Mother Nature's Son" ("sings a lazy song beneath the sun"), "It's All Too Much" ("sail me on a silver sun"), "I've Got a Feeling" ("everybody saw the sun shine"), and "Two of Us" ("standing solo in the sun"). Also, allusions can be found in "The Word" ("it's so fine, it's sunshine") and because of the many panes of sun-drenched glass, "Across the Universe" ("images of broken light").

94. **The cemetery** The bird flies into a cemetery. A general reference to "Eleanor Rigby" can be cited just from the location: "buried along with her name."

95. **The statue** We next see a statue of the Blessed Virgin Mary, alluding to the song "Lady Madonna" as well as the line "Mother Mary comes to me" from "Let It Be." As the bird flies by, the statue turns its head to follow it. This could be a reference to the line "watching her eyes and hoping I'm always there" from "Here, There, and Everywhere."

96. **The tombstone** Next is Eleanor Rigby's actual grave marker on which is written "In Loving Memory" above her name.

97. **Father McKenzie** The clergyman from the song walks away from the grave, illustrating the line from "as he walks from the grave" from "Eleanor Rigby."

98. **Martha** As Father McKenzie walks away, a big sheepdog bounds across the grass. This is a reference to Paul's pet, Martha the sheepdog, the canine that inspired him to write the song "Martha My Dear." There is a more obscure reference here as well, specifically to the line, "sheepdog standing in the rain" from "Hey Bulldog."

99. **Paul**   The bird flies over a country road where Paul is jumping around like "A Fool on the Hill."

100. **"She is far away"**   A woman carrying a suitcase is seen walking down the road, visually illustrating the title and lyrics of the song "She's Leaving Home."

101. **The car**   A Rolls Royce is driving away from the woman, another possible reference to "Drive My Car." (The cost of a Rolls has led some fans to see this as an allusion to "Baby, You're a Rich Man.") Other car references include the line "If you drive a car, I'll tax the street" from "Taxman," "he blew his mind out in a car" from "A Day in the Life," and "you were in a car crash" from "Don't Pass Me By."

102. **The road**   Off in the distance is a "long and winding road."

103. **Mountains**   In the distance, far beyond the road, "snow-peaked mountains" are glimpsed which could be an allusion to the image and line from "Back in the U.S.S.R."

104. **Abbey Road**   The bird flies over the famous Abbey Road intersection that appears on the *Abbey Road* album cover. A Volkswagen is parked at the curb, referring to the VW (another "beetle") with the license plate "28IF" on the original cover that was supposed to tell fans that Paul would have been twenty-eight *if* he had lived.

105. **Rita (?)**   A woman is crossing Abbey Road and walking towards the Volkswagen. She is wearing a dress and a hat, but it is unclear whether or not it's a uniform. Since she also appears to be carrying a pad (as in citations pad), this would seem to be Rita the meter maid from "Lovely Rita." (Just before she disappears out of frame, it looks like she veers slightly toward the front of the Volkswagen, as though she was going to write a ticket and place it on the windshield.)

106. **The chairs**   On the balcony above the entrance to the concert hall are *three* chairs, providing another "three" reference and again illustrating the "one and one and one is three" line from "Come Together."

107. **The concertgoers**   The bird follows a group of people into a concert hall. Since we next see the *conclusion* of a performance, we must assume that these people are filing in for the next show, a reference to the line "we hope you will enjoy the show" from "Sgt. Pepper's Lonely Hearts Club Band." They are waiting for "the singer" to "sing a song." (Also, if the concert hall is the Royal Albert Hall, then "A Day in the Life" is being alluded to again.

108. **The joker**   A joker in a pointed hat is briefly seen backstage, alluding to "don't you think the joker laughs at you" from "I Am the Walrus."

109. **The spotlight**   The ukulele player is bathed in a bright white spotlight, a reference to "The Inner Light."

110. **The ukulele player**   He is obviously playing a song from years past, which could be a nod to the line "a song that was a hit before your mother was born" from "Your Mother Should Know."

111. **The curtain**   The curtain comes down on the performer, alluding to "The End."

112. **John and the backwards message**   John is heard saying the words "Made by John Lennon" which, when played backwards, are heard as "turned out nice again, didn't it?"

It certainly did.

The song   The years 1995 and 1996 were busy ones for the late John Lennon. He had two new songs out and also appeared in a 10-hour documentary.

When Yoko gave John's cassette demo of the incomplete song "Free as a Bird" to Paul, George, and Ringo in 1994, they went to work, actually writing additional new material for the song and putting together an ingeniously complex and referential video.

"Real Love," on the other hand, was a completely finished song when Yoko turned over the tape to the other Beatles. John recorded the entire song alone at the piano and later added a second vocal line and a drum machine. The finished version of "Real Love" as it appears on *Anthology 2* is credited to John Lennon alone. ("Free as a Bird" is likewise credited to John Lennon as an "original composition," but the "Beatles version" is credited to all four Beatles.) "Real Love" is an infectious tune that John recorded at home in late 1979 during his "househusband" years. ("Beautiful Boy," the gorgeous *Double Fantasy* ballad, was also recorded at home during this period.)

John recorded seven almost identical demos of "Real Love" (which for a time had the working title of "Real Life"). Take 6 had previously been released on the *Imagine: John Lennon* soundtrack and it isn't known what take Yoko turned over to the other Beatles, although it probably doesn't make that much difference if the takes were all essentially the same.

Paul, George, and Ringo are at the top of their game with their work on "Real Love." According to the liner notes for *Anthology 2,* they started working on the song about a year after they finished "Free as a Bird."

Paul and George added acoustic guitars, George played lead guitar, and Ringo played drums. Paul played not one, but two bass tracks for the recording, one of which was performed on the original stand-up double bass that Bill Black had played on Elvis's song "Heartbreak Hotel." (How's that for a musical lineage?) Backing vocals were sung by Paul and George, and Paul also sang behind John's part to bolster the "occasionally thin" sound of John's lead vocal.

There are some especially nice musical touches in "Real Love," most notably Ringo's absolutely perfect drumming, George's lead guitar work, and the harmonies. Music can be heard in the last few seconds of the song that sounds like a banjo, but which is probably a honky-tonk piano. Nonetheless, it's a nice touch and is representative of the care and musical skill put into transforming a hissy, clicking, buzzing demo tape into a *Beatles record*—and a *damn good* Beatles record at that. Credit is due Jeff Lynne.

The video   Work on recording "Real Love" (the song) began in February 1995 in Paul McCartney's home studio, The Mill. The video for this song, directed by Kevin Godley, was nowhere near as elaborate as that for "Free as a Bird" and consisted mainly of scenes from the "Real Love" recording sessions interspersed throughout with Beatles career footage (*Magical Mystery Tour, Let It Be,* the "Hello, Goodbye" video, the *Our World* performance, etc.) and clips from *Imagine.*

Paul McCartney has an incredible home recording studio and one of the real thrills for Beatles fans is the chance to see inside this hallowed *sanctum sanctorum.*

The "Real Love" video is probably as close as we're going to get to a guided tour of The Mill and, as such, it is great fun to watch.

The video begins with John's white piano rising into the skies above the Liverpool docks (to heaven?) and the video focuses heavily on John throughout its four minutes. The editing in this video is brilliant. There is a line in "Real Love" where John sings "accept you where my life will go." The editors found a clip of John from the *Let It Be/White Album* days where he is singing words that perfectly match the last three of four syllables of the "Real Love" line, giving the impression that John was in the studio recording the song with the other Beatles—an extremely powerful moment. (They also use an early clip of John strumming a guitar in time to "Real Love" that works just as well.)

I personally would have preferred more scenes of Paul, George, and Ringo recording the song in the studio. A couple of times we see George playing the actual riff we're hearing, or we see Ringo playing the drum track to the song in real time and these, without question, are the most memorable moments in the video. Actually seeing the Beatles performing together again live in a studio is an experience that cannot be adequately described by most fans. We could have used more of that.

Overall, the "Real Love" video is a wonderful companion piece to "Free as a Bird" and what these two marvelous Beatles creations do is make us want more. If I had one "Beatles" wish, it would be that Paul, George, and Ringo somehow find a way to work on the more than two dozen surviving unreleased John Lennon compositions and do a whole album of brand new Beatles songs, in the tradition of "Free as a Bird" and "Real Love." Yoko has the tapes, the three surviving Beatles are all back on good terms with her and each other. The success of the *Anthology* and the new tunes might spur them all to go even further with John's demo tapes.

If they did, the world would receive a gift of a *brand new Beatles album*.

Imagine.

He Blew His Mind Out
in a Car . . .

37. "Paul Is Dead"

CHRIS FARLEY   You remember when you were with the Beatles and you were
    supposed to be dead? And . . . uh . . . there was all these clues, that . . . like
    . . . you play some song backwards and it'd say . . . like . . . "Paul is dead."
    And . . . uh . . . everyone thought you were dead . . . or somethin' . . .
PAUL McCARTNEY   Yeah.
CHRIS FARLEY   Uh, that was a hoax, right?
PAUL McCARTNEY   Yeah, I wasn't really dead.
CHRIS FARLEY   Right.

> —From an interview with Paul McCartney on
> "The Chris Farley Show" segment of the
> February 13, 1993, *Saturday Night Live*

41 "PAUL IS DEAD" CLUES

Paul McCartney is not dead, okay?

No, really.

He's *not* dead.

Yeah, I know that the cover of *Abbey Road* is a symbolic reenactment of his
funeral procession. You did know that corpses are buried barefoot, now, didn't you?
Paul was actually wearing sandals the day they took the picture and for one of the
shots, he decided to walk across the intersection barefoot.

Honest.

Yes, I know that in the promotional booklet that came with the *Magical Mystery Tour* album, Paul is the only Beatle wearing a black carnation instead of a red
one during the "Blue Jay Way" sequence. The truth is that the florist simply ran
out of red carnations the day they shot the picture and Paul just happened to be the
one who got the black one.

Paul McCartney is most assuredly alive and well. At this writing, his new CD,
Flaming Pie, a brilliant album containing some of his strongest work in years (with
the band made up entirely of *Paul* sounding incredibly Beatlesque if the truth be
told), recently debuted in the number-two spot on the charts, having sold 121,000
copies in its first week of release.

There is no denying that finding and analyzing all the "Paul Is Dead" clues is an enormous amount of fun. It is probably what prolonged the worldwide frenzy back in September, October, and November of 1969 when the rumor that Paul had died in a car crash first surfaced thanks to an intentionally satirical review of *Abbey Road* in a college newspaper. That paper alleged to find all kinds of secret messages and clues planted by the surviving Beatles to tell the world that Mr. McCartney was no longer with us.

The article that started it all was written by University of Michigan sophomore Fred LaBour. LaBour was inspired to write the review after Detroit's WKNR-FM disk jockey Russ Gibb received a call from a guy named Tom who claimed to have found secret messages on Beatles records revealing that McCartney was dead.

LaBour heard Gibb's conversation with the caller and decided to deliberately expand on the "Paul Is Dead" thesis in his *Abbey Road* review for the University of Michigan's school newspaper, the *Michigan Daily*.

John Gray, the editor of the *Daily,* personally introduced LaBour's article:

> Mr. LaBour was originally assigned to review *Abbey Road,* the Beatles' latest album, for the *Daily*. While extensively researching *Abbey Road*'s background, however, he chanced upon a startling string of coincidences which put him on the trail of something much more significant. He wishes to thank WKNR-FM, Louise Harrison Caldwell, and George Martin's illegitimate daughter Marian for their help. Mr. LaBour says it's all true.

LaBour's article began:

> Paul McCartney was killed in an automobile accident in early November 1966 after leaving EMI recording studios tired, sad, and dejected.
>
> The Beatles had been preparing their forthcoming album, tentatively entitled *Smile,* when progress bogged down in intragroup hassles and bickering. Paul climbed into his Aston-Martin, sped away into the rainy, chilly night, and was found four hours later pinned under his car in a culvert with the top of his head sheared off. He was deader than a doornail.

LaBour's article discussed the most common "Paul Is Dead" clues, including Paul's "O. P. D." ("Officially Pronounced Dead") jacket patch on the *Sgt. Pepper* album; the "I buried Paul" fadeout on "Strawberry Fields Forever"; all the appearances of hands above Paul's head in Beatles photographs; the *Abbey Road* funeral procession; and the backwards message "Turn me on, dead man" in "Revolution No. 9."

The myth immediately took hold and blossomed. It was learned that the surviving Beatles decided that they would *not* reveal this terrible tragedy to their fans but instead, replace Paul with a double, a musical doppelgänger.

Paul's "replacement" was a guy by the name of William Campbell, a lucky bloke who just so happened to be the winner of a Paul McCartney look-alike contest. Not only was Campbell the spitting image of the "cute" Beatle, he was also musically and vocally gifted enough to be able to duplicate Paul's writing, playing, and singing abilities. After a period of "training" by John, George, and Ringo, Campbell took Paul's place in the Beatles.

Even though the Beatles did not want to shock the world by revealing the truth about Paul's violent death, they had too much respect for their fans not to let them somehow know of his death. So they began planting "clues" on Beatles albums that would alert the attentive fan to the terrible reality.

The rumors surrounding Paul's alleged death grew into a cottage industry. Special edition magazines and TV and radio programs were devoted to the rumors, and countless newspaper articles fueled the fervor. I can remember trading clues with fellow Beatles fans when I was in my teens, aghast at the thought that the rumors might actually prove to be true. They weren't, as we now know, and it would be another decade before we actually would have to go through the *real* death of a Beatle.

This feature compiles some of the more intriguing "hidden" clues. I have concentrated here on primarily visual clues found on record albums and on aural clues heard in the Beatles' songs. I have not focused on song lyrics because they are open to a wide range of interpretation—almost anything can be read into a line from a song. I do, however, examine song lyrics that seem to be a deliberate attempt by the Beatles to address the whole "Paul Is Dead" phenomenon (such as the "walrus was Paul" line in "Glass Onion.")

1. **The two *Yesterday and Today* album covers**   *Yesterday and Today* was the first Beatles album released after Paul's rumored death. The two versions of the album's cover are supposed to contain the first of the hidden messages from the Fab Four.

    The first cover, the infamous recalled "butcher" cover, is supposed to contain the most blatant acknowledgment of Paul's death. (The "butcher" cover was originally shot for the "Paperback Writer" single and added to the album as an afterthought. This cover, which is now an extremely valuable collectible, shows the four Beatles in white butcher coats, covered with decapitated dolls and bloody meat.) The clues here are that the two headless dolls in the picture are resting on Paul's right and left shoulders and a doll's head sits in his lap. (George holds the other severed head.) This is supposed to be the Beatles' way of visually illustrating the bloody results of Paul's car crash. There is a pair of false teeth on Paul's right arm, apparently indicating that his teeth were knocked out during the accident and they could not identify his body from dental records.

    The second cover—the "trunk" cover—shows us Paul sitting in a trunk that is standing on its side with its cover open. This trunk is supposed to symbolize a coffin and indicate that Paul is buried somewhere. In the picture, none of the Beatles are smiling and John, George, and Ringo are all standing above the trunk supposedly looking down into Paul's casket.
2. **The *Rubber Soul* album cover**   This cover is supposed to be a photograph taken from inside Paul's grave looking up. The four Beatles are all seen from below in sort of a fisheye view and it is their way of telling fans that Paul is dead. The title *Rubber Soul* is also their way of hinting at the bogus nature of the Paul replacement.
3. **The *Revolver* cover**   This cover, designed by Beatle pal and fellow Brian Epstein client Klaus Voorman, consists of a collage of line drawings and black-

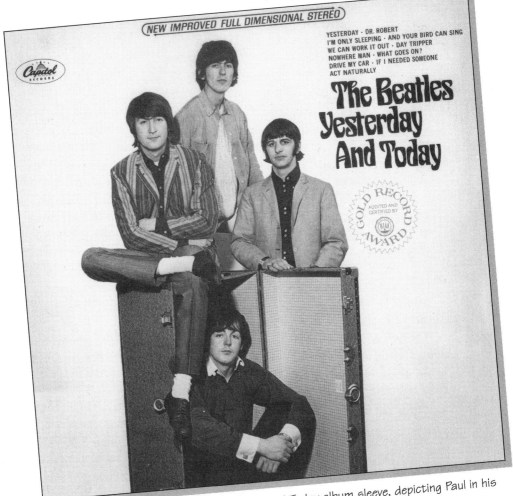

NEW IMPROVED FULL DIMENSIONAL STEREO

Capitol RECORDS

YESTERDAY · DR. ROBERT
I'M ONLY SLEEPING · AND YOUR BIRD CAN SING
WE CAN WORK IT OUT · DAY TRIPPER
NOWHERE MAN · WHAT GOES ON?
DRIVE MY CAR · IF I NEEDED SOMEONE
ACT NATURALLY

The Beatles
Yesterday
And Today

GOLD RECORD AWARD
AUDITED AND CERTIFIED BY RIAA

The "bloodless" version of the Yesterday and Today album sleeve, depicting Paul in his coffin/steamer trunk. (Photofest)

and-white photos of the four Beatles. The death clue? The line drawing of Paul's face is the only one shown in profile; all the others are seen full face. Why this means Paul is dead baffles the mind, but cluesters have considered this to be one of the hints.

4. **The "Strawberry Fields Forever"/"Penny Lane" single sleeve**   This sleeve has a framed photo of the Beatles on a stage. Four stage spotlights highlight the boys: one above John's head, one above Ringo's head, and one to the left of George. Paul's spotlight, however, emanates from a mirror directly in front of him, indicating, presumably, that he is on another plane, and that his "inner light" is in a mirror world somewhere. Quite clever, wouldn't you say?

5. **The "Strawberry Fields Forever" video**   Paul is seen in a tree looking down on the other three, symbolically representing once again that he has risen above the survivors to another plane.

There are several visual clues on the cover of *Sgt. Pepper* that indicate that the Beatles are trying to tell the world that Paul is dead.

6. **Funeral photo**   The first and most obvious *Sgt. Pepper* clue is that the cover photo depicts a funeral. Whose? Why, Paul's of course!

   Is it too much of a stretch to read sadness in the faces of the wax Beatles figures as they morosely stare down at Paul's "grave"? Just asking.

7. **The flower guitar**   In the foreground is a bass guitar made of flowers that has only three strings. This is Paul's bass and the three strings symbolize the three remaining Beatles. Some people also claim that they can see "Paul?" spelled out in the flowers.

8. **The propped-up Paul**   Paul is the only one facing front and the other three Beatles are all turned towards him as though they were holding him up. If he were dead, he would need to be held up, right? (Shades of *Weekend at Bernie's!*) Outtakes of the *Sgt. Pepper* photo shoot session show Paul in a variety of positions and locations on the set, including sitting down.

9. **Paul's black instrument**   John, George, and Ringo are all holding brass instruments. Paul's is black, symbolizing his death.

10. **The doll and her car**   There is a doll to the left of the Beatles wearing a dress that reads "Welcome the Rolling Stones." On the doll's lap is a toy car that is supposed to be either on fire or filled with blood. This represents the Aston-Martin that Paul was driving when he had his fateful accident on November 9, 1966. There appears to be streaks of blood running down the doll's dress.

11. **The secret message on the bass drum**   If you take a mirror and place it so that you split the words "Lonely" and "Hearts" horizontally, the resulting "words" spell out the secret message "ONE HE DIE." This is a stretch but this message can actually be seen if you're generous about interpreting certain symbols and curves as letters. The actual text that appears if you cover the bottom half of the letters so that the top halves are doubled and reversed is "1ONE1X HE|DIE."

12. **The hand above Paul's head**   There is an open palm above Paul's head. According to the "Paul Is Dead" mythology, this is supposed to be an Eastern gesture that is made over someone about to be buried. No such symbology exists.

13. **The Shiva doll**   A four-armed Indian Shiva doll points his "death" hand (the left rear hand) at Paul.

14. **George's message**   On the back cover of the *Sgt. Pepper* album, George can be seen pointing directly at the lyric "Wednesday morning at five o'clock" in "She's Leaving Home." This was supposed to be the time and day of Paul's fatal accident.

15. **Without Paul?**   Paul's head touches the words "Without You" from George's song, "Within You Without You," indicating that the Beatles and the world must survive without the esteemed Signore McCartney.

16. **Paul's back?**   On the back cover of the *Sgt. Pepper* album, Paul is the only one with his back to the camera. This means that he is dead. There are conflicting stories explaining why Paul is, indeed, seen only from behind. One explanation was that it wasn't even Paul in the picture. In *The Long and Winding Road: A History of the Beatles on Record*, Neville Stannard wrote:

Also on the back cover is a small picture of the Beatles, but one Beatle has his back turned. This is because it isn't a Beatles at all, and is, in fact, Mal Evans—Mal deputized for Paul, who was in America to be with Jane Asher on her twenty-first birthday . . . As the sleeve had to go into production by the end of April, before Paul was due to return, Mal donned Paul's Sgt. Pepper gear and stood in for him, but turned his back so that people would not suspect that Paul was absent.

To further confuse matters, Paul himself has talked about his backwards pose on the cover. Paul claims that he is, in fact, the person seen in the photograph. In 1980, he told *Musician* magazine, "[I]t was just a goof when we were doing the photos. I turned my back and it was just a joke."

In Mark Lewisohn's essential *The Beatles Recording Sessions,* there are several rare, full-color outtakes from the same *Sgt. Pepper* photo shoot and Paul is in every one of them.

17. **Paul's "O. P. D." patch**   On the inside album cover, Paul is seen wearing a patch on his jacket that reads "O. P. D.," initials which supposedly stand for "Officially Pronounced Dead," the British equivalent of the American phrase "Dead on Arrival." This was allegedly a very blatant way for the Beatles to tell us that Paul was dead. The truth is that the patch actually reads "O. P. P.," which stands for "Ontario Provincial Police." The garment has a fold in it which makes the last *P* look like a *D* to some people. All of the Beatles received these patches as a gift during their 1965 North American tour. (The Fab Four played the Toronto Maple Leaf Stadium on August 17, 1965.)

18. **Paul's Medal of Valor**   In the inside photo, Paul is wearing a British Medal of Valor. This was alleged to be the surviving Beatles' way of telling his fans that he died a heroic death. The only trouble with this clue is that the medal he (and George, for that matter) are wearing is not a British Medal of Valor. What *does* the medal represent? Who knows?

19. **The bloody sleeve**   Some fans have noted that the original inner sleeve of the *Sgt. Pepper* album is colored red at the bottom and gets progressively lighter as the color rises to the top of the sleeve. This is supposed to mean that the album was standing in blood and the red liquid seeped its way up through the paper. Does this mean that Paul is dead? Of course it does!

20. **Selected *Sgt. Pepper* lyrics**   To many "Paul Is Dead" cluesters, *Sgt. Pepper* is the album that includes the most candid lyrical admissions that Paul died and was replaced by look-alike William Campbell. The first clue comes in the first song, "Sgt. Pepper's Lonely Hearts Club Band" in which "Paul" sings "so let me introduce to you the one and only Billy Shears." "Billy Shears" is supposed to be the words "Billy's here," revealing that Paul has been replaced by William "Billy" Campbell.

In "She's Leaving Home" is the previously mentioned line "Wednesday morning at five o'clock" which is supposed to be the time of Paul's fatal car accident.

In "Lovely Rita" Paul tells us that he "caught a glimpse of Rita" and was so distracted that he "took her home" and "nearly made it." This leads us to the line telling us that he "didn't notice that the light had changed" from "A Day in the Life." We are also told in "A Day in the Life" that "he blew his mind out in a car."

In "Good Morning, Good Morning," we again are told the time of Paul's accident: "People running 'round, it's five o'clock."

In "Within You Without You" we are told that life goes on "without you [Paul]."

21. **In the British groove**   On the inner groove of side two of the British *Sgt. Pepper* disk and subsequently at the end of the *Sgt Pepper* CD, the words "never could be any other way" are repeated over and over. This is supposed to be the Beatles' way of telling Paul's fans to accept his death.

22. **Really?**   On mono pressings of the album, during the reprise of the title cut, a voice can be heard shouting, "Paul McCartney is dead, everybody! Really, really dead!"

23. **Paul's where?**   On European pressings of *Sgt. Pepper*, after "A Day in the Life," there are two seconds of chatter which apparently can be interpreted as the phrase "Paul's found heaven."

THE *MAGICAL MYSTERY TOUR* ALBUM

24. **Cover phone number**   The word *Beatles* is written in stars on the cover of the *Magical Mystery Tour* album. If you read the word upside down it reveals the phone number 537-1038, or the phone number 231-7438, depending on how you interpret certain "digits." According to the "Paul Is Dead" mythology, if you called this number at a certain time (revealed in the lyrics of "She's Leaving Home"), you would be connected with none other than Billy Shears himself (actually Paul's replacement William Campbell), who would then tell you the truth about Paul's death. (Where, one wonders, might we find clues revealing the area code?)

25. **The magical Beatles**   On the inside cover of the *Magical Mystery Tour* album, there is a drawing of the four boys dressed as magicians. Paul's hat has black flowers on it which, of course, means that he is dead.

26. **The walrus was Paul?**   On the *Magical Mystery Tour* album cover, Paul is dressed as a black walrus, supposedly a symbol of death in some Scandinavian cultures. This is totally inaccurate. There is no connection between the symbol of the walrus and the concept of death in any of the Scandinavian mythologies.

27. **Paul was?**   On page 3 of the souvenir booklet that came with the *Magical Mystery Tour* album, Paul is sitting behind a desk that has a sign on it that reads "I WAS." Some people interpret this sign as reading "I YOU WAS." Whatever. This sign means, of course, that Paul is dead.

28. **The black flower**   As mentioned in the introduction to this chapter, in the "white tails" photograph in the *Magical Mystery Tour* photo booklet, John, George, and Ringo are wearing red carnations and Paul is wearing a black one. This means that he is dead, even though he just happened to be the Beatle who got the black flower after the florist ran out of red ones. Can you imagine the confusion if one of the other Beatles had worn the black one for that picture? The "Paul Is Dead" legend would have entered a whole new phase and befuddled fans who were certain they had already figured the whole shebang out!

29. **Another hand over Paul's head**   On page 24 of the booklet, a man in a bowler hat holds his hand above Paul's head (see number 12).

30. **"Your Mother Should Know"**   If this *entire song* (sheesh) is played backwards, it supposedly contains such lines as "Why doesn't she know me dead?" and "I

shed the light." Tell you what: You play the song backwards and listen for recognizable English and let me know, okay?

31. **John buried Paul** At the conclusion of "Strawberry Fields Forever," John can be heard saying, "I buried Paul." What he is actually saying is "cranberry sauce" (as can be plainly heard in the "Strawberry Fields" alternative takes on the *Anthology*.)

THE *WHITE ALBUM* CLUES

32. **"Glass Onion" means casket handles?** Russ Gibb claimed that the term "glass onion" was British slang for casket handles because that's what the old-style handles looked like. There is no historical documentation that confirms this theory.

33. **"The walrus was Paul"** When John sang this line in "Glass Onion," fans saw this as a confirmation of Paul's death because of the mistaken interpretation of the walrus being a symbol for death.

34. **The end of "I'm So Tired"** If you play backwards the mumbling at the conclusion of John's "I'm So Tired" on the *White Album* and listen carefully, you can hear, "Paul is dead, man, miss him, miss him." In Mark Lewisohn's important chronicle of the Beatles in the studio, *The Beatles Recording Sessions*, he reveals that John actually muttered (in *forward* speech, of course), "Monsieur, monsieur, how about another one?"

35. **George's lament** At the end of "While My Guitar Gently Weeps," George cries out "Paul, Paul, Paul." This meant that Paul was dead. What George actually sings/moans is "oh, oh, oh."

36. **"Number 9. Number 9. Number 9. Number . . ."—oh, forget it** This is a spooky one. When the "Number 9" mantra from "Revolution 9" on the *White Album* is played backwards, it *really* does sound like "Turn me on, dead man." John Lennon admitted that all the EMI recording engineers would say the take number onto the tape before beginning a recording and John just happened to like the sound of the guy saying, "Number 9." Andru Reeve, in his definitive "Paul Is Dead" book, *Turn Me On, Dead Man*, suggests that the phonetic reversal might have been intentional; that John played "Turn me on, dead man" backwards and decided it sounded enough like "Number 9" to ultimately work. John Lennon himself refutes this theory but, then again, maybe *John's denial* was part of the conspiracy, too! (Only kidding.)

YELLOW SUBMARINE

37. **Yet *another* hand over Paul's head!** On the *Yellow Submarine* album cover, John is holding his hand over Paul's head (see numbers 12 and 28).

ABBEY ROAD

38. **The funeral procession** The *Abbey Road* album cover was the visual confirmation of Paul's death that really pushed many fans over the edge. The photo of the Beatles crossing Abbey Road supposedly contained scads of "how can it not be so!" clues that drove "Paul Is Dead" theorists nuts.

133

First, the Beatles' attire tells the tale. John is dressed in all white. This meant that symbolically he was the priest at Paul's funeral. Ringo is dressed in a tai-

A clue from the Magical Mystery Tour souvenir booklet. Paul was, wasn't he?! (Editor's collection)

lored black suit. This meant he was the funeral director. George is in denim, meaning he was the grave digger. Paul was dressed in a suit, but barefoot, out of step with the others, with his eyes closed, and carrying an unlit cigarette in the wrong hand. Of course, this meant that he was the corpse. In addition to the Beatles themselves, other clues include the Volkswagen "Beetle" parked on the street. This vehicle has the license plate "LMW 28IF." The "LMW" was supposed to translate as "Linda McCartney Weeps" and the "28IF" meant that Paul would have been twenty-eight *if* he had lived.

All of these "clues" have been quite effectively debunked, but the fact that fans were able to come up with such detailed interpretations from one photo illustrates the rabid interest the "Paul Is Dead" theory provoked in Beatles watchers.

The clothes were just what each Beatle happened to wear the day the picture was taken. (During a 1969 radio interview, John said, "We all decided individually what to wear that day for the photograph.") Paul being barefoot is coin-

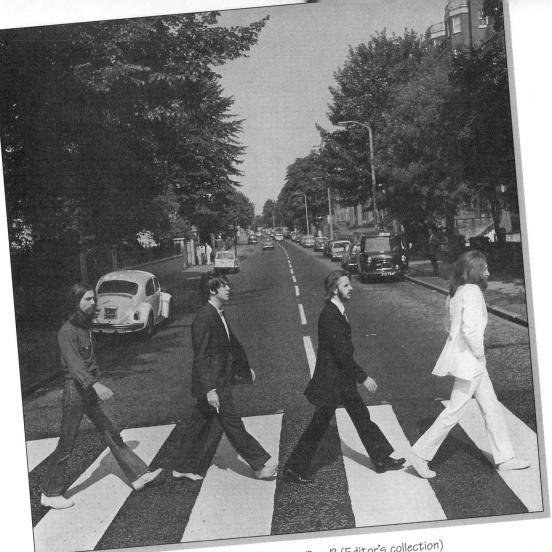

Can you spot all the clues on the cover of *Abbey Road*? (Editor's collection)

cidence: He showed up for the shoot in sandals and decided to take them off for one shot. There are five outtakes from this session in which Paul is seen crossing the street wearing the sandals in two of them.

The VW just happened to be parked there and couldn't be moved. (This car sold for $4,000 at auction in 1986.) The license plate was the car's actual plate.

39. **We've just seen a face?**   On the back of the *Abbey Road* album cover, a girl in a blue dress is passing in front of the wall on which "The Beatles" is written. If you look carefully, you can see Paul's face (actually his nose and mouth) in the girl's elbow. To be fair, there *is* something in the photo that can be interpreted as a face, but who the hell would have seen it if no one believed Paul was dead? Also on the back cover, in the upper-left-hand corner, are a series of eight dots that form the number 3 when connected with a pen or marker. This was how the surviving Beatles told us that there were only three of them left. In reality, the number could also be seen as a 5 which would add whole new dimension to the rumor, wouldn't it?

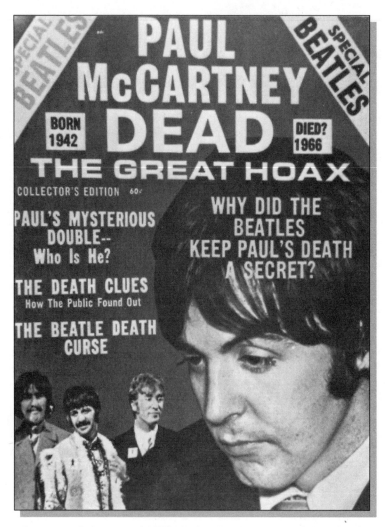

The cover of the special 1978 *Paul is Dead* magazine. (Photofest)

40. **One and one and one . . .** This was blatant. In "Come Together," John sang the line, "one and one and one is three," yet another "three" message about the loss of one Beatle.

41. **"Octopus's Garden"** Supposedly, the term *octopus's garden* is a slang British naval term for burial at sea from either drowning or as an intentional interment similar to *Davey Jones' locker.* This was Ringo's way of telling us that Paul was dead.

In a 1996 interview, Ringo talked about writing "Octopus's Garden" and revealed that someone once told him that it was common for octopuses to collect shiny things from the ocean floor and neatly arrange them in their nest . . . almost like flowers in a garden. Ringo thought it was the "happiest" thing he had ever heard and was inspired to write the song.

To sum up the whole "Paul Is Dead" fiasco, I turn the microphone over to Barbara Suczek, former sociology lecturer at San Francisco State University. In 1972, when Suczek was a graduate student, she wrote an especially astute article—scholarly yet completely accessible—about the "Paul Is Dead" phenomenon called "The Curious Case of the 'Death' of Paul McCartney" that was originally published in the sociology journal, *Urban Life and Culture*.

Her final paragraph puts the whole bloody circus into perspective:

> The public stir attending the "death" of Paul McCartney was obviously an amusing but trivial social phenomenon: shortlived and probably inconsequential. That it should have spread as widely and as rapidly as it did, however, suggests that there are processes of social interaction at work that it might well behoove us to examine more carefully. However foolish its guise, the McCartney rumor clearly indicates that there is a potential for irrational belief and action—be it constructive or be it destructive to what or whose values—that is alive and well in the modern, industrialized, "enlightened" world.

THE CONTENTS OF THE *PAUL McCARTNEY DEAD—THE GREAT HOAX* MAGAZINE

The "Paul Is Dead" maelstrom took place over a three-month period in late 1969. When Paul appeared on the cover of Life magazine on November 7, 1969 (the article was titled "Paul Is Still With Us"), it was hoped that the question of Paul's existence would be finally resolved.

Think again.

Nine years later, the controversy still raged, and the subject of this feature gives ample evidence that there were still a great number of Beatles fans who still doubted that Paul was alive. Here, then, is a look at the table of contents of a special magazine published in 1978 solely to fan the fires of speculation as to whether the very-much-alive Paul McCartney was, in fact, still among the living.

Paul McCartney Is Dead!
The Accident That Took Paul's Life
Why Did the Beatles Keep Paul's Death a Secret?

The Mysterious Double
Who Is He?
How He Impersonates Paul
Paul's Wedding: Who Did Linda Eastman Really Marry?

The Death Clues—How the Public Found Out
How the Beatles Sang About Paul's Death
How the Album Covers Showed Paul's Death
Paul McCartney: 1942–1966? "I Am Dead"
The Beatles Death Curse
The Face of Paul McCartney—When Did the Imposter Take His Place?

The Great Hoax
Do the Beatles Really Mourn Paul's Death?
Paul's Fans Cry: "It's a Cruel Joke—Paul Is Alive"
. . . And Those in Tears Ask: "Why Did Paul Die?"
Paul Died and Was Reborn
Paul Speaks
Rejoice! Paul "Lives"

THE 2 FUNNIEST "PAUL IS DEAD" CLUES OF ALL TIME

In the October 1977 issue of *National Lampoon* magazine, there was an article entitled "He Blew His Mind Out in a Car: The True Story of Paul McCartney's Death."

This scathingly satirical piece was brutal in its no-holds-barred Paul (and Linda) bashing—all done with the ostensible intent to prove that Paul was dead and had been replaced with a doppelgänger. To wit:

> The ego-seeking dominance of "McCartney" during the Apple phase, his cantankerous demands over the stewardship of Allen Klein, his marriage to an unattractive and snobbish opportunist, and his current obsession with easy money, outdated social pretension, and the lowest forms of elevator music, are ample evidence of an exploitation of the original Paul's reputation and talent, which only time and an informed public can curtail.

The article went on to sample some of the planted "clues" in the Beatles oeuvre, citing some genuine hints, while gleefully inventing others, two of which are the subjects of this list.

They are:

1. To inform their fans of Paul's death, the Beatles sealed an entire *Requiem Mass* inside the first one thousand pressings of *Abbey Road*. (The author did not indicate whether it was Mozart's or Verdi's.)

2. John and Yoko willingly participated in the "Paul Is Dead" master plan with their infamous *Two Virgins* album. The only way for fans to glean the morbid hidden messages was to remove the existing cuts of the Lennon/Ono collaboration with a carving knife or belt sander. Only then would the details of Paul's death be revealed.

(Photofest)

Then We Will Remember . . .

38. 78 "Toppermost of the Poppermost" Moments From *The Beatles Anthology*

A guitar's all right for a hobby, but it won't earn you any money.
—A Lennon family adage bandied about when
young John was just learning how to play guitar

The Beatles Anthology is probably the most important document about the most important rock band in the history of popular music.

Fans had three versions of the *Anthology* to choose from: a 6-hour TV mini-series; a 10-hour, 8-volume videotape series; and a 3-volume, 6-CD set of music and interviews.

Of course, most serious fans opted for all three tellings of the tale.

The Beatles Anthology is the story of the Beatles told *by* the Beatles, with contributions by a few important members of their inner conclave—most notably, Brian Epstein, Neil Aspinall, and Derek Taylor.

The *Anthology* series boasts performance footage (some of which had never been seen before), press conferences, rehearsal video, and home movies gleaned from the personal archives of the Beatles themselves.

There is much to see and hear in the *Anthology* and the ultimate way to view it is in order, one tape at a time, until you have watched all ten hours of the series.

That is often not possible, however, and so, this feature compiles and discusses seventy-eight of the more notable moments in the series.

(On a personal note, if I absolutely had to pick a favorite installment of the series, I'd have to go with Volume 6. It includes Paul's performance of the introduction to "Strawberry Fields Forever," a moment that blew away this fan of the Fabs. Volume 8 is pretty cool, too, although, to be fair, we're talking minor gradations of appeal here. The whole *Anthology* series is brilliantly produced, sublimely entertaining, and absolute must-viewing for Beatles fans the world over.)

THE BEATLES ANTHOLOGY 1

1. **The clip from *The Wild One*** *The Beatles Anthology* begins with a clip from the 1954 Marlon Brando film *The Wild One* in which Brando shouts, "The

Beetles missed you! All the Beetles missed you!" Even though the name of the biker gang was spelled with an "e," it is still quite an extraordinary moment to hear Brando shouting the name of the Fabs in a movie that came out years before John and Paul ever met.

2. **The "young/old" photo montage**   There is a very nice sequence showing the individual Beatles from the early "matching suits" phase of the band right up through shots of them from the *Let It Be* era, when it was essentially all over.

3. **The regression montage**   After a collage of scenes from the Beatles' career, we see a *very* rapid series of photos of the Fabs that begins in their final years and goes all the way back to shots of them as infants. (Use slow motion and freeze-frame this sequence so you can get a good look at each of these memorable photos.)

4. **Memorable Quote 1 (Rewriting History)**   When talking about his birth, Ringo tells his interviewer, "My mother used to say that because I was born, the Second World War started."

5. **Paul's ukulele fetish**   Paul tells us that because John's mother Julia played the ukulele, throughout his life Mr. McCartney has always loved any adult that played the ukulele. (Even Tiny Tim?!)

6. **The Beatles' influences**   In *Anthology 1,* each of the Beatles reminisces about some of the musical influences that shaped their playing and writing styles. Paul cites Buddy Holly and his song "Peggy Sue," the song "Searchin'," and the movie *The Girl Can't Help It.* John mentions early blues, Elvis and his song "Hound Dog," as well as Elvis's movies. ("*That's* a good job," he remembered thinking.) George remembers hearing Fats Domino and Jimmie Rodgers when he was twelve or thirteen, and also mentions the song "Rock Island Line" by Lonnie Donegan as being an inspiration. Ringo recalls being excited by Bill Haley and the Comets as well as by Frankie Laine.

7. **The B7 trip**   Paul tells a fascinating story about taking two buses to meet with a Liverpool guy who knew how to play a B7 chord. He and John already knew an E chord (E-G#-B) and an A chord (A-C#-E), but they needed the elusive B7 (B-D#-F#-A) to complete rock's hallowed (and, let's face it, overused) 1-4-5 sequence.

8. **Memorable Quote 2 (Paul and George)**   Beatles fans have long known about the on-and-off tension between Paul and George. In *Anthology 1,* Paul addresses this issue and acknowledges that it may have started way back in their early years together. "It might have been a failing of mine to tend to talk down to him because I'd known him as a younger kid," Paul admits. Paul, who is nine months older than George, at one point says he is a year-and-a-half older than George. George then comments, "Even *now,* he's nine months older." (Sounds like good old-fashioned sibling rivalry, now doesn't it?)

9. **John and Paul's first meeting**   In this installment of the *Anthology,* we see the original program from the St. Peter's fete at which John performed with the Quarry Men on the day he met Paul. Paul remembers specific songs John performed and what he was wearing. The overall impression is that this somewhat casual meeting manifested an intense vibe that the participants were aware of. Paul repeats the anecdote about John being impressed with the fact that Paul knew all the words to Eddie Cochran's "Twenty Flight Rock," and then, forty years later, Paul performs the song *flawlessly* for the *Anthology* cameras. Too cool.

John in his "leather" phase during the early years of the Beatles. (Photofest)

10. **Memorable Quote 3 (life without a drummer)**   In the Quarry Men's early days, Paul had to convince club owners who were skeptical about hiring a band without a drummer that they could play without a percussionist and still rock. Paul remembers telling them, "The rhythm's in the guitars!"

11. **Memorable Quote 4 (hiring Stu Sutcliffe)**   Paul talks about how the guys in the band convinced Stu Sutcliffe to spend the 75 quid he received for selling a painting to buy a Hoffner bass—even though Stu couldn't play a lick. George remembers, "It was better to have a bass player who couldn't play than to not have a bass player at all."

12. **Beatles with an A**   In this segment of the *Anthology,* John says, "Well, I had a vision when I was twelve and I saw a man on a flaming pie and he said, 'You are Beatles with an *A,* and we are." This is a variation of John's original use of the image of a flaming pie (which Paul eventually borrowed over thirty-five years later for the title of his 1997 CD *Flaming Pie*). John's original use of the term appeared in his 1961 *Mersey Beat* essay, "Being a Short Diversion on the Dubious Origins of the Beatles." In that essay, John wrote, "It came in a vision—a man appeared on a flaming pie and said unto them 'From this day on you are Beatles with an *A.'* Thank you, Mister Man, they said, thanking him."

13. *Also* **known as . . .**   When the Beatles Ur-group Long John and the Silver Beatles toured Scotland in 1960, they were offered work backing up singer Johnny Gentle. They accepted the gig and temporarily changed their names for it. Paul

became Paul Ramon; George became Carl Harrison; and Stu became Stu De Stael. John was known simply as Long John.

14. **Memorable Quote 5 (John's pep talk)**   During the 1960 Scotland tour (which George remembers as "pretty pathetic"), John tried to boost everyone's spirits by asking them, "Where are we goin', fellas?" to which they replied, "To the top, Johnny!" John would tell them that they were all going to "The Toppermost of the Poppermost!"

15. **Memorable Quote 6 (If only . . .)**   John reveals, "Our best work was never recorded."

16. **Memorable Quote 7 (It was meant to be)**   George believes that Ringo was always meant to be a Beatle: "Ringo kept sitting in with the band and every time Ringo sat in with the band it just seemed like this was it." Later in this installment, George says he believes that Ringo was the drummer for the band even before he joined: "It's just that he didn't enter the film until that particular scene."

17. **Brian knew**   Early on, Brian Epstein believed the Beatles could be great even though he initially felt they were "lacking in presentation and attire." He always felt, however, that "something great came through."

18. **That suits them**   What makes the *Anthology* so intriguing is hearing the participants' different versions of how things happened. During the segment on Brian Epstein, we're initially told that it was Brian who decided to dress up the Beatles in matching suits, but then Paul tells his interviewer that it was *he* who came up with the idea of the suits.

THE BEATLES ANTHOLOGY 2

19. **"Tomorrow Never Knows"**   The second installment of the *Anthology* opens with clips of George, John, and Paul from the early sixties talking about how they each foresee the future of the Beatles. George pretty accurately sees down the long and winding road: He tells a reporter he thinks they'll be in the music business as a group "at least four more years." John is a tad cynical, saying, "You can be bigheaded and say we'll last ten years—but we'll be lucky if we last three months." Paul is realistic, hedging on just how long he thinks the Beatles will last. He tells a reporter that he thinks John and he will always write songs together for other artists "as a sideline" even if the band breaks up and they do not perform their stuff solo. This makes all the sense in the world when we consider that throughout their early years, John and Paul were writing songs for other singers and groups to perform. (See the chapter "24 Songs Written by John Lennon, Paul McCartney, or George Harrison That Were Recorded by Other Musicians.")

20. **George's embarrassment**   George admits that he was a little embarrassed during the Beatles' 1963 tour with British singer Helen Shapiro. Shapiro was the headliner on the tour but the crowds all came to see the Beatles. "Please Please Me" had just hit number one and the U.K. audiences already had an early touch of Beatlemania.

21. **Case closed**   George Martin admits that he didn't think John and Paul could write a hit song until they came in with "Please Please Me."

22. **A minor development**   Paul talks about how the switch to a minor 7th chord for the bridge of "From Me to You" was something he and John discovered

how to do and which they considered a step forward in their songwriting abilities.

23. **Everywhere there are lots of piggies**   Ringo talks about the days when they constantly watched the music trade papers and each time one of their records moved up the charts, they would go out for a celebratory dinner. He remembers that in the first eighteen months or so when their records were getting a great deal of radio airplay and were doing very well, the Beatles got fat. Ringo recalls that this was when he personally discovered the joys of smoked salmon.

24. **Memorable Quote 8 ("You know that we're as close as can be, man")**   George on the Beatles as friends: "We were tight. That was one thing to be said about us. We were really tight, you know, as friends. We could argue a lot amongst ourselves but we were very very close to each other."

25. **Workin' like a dog, Part 1**   John reveals that the Beatles used to complete a single in twelve hours because the powers-that-be wanted a new Beatles record in the stores every three months.

26. **I can change it 'round**   Paul talks about how the song "She Loves You" was a major shift in his and John's *thematic* approach to songwriting. Prior to "She Loves You," most of their songs were from an I-centered point of view: "Please Please *Me*," "*I* Saw Her Standing There," "Ask *Me* Why," "Love *Me* Do," "From *Me* to You," etc. With "She Loves You," John and Paul's songwriting perspective became that of an observer reporting a conversation to a lovesick friend and offering advice on how to win back the woman the poor bloke loves. This move away from the song as a personal message signaled a maturing narrative sensibility that would provide John and Paul with more opportunities for song subjects.

27. **Memorable Quote 9 (Ringo as Thomas Wolfe)**   Ringo poignantly talks about how, after they all became enormously famous, "It was impossible to go home." Later in this installment Ringo relates an anecdote about visiting a beloved aunt after Beatlemania took hold of the world. He remembers accidentally spilling some tea and everyone in the room jumping up to tend to him. Prior to the Beatles, Ringo would have been left to fend for himself if he spilled something, but as George so aptly puts it, "People are so in awe of fame, [they] forget how to act normal."

Well, who else is there? There's nobody else. [There's] Elvis and [there's] us. Everyone can relate to the Beatles, you know, children who weren't born relate through the music.

We always did songs which related to everybody from children to our parents and grandparents. And now we're the parents and my mother is a grandparent and she still relates. I mean, the melody lingers on—everyone relates to "Yesterday" and half the people still relate to "I Am the Walrus." We were the monsters. There's been a lot of biggies and very few monsters. That's the difference.

—Ringo, talking in 1976 about the enduring popularity and importance of the Beatles

---

28. **Memorable Quote 10 (It *Does* Come Easy)**   John was apparently surprised by the overwhelming success of the group in America. "We thought," he admits, "we'd have to work a little for this notoriety." When asked at a press conference about the secret of their success, he jokes that if they knew the answer to *that* question, they'd all be managers instead of musicians.

29. **Give peace a chance**   George remembers being told that during the ten minutes or so of their first *Ed Sullivan Show* appearance, there was no reported crime in the United States. Even though that is a bit of an exaggeration, crime actually did drop significantly during their performance.

30. **Beatles in the round**   One of the most dramatic illustrations of just how far performing and live sound technology have evolved since the Beatles toured is the footage of their February 11, 1964, concert at the Coliseum in Washington, D. C. This footage is included in the *Anthology* series and is also available on the GoodTimes videotape *The Beatles Unauthorized*.

    The staging of this show is so primitive, it almost comes across as a *parody* of a live concert. The Beatles perform on a stage surrounded on all four sides by the audience. They are required to face a different side of the crowd after each song or two and this requires that they drag wires and move microphone stands themselves to whatever side of the stage on which they had to perform.

    Ringo's drums are on a revolving platform that got stuck and, during one "repositioning," wouldn't turn at all. Two or three nerdy looking guys in suits jump onto the stage and struggle to rotate the platform so Ringo would be facing the proper side.

    Watching this ludicrous bumbling by these "stagehands" is a hilarious experience which comes off as both surreal and pathetic at the same time. These are the bloody *Beatles* for heaven's sake and yet their stage accommodations are as primitive as something a high school garage band might use on one of their first forays into live performing. Another ridiculous moment occurs when Ringo has to sing "Act Naturally." Instead of providing Ringo with a boom mike, they simply place an upright mike stand between his legs and make him sing—and play the drums of course—like that. (Another example of this kind of prehistoric staging is the Beatles being forced to *share* microphones on stage. Sometimes John, Paul, and George end up singing into *one* mike.)

31. **Meet the wife**   When the Beatles were touring, it was thought that their fans (primarily their *female* fans) would reject them if they learned that any of them were married. John's flustered answer to a reporter's question about whether or not his wife liked visiting America is seen today as very funny. It effectively illustrates how musicians' and actors' images were very carefully monitored and controlled back in the fifties and sixties according to some rather strange guidelines.

THE BEATLES ANTHOLOGY 4

32. **Cautious George**   The idea of a ticker tape parade for the Beatles is discussed as part of the hoopla surrounding their summer 1964 return to the United States for their Hollywood Bowl concert. George refused to go if the parade idea were approved. Why? Because it had only been a year since J. F. K. was shot in a Dallas motorcade and George obviously felt uneasy about the idea of

the Beatles riding through the streets in open cars. (One also gets the sense that he felt it would be a little unseemly for a pop group to be honored in a motorcade after a U.S. president was recently killed in one.)

33. **Memorable Quote 11 (Ringo had fun)**   Ringo admits that the mania surrounding the group (something John describes as being in the "eye of the hurricane") tickles him: "I loved it," he said in the *Anthology*. "I loved all the decoy cars and all these intricate ways of getting us to the gigs."

34. **The Dylan influence**   Everyone knows that Bob Dylan influenced the Beatles and that the *Rubber Soul* album was the first manifestation of his style being evident in Beatles songs. As is common in the *Anthology*, we learn of the different interpretations of events by individual Beatles. When it comes to Dylan, Paul describes him as an "idol." The more circumspect George says he was not an idol, but that his records did give them a "buzz."

35. **Paul's secret to life**   "There are seven levels." He discovered this one night when he was drunk. Paul has never publicly elaborated on what the seven levels actually are or were.

36. **Memorable Quote 12 (Ringo still having fun)**   When asked about pot, Ringo remembers, "I laughed and I laughed and I laughed. It was fabulous."

37. **John's safe haven**   Paul remembers that John used to say that he always felt safe on stage—even when they performed in a venue in which they could easily be picked off by a sniper hidden away in some high perch. (A sniper was something that George Martin especially worried about.)

38. **Workin' like a dog, Part 2**   The Beatles' 1964 summer tour of America consisted of thirty-two shows in thirty-four days in twenty-four cities. Give those boys a pillow!

39. **Memorable Quote 13 (John's legacy)**   During a discussion of the revolutionary feedback introduction to "I Feel Fine," George sums up John's contribution to modern rock with four simple, yet profound words: "He invented Jimi Hendrix."

40. **Script doctoring**   The Beatles admit that they asked the creative team behind *Help!*—writers Charles Wood and Marc Behm and director Richard Lester—to write the Bahamas scenes and skiing scenes into the movie because none of them had ever been to the Bahamas, nor had they ever been skiing. Of their escapades, George understatedly comments, "We had fun in those days."

41. **The story of "Yesterday"**   Paul tells *Anthology* viewers exactly how the most covered song of all time actually happened: "I had a piano by the bed and I just woke up one morning with this tune in my head . . . I went to the piano and found the chords to it . . . I made sure I remembered it. And then I just hawked it 'round to all my friends and stuff and said, 'What's this? It's got to be something.' It's like a good little tune and I couldn't have written it, 'cause I just dreamed it. You don't get *that* lucky."

42. *Embarrassed* **by "Yesterday"?**   Paul admits that the reason "Yesterday" was never released in the United Kingdom as a single was because they were a little embarrassed by such a gorgeous and lush ballad coming out of a rock-and-roll band.

43. **Memorable Quote 14 (Working with Lennon and McCartney, Part 1)**   John talks about George's songwriting, frankly admitting that it was very difficult to compete with him and Paul (something Ringo acknowledges later on in *Anthology 5* as well): "[George] just wasn't in the same league for a long time," John said. "That's not putting him down. He just hadn't had the practice of writing that we had."

44. **Frank Sinatra's "favorite Lennon/McCartney song"**   It's George Harrison's song, "Something." (Good one, Frank.)

THE BEATLES ANTHOLOGY 5

45. **The mother of invention**   Vox had to build special 100-watt amplifiers for the Beatles' Shea Stadium concert. (The Fabs had previously used Vox 30-watt amps on stage.)

46. **Visiting Elvis**   Ringo was excited. John says he jammed with Elvis, the others say he didn't. Derek Taylor says that Priscilla came in wearing a tiara in her hair, Paul says it was a bow. George says he doesn't remember because he was too busy trying to score some reefer off the Memphis Mafia. Paul also admits that meeting Elvis "was one of the great meetings of my life," but Ringo throws the whole relationship into perspective when he reminds us that Elvis actually tried to have the Beatles banned from America.

47. **Memorable Quote 15 (We all wanna change the world?)**   George sums up the global influence of the Fabs thusly: "They used us as an excuse to go mad, the world did, and then blamed it on us."

48. **Memorable Quote 16 (Working with Lennon and McCartney, Part 2)**   Ringo talks about writing songs on his own and his trepidation at bringing them in for the others to hear: "It used to be just *hard* to bring your songs in when you had *Lennon and McCartney.*"

49. **Musicianship**   During a discussion on how difficult it was to perform the opening a capella "Nowhere Man" harmonies live, a clip is shown of a live performance of the song. The professionalism and musicianship of the Beatles is evident during this clip in one brief moment that actually amounts to nothing more than a single note. As the boys begin singing "He's a real nowhere man, sitting in his nowhere land," in demanding three-part harmony, Paul senses after only a few seconds that their complex harmony is drifting off key. He immediately plays one single note on his bass to give them all a pitch anchor so they can stay together and they finish the introduction with no audible clunkers.

50. **Memorable Quote 17 (birth of the video)**   One of the really interesting features of the entire *Anthology* series is the inclusion of rare music videos (they were called "promo films" back then) that the Beatles produced to send out to TV stations when a new record was released. These were essentially early music videos, most of which could easily be played now and fit right in with what's being aired today. George bemusedly sums up their foray into videos by telling his interviewer, "In a way, we invented MTV."

Even now I look back and I can see, relative to a lot of other groups or pop music in general, the Beatles did have something. But that's relative to that. Relative to something else . . . I can accept whatever the Beatles were on those terms. But it's a bit too much to accept that we're supposedly the designers of this incredible change that occurred [in the sixties]. In many ways we were just swept along with everybody else.

—George, November 1987

---

51. **The Philippines** There is some interesting background on the Beatles disastrous July 1966 trip to the Philippines. Ringo says he hated it there, and George admits he felt a "negative vibe" as soon as they landed. The Beatles inadvertently snubbed Imelda Marcos and the royal family by not showing up for a state dinner and on their way to the airport for their return flight home, they were booed and things got ugly. Before they were allowed to leave, Brian Epstein and Mal Evans were pulled off the plane and forced to give back the money the Beatles were paid for their performance.

52. **Christ, you know it ain't easy** There is an extended segment on John's "we're more popular than Jesus" comment and the furor it caused in the United States. There is amazing film footage of rednecks in the Bible Belt burning "Beatle trash" in mass bonfires that today come across like something filmed in a despotic foreign country instead of the United States. Brian Epstein's August 6, 1966, statement to the press in which he tries to smooth the waters is also shown: "The quote which John Lennon made to a London columnist more than three months ago has been quoted and misrepresented entirely out of context." George remembers, "The repercussions were big." One astonishing interview with a Ku Klux Klansman in full regalia is shown in which the Klansman hints at some of the ways his "religious" organization can disrupt Beatles concerts in the future because of John Lennon's "blasphemy." Whoever thought "there'd be days like this?" Indeed. (See the March 4, 1966, entry in the chapter "Important Events in the History of the Beatles" for more details on John's remarks.)

53. **We hope you have enjoyed the show** *Anthology 6* shows the preparations for the Beatles' final live concert on August 29, 1966, in Candlestick Park, San Francisco. By now, as George admits, Beatlemania "[had taken] its toll," and "It was no longer fun anymore." (He also uses words such as *madness* and *chaos* to describe the mood of the times.)

54. **"Come Together"** John tells a reporter that the Beatles will always be getting together for one reason or another. Ringo echoes these sentiments, as does George. Paul is then seen talking about how in the mid-sixties the quality of their performances started going downhill and that was when they decided that they wanted to spend most of their time in the studio. "Now our performance is that record," he says. He later talks about how they considered sending the *Sgt. Pepper* album out on tour instead of the band itself, revealing that they got the idea from Elvis, who had recently sent his gold-plated Cadillac out on tour. The car was very successful.

55. **Itself worth the price of admission** Other than Jimi Hendrix's performance of "Sgt. Pepper's Lonely Hearts Club Band," one of the most breathtaking moments in the *Anthology* is a scene of Paul actually in the studio beautifully playing the mellotron introduction to John's "Strawberry Fields Forever" and then singing a few lines of the classic.

56. **Memorable Quote 18 (Paul on John)** When discussing his first hearing of John's brilliant song, "A Day in the Life," Paul touchingly admits, "I was a big fan of John's" and recalls not being able to wait to "get his hands on" the song and see what else could be done with it.

147

57. **Perhaps the single greatest piece of Beatles trivia ever**   Paul talks about being blown away when he and some of the others went to see Jimi Hendrix in concert in London on Sunday, June 4, 1967, and Jimi opened his show with a kick-ass rendition of "Sgt. Pepper's Lonely Hearts Club Band." What was so special about Jimi doing a cover of a Beatles song? The *Sgt. Pepper* album, Paul recalls, had been released the previous Friday—only two days before Jimi's concert—and he had already learned the song from the record and thought enough of the tune to open his show with it.

58. **Not everyone was happy**   George was not especially thrilled with working on the *Sgt. Pepper* album. He had only one song on the LP and he admits that he found working on the record tiring and a bit boring. He muses that part of the reason was because his "heart was still in India."

59. **Memorable Quote 19 (George spells it out)**   By the time of the *Sgt. Pepper* album, George admits that he "was losing interest in being Fab."

THE BEATLES ANTHOLOGY 7

60. **Well, did he or didn't he?**   *Anthology 7* opens with a look at the 1967 "Summer of Love" *Our World* satellite TV show on which the Beatles performed "All You Need Is Love" for a huge global audience of four hundred million viewers. George Martin says that John wrote the song specifically for the show and Ringo agrees. Paul, on the other hand, says he *doesn't* think it was written for the show. In any case, Ringo remembers that "it was a fabulous time, musically and spiritually." The more cynical George, however, puts a slightly different spin on this period and the whole Haight-Ashbury scene: "A lot of that was bullshit," he says. Haight-Ashbury, instead of being a Mecca for glowing, peace-loving young people, was filled with "horrible, spotty, drop-out kids on drugs."

61. **Brian's death**   George describes Brian's death as leaving a "huge void" and admits that the four of them knew nothing about their own finances or business affairs. Ringo describes the Beatles after Brian's death as "chickens without heads."

62. **The Beatles' telegram to Ed Sullivan**   A clip is shown of Ed Sullivan reading a telegram from the Beatles that they sent to him along with the video of their new single, "Hello Goodbye." The telegram reads, "Dear Ed, winter has come again to our Great Britain and we sit by our fires warming our feet. Stop. We send all love to you and everyone looking in. We are happy to be on your show, too. Stop. Have a beautiful Christmas and a sincere New Year. Love, the Beatles."

63. **The Apple boutique**   According to a news announcer of the times, the Beatles' new shop would sell "books, jewelry, paintings, and hippie clothes, as well as furniture."

64. **"Very John"**   Paul remembers that when the opportunity arose while in India to take a helicopter ride with the Maharishi, John leaped at the chance. His reason? John hoped that during the flight the Yogi would "slip him the answer." Paul laughs that this was "very John."

65. **The young JT**   A short clip of James Taylor's audition for his Apple recording contract is shown and it is fascinating to hear how much more nasal and whiny his voice was back in the late sixties. Even then, though, he could most definitely write incredible songs.

George mugging for the camera: was Beatlemania getting to him? (Photofest)

66. **George on Apple** George now feels that the whole Apple company fiasco was "John and Paul's madness, ego, running away with themselves."

67. **Memorable Quote 19 (John on John and Yoko)** "We just wanted to be together all the time."

THE BEATLES ANTHOLOGY 8

68. **The Outsiders** A sign of just how fragmented and restless the Beatles had become is illustrated by the segment that opens *Anthology 8*. George talks about leaving the band temporarily. Ringo remembers that it was because he felt like it was him against the other three that *he* wanted to leave. When the others learned of this, they all admitted that they felt the same way. Each felt that he was the outsider and the other three—in all the different configurations—were against *him*.

69. **The *White Album*** George Martin reveals that he did not think that all the material ultimately released as the 2-disc *White Album* was of sufficient quality to warrant a double album. He wanted to do one *great* album instead. Ringo disagrees about the quality of the songs, but feels that they should have done two separate albums instead of one double. George says he thinks they included

everything because there was a lot of ego in the band by this time. Paul sums up the debate and effectively closes the discussion by exclaiming, "It's the bloody Beatles' *White Album!* Shut up!"

70. **The end**   This final installment of the *Anthology*, by necessity, covers the dissolution of the band. John describes their breakup as a "slow death." Ringo describes it as "like a wind-down to a divorce." George says, "It started stifling. It had to self-destruct." Paul later says that the movie *Let It Be* shows how a group breaks up.

71. **At Twickenham**   The misguided attempt to film the Beatles rehearsing and recording an album began with moving them to Twickenham Film Studio, a cold and horrid place that no one liked. When the ongoing personality conflicts among the Beatles were added to the mix, it made for a miserable time. George especially did not like the experience. He talks about having just spent six wonderful months working with Bob Dylan and the Band and returning to the tension and unhappiness of the Beatles at that time was just horrible for him.

72. **Paul and George**   There was palpable tension between Paul and George at Twickenham and the camera captured it all. It is obvious that no one wanted to be doing what they were doing, except perhaps for Paul, and the friction escalated.

73. **The dream is over**   There are a couple of very revealing scenes of John and George arriving separately at the Saville Row Apple Studios. Some female fans are standing on the sidewalk outside the studio, watching the boys arrive and enter the building. John and George each turn and look at the girls but neither of them speaks to these fans, nor do they even smile at them. Instead, there is a noticeable wariness on their faces. Neither of them has a bodyguard with him, but the openness and easy approachability of their early years is most assuredly gone.

74. **Memorable Quote 20 (Ringo on the Beatles' work ethic)**   "When we were working on something good, the bullshit went out the window."

75. **Memorable Quote 21 (Paul on the Beatles' legacy)**   "To me, the Beatles were always a great little band, nothing more, nothing less—for all our success. When we sat down to play, we played good. When we first got Ringo into the band, it really jelled. We played good. And we never had too many of those times where it's just not working."

76. **Memorable Quote 22 (Ringo on the Beatles' legacy)**   "It was magical. An amazing closeness. We were four guys who really loved each other."

77. **Memorable Quote 23 (George on the Beatles' legacy)**   "The Beatles gave their nervous systems."

78. **The final word**   One of the final sound bites in the *Anthology* is an insightful comment by John Lennon. He gives what is perhaps the best advice possible to Beatles fans everywhere: "You have all the old records there if you want to reminisce."

Amen.

No matter how much we split, we're still very linked. We're the only four people who've seen the whole Beatlemania bit from the inside out, so we're tied forever, whatever happens.

—Paul, April 1970

The Greatest of Them All . . .

39. 18 Beatles Grammy Awards

1964 Best New Artist   The Beatles

1964 Best Performance by a Vocal Group   "A Hard Day's Night" by the Beatles

1966 Best Contemporary Pop Vocal Performance, Male   Paul McCartney performing "Eleanor Rigby"

1966 Best Album Cover   *Revolver* by the Beatles

1966 Song of the Year   "Michelle" by the Beatles

1967 Album of the Year   *Sgt. Pepper's Lonely Hearts Club Band* by the Beatles

1967 Best Contemporary Rock-and-Roll Recording   *Sgt. Pepper's Lonely Hearts Club Band* by the Beatles

1967 Best Album Cover   *Sgt. Pepper's Lonely Hearts Club Band* by the Beatles

1967 Best Engineered Recording   *Sgt. Pepper's Lonely Hearts Club Band* by the Beatles

1969 Best Engineered Recording   *Abbey Road* by the Beatles

1970 Best Original Score Written for a Motion Picture or TV Special   *Let It Be* by the Beatles

1975 Hall of Fame   The Beatles

1990 Lifetime Achievement Award   Paul McCartney

1991 Lifetime Achievement Award   John Lennon

1995 Lifetime Achievement Award   George Martin

1996 Best Pop Performance by a Duo or Group With Vocal   "Free as a Bird" by the Beatles

1996 Best Music Video, Short Form   "Free as a Bird" by the Beatles

1996 Best Music Video, Long Form   *The Beatles Anthology* by the Beatles

40. The 3 Beatles Albums in New York's WNEW Top Ten Rock Albums of All Time

In July 1997, the premier New York FM radio station WNEW (102.7) conducted a Listener's Survey to determine the 102 greatest rock albums of all time. The Beatles had *three* albums in the Top Ten (including *two* in the Top Five)—thirty years after the band broke up. Here is the complete Top Ten.

> *Dark Side of the Moon*   Pink Floyd
> ***Sgt. Pepper's Lonely Hearts Club Band***   **The Beatles**
> *Who's Next*   The Who
> ***Abbey Road***   **The Beatles**
> *Led Zeppelin IV*   Led Zeppelin
> *Born to Run*   Bruce Springsteen
> ***The Beatles*** (the ***White Album***)   **The Beatles**
> *Tommy*   The Who
> *The Wall*   Pink Floyd
> *Aqualung*   Jethro Tull

(Editor's collection)

Nice Apple Tart . . .

41. 25 Artists Other Than the Beatles Who Released Music on the Apple Label

The aim of the company isn't a stack of gold teeth in the bank. We've done that bit. It's more of a trick to see if we can get artistic freedom within a business structure; to see if we can create things and sell them without charging three times our cost.

—John Lennon on May 15, 1968, at the launch
of Apple Records in New York

Apple was the Beatles' dream company. Apple Records would provide an opportunity for struggling musicians to make the records they wanted to make—without (as John so vulgarly put it at an Apple press conference) having to go on their knees in somebody's office. To give the Beatles credit, the idea was honorable and their intentions noble. The Apple raison d'être was art for art's sake, but unfortunately, art must also be viewed as merchandise—if the artists and their sponsoring companies want to stay in business.

Apple Records (and, by extension, the entire Apple organization) could have been a huge success, but the Fabs dived headfirst into the endeavor without any real game plan. They had only an idealistic vision of happy creative people turning out music and art that would be eagerly anticipated and warmly embraced by people all over the world. All you need is love, right?

Wrong.

Apple was mismanaged from the start and it is amazing that the record company produced what it did. It seems the Apple powers-that-be could handle producing records all right; they just didn't know how to promote them and balance the books. Nonetheless, Apple was a grand idea. That it didn't work does not diminish the greatness of the *concept* of Apple.

Here is a look at the twenty-five artists who released records on the Apple label from 1968 to 1976 (in addition, of course, to Apple's biggest band, the Beatles themselves).

1. **Badfinger**   Badfinger was Apple's premier group (James Taylor's popularity grew later after he left Apple) and today, CD compilations of their hits and

rereleases of their albums are still in the stores. Mal Evans brought in their tapes to the Beatles and they were signed to Apple in April 1968. Their first single on the label was the unsuccessful "Maybe Tomorrow" but they are probably best known for their Paul McCartney-penned hit "Come and Get It." (Check out the *Anthology 3* CD for Paul's amazing "one-man band" demo version of this song.) Other Badfinger hits were "No Matter What," "Without You," and "Day After Day." Their albums *No Dice* (1970) and *Straight Up* (1971) are extremely entertaining and contain some very Beatlesque cuts. They still hold up today and, in the end, that is probably the ultimate judgment of just how good Badfinger really was. Badfinger founding members Pete Ham and Tom Evans both committed suicide.

2. **The Black Dyke Mills Brass Band**   This band launched their shortlived Apple career with a song written by Paul McCartney called "Thingumybob." This was the extent of their time with Apple although this group is still alive and kicking in the United Kingdom even today.

3. **Richard Brautigan**   Yes, this is the writer Richard Brautigan, author of *Trout Fishing in America*. His only release on Apple's Zapple imprint was a spoken word LP of his reading from *Trout Fishing in America*.

4. **Brute Force**   Brute Force was actually a singer/songwriter named Steven Friedland. His only release on Apple was a strange song called "The King of Fuh." It was less than successful.

5. **Delaney and Bonnie**   This popular duo did only one album for Apple. It was called *The Original Delaney and Bonnie (Accept No Substitutes)* and it was released in the United States in May of 1969.

6. **Elephant's Memory**   This band was a tight New York group that worked with John and Yoko for a year and released one John Lennon-produced album on the Apple label called *Elephant's Memory*.

7. **Bill Elliott and the Elastic Oz Band**   This was actually another incarnation of the Plastic Ono Band. John changed the name of the group for one single, "God Save Us," which he wrote especially to benefit the defendants in the 1971 Oz Obscenity Trials in the United Kingdom. (The reason he changed the name was because he did not want the record to be known as "the new John Lennon single.")

8. **Grapefruit**   This group released one single, "Dear Delilah," through the Apple Publishing Company in 1967 before Apple Records was formed. That was the extent of their involvement with Apple. (The name of the group was a tribute to Yoko Ono's 1964 book of poetry called *Grapefruit*.)

9. **Chris Hodge**   Hodge released two singles with Apple called "We're on Our Way" (1972) and "Goodbye Sweet Lorraine" (1973) and then vanished. There was a rumor that Hodge was working with eccentric filmmaker Nicholas Roeg (*Performance, The Man Who Fell to Earth*) for a time but this was never confirmed.

10. **Mary Hopkin**   This sweet-voiced British singer was Paul McCartney's protégée and one of Apple's biggest success stories. Her first big hit was the single "Those Were the Days," which was released in 1968 and became an instant smash. Her first album, *Postcard* (1969), was produced by Paul McCartney and did very well. Her second single was a John Lennon/Paul McCartney composition called "Goodbye," which was a Top Twenty hit in both the United Kingdom and the United States. Mary left Apple in 1972 and never again achieved the recognition or success she had attained while with the Beatles' company.

11. **The Hot Chocolate Band** The only record this group (actually two songwriters) released with Apple was a reggae version of John's "Give Peace a Chance."

12. **Jackie Lomax** A singer who never quite hit the heights everyone expected he would—even with the star-studded lineup that played on his first single, "Sour Milk Sea," a George Harrison composition. The Apple single "Sour Milk Sea" boasted Paul McCartney on bass, George Harrison on rhythm guitar, Ringo Starr on drums, Nicky Hopkins on piano, and Eric Clapton on lead guitar. (Sounds like a bloody Beatles record, eh?) Jackie later signed with Warner and then, Capitol, but never took off despite his unquestionable talent.

13. **The Modern Jazz Quartet** This respected jazz group did two LPs with Apple (*Under the Jasmine Tree* and *Space*) and then left the label. They were originally signed to broaden the range of the company's artist roster.

14. **Yoko Ono** Mrs. Lennon had several releases with Apple, some of which were the B-sides of Plastic Ono Band singles ("Remember Love," "Don't Worry Kyoko [Mummy's Only Looking for Her Hand in the Snow]," and "Who Has Seen the Wind?") and some of which were her solo albums (*Approximately Infinite Universe* and *Feeling the Space*).

15. **David Peel** A pot legalization advocate and New York street singer whose 1972 Apple LP *The Pope Smokes Dope* was produced by John and Yoko and included the Lennon/Ono composition "The Ballad of New York City." Peel was beyond eccentric and, thus, got very little airplay—but John liked him. Visit Strawberry Field in New York's Central Park today and you just might catch an impromptu Peel performance.

16. **Billy Preston** In addition to playing on the Beatles' *Let It Be* album, Billy Preston released his own records with Apple, most notably, the single "That's the Way God Planned It" with its great "Let It Be" chord progression. Billy also released two albums with Apple, *That's the Way God Planned It* and *Encouraging Words*, which were coproduced by George Harrison. His biggest post-Apple hit was the single "Will It Go 'Round in Circles," which earned a Gold Record.

17. **Radha Krsna Temple** This "group" consisted of members of London's Radha Krsna Temple and their Apple releases were intended by George to promote Krishna consciousness throughout the world. Thus, their first Apple single (1969) was the "Hare Krishna Mantra," which was produced by George. Their 1971 album *The Radha Krsna Temple* (also produced by George) was kind of a "how-to" of Krishna consciousness and included mantras, chants, and spoken word features.

18. **Ravi Shankar** Ravi was an established musical artist on several labels when he signed with Apple and his involvement with the company was due to George's enthusiasm for the sitar and his friendship with Ravi (a relationship that continues to this day).

19. **Phil Spector and Ronnie Spector** Legendary producer Phil Spector worked on Ronnie Spector's 1971 Apple single "Try Some, Buy Some" (written by George Harrison) and also put together *Phil Spector's Christmas Album* (1972) for the label.

20. **Sundown Playboys** This group consisted of two musicians who worked full-time jobs during the day (one worked in an oil refinery and one serviced candy vending machines) and played Louisiana French Cajun music at night. They released one Apple single in 1972 called "Saturday Night Special."

21. **John Tavener**   Apple's only classical musician. Tavener was a British conductor/composer who released two classical albums with Apple: *The Whale* (1970) and *Celtic Requiem* (1971).

22. **James Taylor**   James Taylor released his only album before *Sweet Baby James* on Apple and then left the company. The album—*James Taylor*—went nowhere, but it did include the sublime "Carolina in My Mind," a song James still performs in concert today. *James Taylor* also included the song "Something in the Way She Moves," which George Harrison has admitted influenced the lyrics of his classic song "Something."

23. **Trash**   This Scottish group was originally known as the Pathfinders but changed their name to White Trash when they signed with Apple. When no one would play their records because the name "White Trash" was racially offensive, they shortened it to Trash. Their first Apple single "Road to Nowhere" bombed and so the band was allowed to preview the Beatles' *Abbey Road* album and pick any song off the record to cover. They chose "Golden Slumbers"/"Carry That Weight" but that, too, tanked because it was released right after the real thing hit the stores. After this, Trash was trashed. (In my never-to-be-humble opinion, they might have had a better chance with *really good* cover versions of "Come Together" or "Here Comes the Sun.")

24. **Doris Troy**   A rhythm-and-blues singer whose first Apple single was the George Harrison song "Ain't That Cute." Because of a lack of promotion, record buyers did not know that George, Ringo, Steven Stills, Jackie Lomax, and Klaus Voorman played on her album *Doris Troy* and the record sank quickly. Troy never recorded with Apple again.

25. **Lon and Derrek Van Eaton**   These two brothers from New Jersey released their first single, the George Harrison-produced "Sweet Music," and their first album *Brother* on Apple, but then quickly signed with A&M. They have appeared on several Beatles solo records as backup musicians.

Apple was a manifestation of Beatle naivety, collective naivety. We said, "We're going to do this and help everybody" and all that and we got conned on the subtlest and bluntest level. We really didn't get approached by the best artists, we got all the bums from everywhere else. All the ones that everyone had thrown out. The ones who were really groovy wouldn't approach us because they were too proud.

—John, after the demise of the original
Apple Records

---

42. The First Solo Singles Released by Each of the Four Beatles

This is a rundown of the first U.S. *solo* releases by each Beatle. Ringo, George, and Paul released their singles after the *Let It Be* album came out in mid-1970. John's first solo single came out a year earlier.

1. **July 1969—John and the Plastic Ono Band**   "Give Peace a Chance"/"Remember Love." John followed this hit with "Cold Turkey" and "Instant Karma," both by the Plastic Ono Band and released before the "official" breakup of the band. "Mother" was actually his first *post-Beatles* single.
2. **October 1970—Ringo**   "Beaucoups of Blues"/"Coochy-Coochy"
3. **November 1970—George**   "My Sweet Lord"/"Isn't It a Pity"
4. **February 1971—Paul**   "Another Day"/"Oh Woman, Oh Why"

43. 5 John Lennon Solo Recordings That Included a Free Poster

Wedding Album (album)
Imagine (album)
Double Fantasy (album)
"Borrowed Time" (single)
"Never Say Goodbye" (single)

An Apple publicity shot from John's early solo days. (Photofest)

44. 3 James Taylor Songs on Which Paul McCartney Performs

1. **"Carolina in My Mind"** Paul plays bass guitar on this beautiful song (one of James's personal favorites and a standard at his live performances), which appears on James's debut album *James Taylor* (his only Apple Records release).
2. **"Let It Fall Down"** Paul and Linda McCartney sing backing vocals on this song off James's 1974 *Walking Man* album.
3. **"Rock 'N' Roll Is Music Now"** The second song on James's *Walking Man* album on which Paul and Linda sing backing vocals.

(Photofest)

Everything Money Could Buy . . .

45. The Beatles at Auction

These two lists provide a fascinating look at the world of Beatles collecting and illustrate how rare Beatles items can escalate in value in a very short time. The first Sotheby's auction, June 9, 1982, sold only twenty-five items, the rarest of which were probably Paul's drawing of Pattie Boyd and the signed *Two Virgins* album. The second auction, June 23, 1984, was more representative of just how valuable some Beatles' memorabilia had become in two short years. The most fascinating illustration of this would be item number 31, one of John Lennon's guitar strings. It was appraised at $200 to $250 and ended up selling for $770. Its value today is probably many times that. Check the asking prices as compared to what the items actually sold for.

In fact, there is no way any of these prices would hold up today. Beatles memorabilia has been one of the best investments anyone could have possibly made over the past thirty years. These Sotheby's auctions offered some especially interesting and intriguing material and provide us Beatles fans with a glimpse into a world where the Fab Four are not just art, they're *currency*.

THE 1982 AUCTION

Item	Asking price	Sold for
1. The platinum disc presented to John Lennon for the 1975 album *Rock 'N' Roll*	$6,000–8,000	$7,700
2. The platinum disc presented to John Lennon for the 1974 album *Walls and Bridges*	$6,000–8,000	$7,700
3. The British gold 45 rpm record presented to the Beatles for the single, "Hey Jude"	$600–900	$3,300
4. A complete set of the monthly Beatles fan magazine *The Beatles Book*	$700–1,000	$1,210
5. A copy of John and Yoko's *Two Virgins* album signed by John Lennon	$300–500	$1,045
6. A portrait of Pattie Boyd drawn by Paul McCartney and signed by McCartney	$500–700	$935
7. A group of miscellaneous Beatles memorabilia	$600–900	$715

Item	Asking price	Sold for
8. A copy of the Beatles' album *Help!*, signed by all four Beatles	$700–1,000	$660
9. "A large and comprehensive lot" of miscellaneous Beatles "ephemera," 1963–1977	$800–1,200	$660
10. A signed song sheet for "Scrambled Eggs" ("Yesterday")	$500–600	$550
11. A copy of the Beatles' *Yesterday and Today* album	$200–400	$440
12. A caricature of Ringo Starr drawn by Abe Hirschfeld	$400–600	$440
13. A Beatles wristwatch	$200–300	$412
14. Assorted Beatles sheet music, each sheet signed by a Beatle with a caricature	$350–500	$357
15. A group of Beatles memorabilia	$75–100	$330
16. Miscellaneous promotional material for John Lennon's *Rock 'N' Roll* album	$250–400	$330
17. The Master Record for John Lennon's single "Whatever Gets You Through the Night"	$300–500	$302
18. 2 Italian posters for the Beatles film *Yellow Submarine*	$300–350	$302
19. A group of Beatles memorabilia	$200–300	$302
20. 4 animation cels from Beatles cartoons	$500–700	$275
21. 2 checks made out to "DelMonico's," dated August 28, 1964, and autographed by John Lennon and George Harrison	$400–450	$247
22. 77 black-and-white press photographs of the Beatles	$400–600	$247
23. 2 Beatles Christmas records: their third, issued December 17, 1965, and their fourth, issued December 16, 1966	$200–300	$192
24. The 45 rpm master record for the Plastic Ono band's single "Cold Turkey"	$100–150	$192
25. Miscellaneous promotional material for John Lennon's *Walls and Bridges* album	$100–200	$132

TOTAL AUCTION PROCEEDS: $28,975

THE 1984 AUCTION

Item	Asking price	Sold for
1. John Lennon's Japanese guitar	$1,500–2,000	$19,800
2. A commemorative platinum album presented to the Beatles by Apple Records	$3,000–5,000	$12,100
3. The gold disc presented to the Beatles for their album *Hey Jude*	$7,000–10,000	$11,000
4. The gold 45 rpm record presented to John Lennon for the Beatles single "Yesterday"	$2,500–4,000	$7,150
5. The gold disc presented to the Beatles for their album *Something New*	$3,000–5,000	$6,325
6. The gold disc presented to the Beatles for their album *Help!*	$2,500–4,500	$5,500

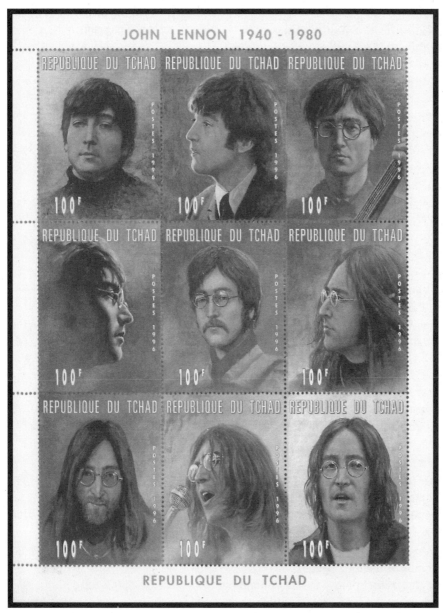

7. The gold 45 rpm record presented to the Beatles for their single "Something"	$1,200–1,600	$3,850
8. The platinum disc presented to George Harrison for the Beatles album *Magical Mystery Tour*	$3,000–5,000	$3,575
9. A concert poster from the Beatles August 23, 1966, appearance at Shea Stadium	$800–1,200	$3,575
10. The Beatles' *Hey Jude* album cover, autographed by the four Beatles	$300–400	$3,080
11. A John Lennon autographed letter	$350–450	$2,970
12. A miscellaneous lot of assorted Beatles material	$900–1,300	$2,750

	Item	Asking price	Sold for
13.	A miscellaneous lot of Beatles autographs	$1,000–1,500	$2,310
14.	A copy of the EMI/Capitol promotional album cover for the Beatles *Yesterday and Today* album	$700–1,000	$2,200
15.	A copy of the Beatles album *Love Songs*, autographed by all four Beatles	$400–600	$1,870
16.	A 1977 British promotional display for *The Beatles at the Hollywood Bowl*	$450–650	$1,870
17.	A miscellaneous lot of Apple promotional material	$700–1,000	$1,760
18.	A photograph of the Beatles, autographed by all four Beatles	$300–400	$1,760
19.	A white planter, inscribed and autographed by John Lennon and Yoko Ono	$600–1,000	$1,540
20.	A photograph of the Beatles from the early 1960s, autographed by all four Beatles	$400–600	$1,430
21.	A copy of the bootleg John Lennon album *John Lennon Sings the Great Rock-and-Roll Hits/ Roots*, autographed and inscribed by John Lennon	$600–800	$1,210
22.	An original proof copy of the Beatles' *Get Back* album	$600–800	$1,100
23.	An original signed Beatles' Y. M. C. A. Jazz Club Membership card from 1962	$600–1,000	$1,100
24.	3 complete sealed sets of John and Yoko's *Wedding Album*, elaborate boxed sets which included a reprint of their marriage license, a photo of a piece of wedding cake sealed in a plastic bag, a postcard, press clippings, and photo booth photos	$175–225	$1,045
25.	2 calendar photographs of John Lennon and Yoko Ono, autographed by John and Yoko	$250–400	$990
26.	The Capitol Records gold album for *The Concert for Bangladesh*	$1,500–2,500	$990
27.	A British autograph book that contained autographs of the four Beatles	$400–600	$935
28.	2 British autograph books, the first containing autographs of the four Beatles	$500–700	$935
29.	33 photographs of the Beatles from the early 1960s	$250–350	$880
30.	5 original tickets from the Beatles' August 29, 1966, concert at Candlestick Park in San Francisco, California	$200–300	$880
31.	One of John Lennon's guitar strings	$200–250	$770
32.	An Apple Records "Our First Four" presentation set	$350–500	$770
33.	A George Harrison autographed letter	$250–350	$660
34.	4 original tickets from the Beatles' August 23, 1966, concert at Shea Stadium in New York	$150–200	$660
35.	The art exhibition "This Is Not Here" by John Lennon and Yoko Ono, originally displayed at the Everson Museum of Art in Syracuse, New York, in 1971	$450–650	$605
36.	2 color progressives for original "Apple" posters	$300–400	$605
37.	A painted plaster life mask of Ringo Starr	$250–300	$550

38.	A roll of Beatles wallpaper from the late 1960s	$150–200	$495
39.	A silver pendant medallion of the August 1, 1971, "Concert for Bangladesh"	$500–700	$495
40.	Approximately 200 Beatles bubble gum cards	$100–150	$467
41.	An official program and ticket from the 1965 *Help!* movie premiere	$250–300	$385
42.	A promotional copy of the Beatles album *Rarities* and an acetate single of "Lady Madonna," sold as a set	$200–300	$302
43.	An unreleased cover design for George Harrison's single "You"	$225–275	$247

TOTAL AUCTION PROCEEDS: $113,491

46. 31 Items of Beatles Merchandise Available in 1997

The Beatles were merchandised like crazy when they were still a band and today, rare Beatles items from the sixties garner big bucks when they become available on the collectors' market. Today, the Beatles are as hot as ever, only the array of Beatles merchandise reflects the changing times (computer mouse pads and CDs are common), and the end is nowhere in sight.

One of the premier marketers of new Beatles memorabilia is Mark Lapidos, the promoter of the highly regarded annual Beatlefest convention. Mark issues a catalog of licensed Beatles merchandise, and the following list gives you a look at the wide variety of Fab Four collectibles (some new, some vintage) that are being sold 30 years after the breakup of the band. (For a free catalog and convention information, call 1-800-BEATLES.)

1. **Mouse pads**   Four Beatles album covers are available as full-color computer mouse pads: *With the Beatles, Sgt. Pepper's Lonely Hearts Club Band, Abbey Road,* and *Let It Be.*
2. **Quartz watches**   All come with straps and offer a wide range of dial designs, including the *White Album* photos, silver and gold Beatles silhouettes, autograph editions, and the *Let It Be, With the Beatles, A Hard Day's Night,* and *Abbey Road* album covers.
3. **Beatles Anthology 24 CD wallet case**   The *Anthology* logo is on the front of the wallet.
4. **Songbooks**   Sheet music collections of everything the Beatles ever recorded, available in a wide range of transcriptions, including piano, guitar, and vocal; one-line "fake" books; and solo guitar. Songbooks for individual albums are also available.
5. **T-shirts and sweatshirts**   All manner of shirts with anything you can imagine Beatles-related on them—logos, album covers, photos, etc. There is even a T-shirt available that comes inside a Beatles lunch box.
6. **Calendars**   For 1998, there were several Beatles calendars available, all boasted a glorious array of Beatles photographs, in every format from small desk calendars to long locker calendars.
7. **Trading cards**   Like sports stars, the Fabs have their own trading cards, including 23K gold *Abbey Road* and *Beatles for Sale* trading cards for $30 each.

LIMITED EDITION MOVIE WATCHES

ONLY $85.00 Each

BRAND NEW

WITH THE B

3621 - A HARD DAY'S NIGHT

3624 - LET IT BE

These three watches each come in the black movie case shown above.

3622 - HELP

3453 - ABBE

3627 - SET OF 4 WATCHES IN LARGE GUITAR CASE - This very Limited Edition comes a 2 foot guitar case with 4 limited edition watches that are unique to this item. There are two each of *Abbey Road and Let It Be* - One each in Gold and the other in Silver. ONLY $320.00

All Watches are water resistant, high quality quartz, stainless steel, and come in a beautiful black guitar case as shown here.

BRAND NEW

402 EAR BEATL IMA

3604 - SILVER SILHOUETTE

3607 - GOLD SILHOUETTE

3651 - LARGE SILVER SILHOUETTE

3653 - LARGE AUTOGRAPHS

3620 - WHITE ALBUM PHOTO

3619 - 4 FACES

ONLY $68.00 Each

4 IM

3612 -

3613 - ABBEY

3611 - LET IT

3616 - WITH THE

3618 - A HARD DAY'S

One our con 100 No

8. **Blankets and towels**   Throw blankets of 100% cotton, 46″ × 67″, that can be used as a throw or hung as a tapestry are available. Designs include the *White Album* photos, the *Rubber Soul* cover, and the *With the Beatles* cover. The 30″ × 60″ towels include a Beatles cartoon design.

9. **Tumbler inserts**   Only the original 1964 drinking tumbler photo inserts were still available—the tumblers themselves were sold out.

10. **Pins**   All manner of Beatles pins were for sale, including some original 1964 pins.

11. **Scarf**   From the Netherlands, this scarf showed four Beatle faces and a guitar.

12. **Neckties**   Over a dozen styles of Beatles neckties were available, some with album covers, some with Beatle faces. There were also several neckties available with specially commissioned artwork inspired by Beatles songs. (I myself have the "Good Day Sunshine" tie—red and black motif—and the "Do You Want to Know a Secret?" tie—blue motif. The "Secret?" tie always elicits compliments. The "Sunshine" tie, not so many. If you see it, you'll know why. Does the word "loud" mean anything?)

13. **Caps**   Of course.
14. **Figurines**   Ringo drum figurines, *Abbey Road* figurines, and more.

as well as . . .

15. Pewter Beatles belt buckles
16. Cloisonné Beatles key chains
17. Beatles refrigerator magnets
18. Embossed metal Beatles signs
19. Beatles gift bags
20. Beatles *Billboard* plaques
21. Autographed Ringo drum sticks
22. Tour programs
23. Beatles enamel plates

24. Beatles numbered prints
25. Beatles posters and lithographs
26. Beatles coffee mugs
27. Beatles puzzles
28. Beatles suspenders
29. Beatles silk vests
30. Beatles greeting cards
31. Beatles post cards

It Took Me Years to Write . . .

47. 28 Books That Would Make Up an Excellent Basic Beatles Library

This admittedly arbitrary selection of Beatles books should nonetheless serve the average Beatles fan well. I chose the most serviceable references available to guarantee that a specific Beatles question could be answered; I selected the most accurate and informative biographies so that any questions on the people, places, and things in the Fabs universe could likewise be resolved.

The books are listed alphabetically by title and I graded them on a 1- to 4-star (★) scale; ★ books can be skipped; ★★ books are worth having but not critical; ★★★ books are "should haves"; ★★★★ books are absolutely essential. Obviously, if you bought all the ★★★★ books on this list, you'd have access to the best and most entertaining Beatles information available.

(Forgive my conceit in including *this* volume, *The Beatles Book of Lists* in this bibliography, but in the book's defense, just the features on "Free as a Bird," the *Anthology* series, and the Beatles covers make this tome a must-have for serious Beatles fans.)

1. *All Together Now* by Harry Castleman and Walter J. Podrazik (Popular Culture, Ink., 1973). The first serious attempt at a comprehensive Beatles discography, this volume will become a reference you will turn to often. I'm not too thrilled with the design of the book, but its gold mine of accurate discographic info makes up for the visual flaws. ★★★★

2. *The Art and Music of John Lennon* by John Roberston (Citadel Press, 1993). A very good account of John's recordings and writings, notable for being one of the first books to acknowledge the existence of "Free as a Bird" and tell us when John recorded the demo that was ultimately transformed into the Beatles first new single in thirty years. Written in chronological order, this book is informative and thorough. No photos; excellent index. ★★★

3. *Beatle! The Pete Best Story* by Pete Best with Patrick Doncaster (Plexus London, 1985). The dumped-Beatles' story. Interesting for its look at the Fabs' early years but one comes away from the book with a "So what?" attitude. Good pictures, no index (which would have made this more useful). ★★

4. *The Beatles Book of Lists* by Stephen Spignesi (Citadel Press, 1998). The book you hold in your hands is included here because not only is it a genuinely fun read, but it is truly up-to-the minute complete, with lengthy features on the "Free as a Bird" video, *The Beatles Anthology,* and late-breaking news about the Beatles and their world. ★★★

5. *The Beatles: A Day in the Life* by Tom Schultheiss (Popular Culture, Ink., 1980). A superb and meticulously detailed diary of a decade in the Beatles' lives and careers. Some pictures; excellent index. ★★★★

6. *The Beatles: The Ultimate Recording Guide* by Alan J. Weiner (Bob Adams, Inc. 1994). An absolutely amazing compendium of Beatles historical and discographic information, presented in chronological order, and organized into "General Chronology," "Recording Chronology," "Discographies," and "Bootlegs and Unreleased Recordings." It also includes appendices on "The Beatles as Supporting Players," "Videocassettes and Laser Discs," "References/Recommended Periodicals," and "Song Title Index." If you could own only one Beatles discography and reference book, this would be the one to buy. ★★★★

7. *The Beatles After the Breakup: In Their Own Words,* edited by David Bennahum (Omnibus Press, 1991). Good selection of quotations by the Fabs, organized by chapter and headings, but not indexed. Nice pix, but the quotations are not attributed to their original sources, which would have been useful. ★★

8. *The Beatles Again?* by Harry Castleman and Walter J. Podrazik (Popular Culture, Ink., 1977). The just-as-good sequel to their first book *All Together Now—*and just as necessary. ★★★★

9. *The Beatles Forever* by Nicholas Schaffner (McGraw-Hill, 1977). One of the first literary companions to the Beatles experience, this volume still holds up today as a valuable resource and an absolutely fascinating read. Great pictures of both the Beatles and Beatles memorabilia, terrific index. ★★★★

10. *The Beatles Recording Sessions* by Mark Lewisohn (Harmony Books, 1988). The definitive chronicle of the Beatles' Abbey Road studio recordings, starting in June 1962 with their infamous "audition" and continuing all the way to the end of their recording career as a group. The book includes a carefully compiled discography, a recording glossary, a wonderfully complete index, and a lengthy interview with Paul McCartney. The book also boasts tons of extremely rare photos and recording session logs, as well as inside information on specific recording sessions. This depth of scholarship does the Beatles justice, but does not make for a dry, academic book. *The Beatles Recording Sessions* is a magnificent accomplishment and an invaluable resource for Beatles fans of all ages. Paul McCartney calls this book the "Bible." He's not kidding. ★★★★

11. *The Beatles: The Authorized Biography* by Hunter Davies (Dell, 1968). The first official Beatles biography, therefore, a must-read. This tome contains good information about the early years of the group and was obviously written from an insider's informed point of view. It suffers, though, from being heavily censored by the Beatles and their families and from the lack of an index. It also includes photos we've seen everywhere. ★★★

12. *The Beatles: The Long and Winding Road: A History of the Beatles on Record* by Neville Stannard (Avon, 1982). An excellent discography, organized into British and American sections, with a good index. This book contains much infor-

mation but could be a little confusing to use due to the way it's organized. Worth having though, if only for the concert playlists and "Christmas Records" tracks listings. ★★★

13. *Beatlesongs* by William J. Dowlding (Fireside, 1989). This is a companion to the Beatles' songs and draws from many sources to present what is probably the most detailed look at the nuts-and-bolts of each Beatles song done to date. Because of the wide range of information offered for each song, you will find this book extremely useful. Dowlding tells us who played what, who wrote what, who sang what, etc. and also includes a nice selection of carefully chosen quotes in which the Fabs talk about specific songs. No pics, but a great index with the main page number that covers a song highlighted in bold type, allowing you to ignore casual mentions of a song and go right to its detailed section. An interesting feature is Dowlding's attempt at assigning a numerical percentage of who wrote what to individual songs. This works for each song ("Birthday" is credited as .7 of the song being written by McCartney and .3 of the song being written Lennon, for example) but the genuinely scientific songwriting credit chart at the end of the book seems a tad over-the-top. ★★★★

14. *A Cellarful of Noise* by Brian Epstein with Derek Taylor (Popular Culture, Ink., reprint edition of 1964 edition). This is Brian Epstein's autobiography, which was actually written by Derek Taylor. Kind of boring and consisting more of Brian's views on show business than an insider's look at life with the Beatles. ★

15. *Collecting the Beatles, Volumes 1 and 2*, by Barbara Fenick (Popular Culture, Ink., 1982 and 1985). If you're a Beatles memorabilia junkie these books provide details on Beatles collectibles you probably never knew existed. Meticulously thorough, but specialized tomes for specialty collectors. ★★

16. *The Compleat Beatles* (Contemporary Books, 1985). The companion book to the documentary. Entertaining and lavishly illustrated, but probably extremely difficult to find. Worth having, though, if you can pick up a copy somewhere. Good interviews, but no index. ★★★★

17. *The Complete Beatles Chronicle* by Mark Lewisohn. This essential volume is an update of Lewisohn's *The Beatles Live!* (which is now out of print), including some information from Lewisohn's *The Beatles Recording Sessions*. This book also includes some new information that makes it an extremely complete chronology of the Fabs' career, from 1957 through 1970. ★★★★

18. *The Encyclopedia of Beatles People* by Bill Harry (Blandford UK, 1997). An absolutely essential compendium of the most important players in the Beatles universe, from Steve Abrams (the Oxford student who arranged for Paul McCartney's 1967 "legalize marijuana" ad in *The London Times*) to Donald Zec (the British *Daily Mirror* entertainment writer who in 1963 wrote one of the first feature articles about the Beatles astonishing rise to fame). Good Beatles chronology, too, as well as some rare, little-seen pix. ★★★★

19. *The End of the Beatles?* by Harry Castleman and Walter J. Podrazik (Popular Culture, Ink., 1985). The third volume in Castleman and Podrazik's Beatles discography series that began with *All Together Now*. ★★★★

20. *Every Little Thing: A Definitive Guide to Beatles Recording Variations, Rare Mixes, and Other Musical Oddities, 1958–1986* by William McCoy and Mitchell

McGeary (Popular Culture, Ink., 1986). Excellent for what it offers, but, let's face it, this is information for the Beatles *fanatic,* not the average fan. Though, if this is stuff you really want to know, then this book is a must. ★★

21. *Here, There, and Everywhere: The First International Beatles Bibliography, 1962–1982* (Popular Culture, Ink., 1982). This book contains highly specialized information for the Beatles researcher, but there is no denying that it certainly is exhaustive and accurate in what it *does* offer. Because of its unique status as an important reference work, we give it two ratings: for the serious Beatles scholar, ★★★★; for the typical Beatles fan. ★★

22. *How They Became the Beatles* by Gareth L. Pawlowski (Plume, 1989). An okay look at the Beatles in the years 1960 through 1964. Good memorabilia and photos, no index. ★★

23. *The Lost Beatles Interviews* edited by Geoffrey Giuliano (Plume, 1996). An excellent compendium of rare and hard-to-find Beatles press conferences and interviews that is a valuable addition to the library of books about the Beatles. Excellent photos and a good index make this worth owning. Everyone from Ravi Shankar to John's uncle Charlie is included in this book, making it an important one, as well as one hell of a read. ★★★★

24. *Nothing Is Beatleproof* by Michael Hockinson (Popular Culture, Ink., 1990). The most amazing compilation of Beatles trivia yet assembled in one place. This is graduate-level Beatles testing and the book (with its multiple indexes), even though ostensibly a quiz book, is also one of the better Beatles reference books. You will undoubtedly learn something about the Beatles that you did not know after browsing through this book. ★★★★

25. *Shout!: The True Story of the Beatles* by Philip Norman (Fireside, 1981). An allegedly "honest" account of the Beatles, yet one that has more errors and unsubstantiated stories than it should. Decent pics and index. ★★

26. *Things We Said Today: The Complete Lyrics and a Concordance to the Beatles Songs, 1962–1970* by Colin Campbell and Allan Murphy (Popular Culture, Ink., 1980). If you were going to own only one collection of Beatles lyrics, then this is the one to buy. Why? In addition to the complete reproduction of the lyrics to every single Beatles song, *Things We Said Today* also includes an amazing concordance that lists in alphabetical order every use of all the words in the Beatles lyrics. Thus, if you wish, you can find every one of the Fab's use of the word *time* in their songs. (By the way, there are 127 uses of the word *time* in the Beatles 189 recorded songs.) This book is irresistible and also extremely valuable. ★★★★

27. *Turn Me On, Dead Man: The Complete Story of the Paul McCartney Death Hoax* by Andru J. Reeve (Popular Culture, Ink., 1994). If you are into the whole "Paul Is Dead" thing, then this is the book for you. Reeve provides what is probably the most complete listing of Beatles "death" clues to date, and also includes many unusual photos illustrating some of the most befuddling visual images. (See the chapter "40 'Paul Is Dead' Clues" for more details on this phenomenon.) ★★

28. *The Ultimate Beatles Encyclopedia* by Bill Harry (Hyperion, 1992). An A-to-Z of Beatledom. Entertaining and informative, and one more Bill Harry home run. ★★★★

48. The 2 Features in the January 1981 Issue of *Playboy* That Make It a Beatles Collectible

This issue featured a lengthy, in-depth interview with John and Yoko.
This issue also had a steamy nude pictorial of the lovely Mrs. Ringo Starr, Barbara Bach. (She was also on the cover of the magazine.)

49. 43 Beatles *Rolling Stone* Magazine Covers

The Beatles defined pop music in the sixties and beyond and yet it wasn't until 1967 that they were featured on the cover of *Rolling Stone* magazine.
They graced the magazine's cover nine times through 1985.

December 14, 1967 ▪ October 26, 1968 ▪ December 21, 1968
November 15, 1969 ▪ October 24, 1974 ▪ July 15, 1976
February 16, 1984 ▪ December 20, 1984 ▪ December 19, 1985

In addition to showing the Beatles as a group, the individual Beatles have also appeared on the cover of *Rolling Stone* a total of thirty-four times:

George Harrison
September 2, 1971 ▪ December 19, 1974 ▪ October 22, 1987
December 17, 1987

Paul McCartney
April 27, 1968 ▪ April 30, 1970 ▪ January 31, 1974 ▪ June 17, 1976
July 12, 1979 ▪ December 8, 1983 ▪ December 22, 1983
August 15, 1985 ▪ September 11, 1986 ▪ December 18, 1986
June 15, 1989 ▪ December 14, 1989 ▪ February 8, 1990 ▪ December 13, 1990

John Lennon
November 9, 1967 ▪ April 27, 1968 ▪ November 23, 1968
February 7, 1970 ▪ January 21, 1971 ▪ February 4, 1971
January 22, 1981 ▪ May 14, 1981 ▪ October 14, 1982
December 23, 1982 ▪ December 22, 1983 ▪ October 20, 1988
December 15, 1988 ▪ August 23, 1990 ▪ December 13, 1990

Ringo Starr
April 30, 1981

JANUARY 21, 1971
50c
UK. 3/-

ROLLING STONE

The
Rolling Stone
Interview:
John Lennon
Part One
**The
Working
Class
Hero**

(Editor's collection)

Singing Songs for Everyone . . .

50. The 37 U.S. Singles

This list, probably more than any other compilation in *The Beatles Book of Lists,* illustrates most dramatically just how colossal the Beatles phenomenon actually was. From April 23, 1962, through May 11, 1970, the Beatles released thirty-seven singles. (Twelve singles were also rereleased—sometimes more than once—to capitalize on the insatiable American appetite for Beatles records. Rereleases are noted in brackets.) Today, it's unfathomable that a musician or group would release twelve singles in one year as the Beatles did in 1964. I recall reading an interview with a musician who remembers one period in the sixties when the top eight records in the Top Ten were Beatles songs. That kind of success has never been equalled.

1962

1. **April 23**   "My Bonnie"/"The Saints" (also January 27, 1964)

1963

2. **February 25**   "Please Please Me"/"Ask Me Why" (also January 30, 1964; August 10, 1964; October 11, 1965)
3. **May 27**   "From Me to You"/"Thank You Girl"
4. **September 16**   "She Loves You"/"I'll Get You" (also May 21, 1964)
5. **December 26**   "I Want to Hold Your Hand"/"I Saw Her Standing There"

1964

6. **March 2**   "Twist and Shout"/"There's a Place" (also August 10, 1964; October 11, 1965)
7. **March 16**   "Can't Buy Me Love"/"You Can't Do That"
8. **March 27**   "Why"/"Cry for a Shadow"
9. **April 27**   "Love Me Do"/"P. S. I Love You" (also August 10, 1964; October 11, 1965)
10. **June 1**   "Sweet Georgia Brown"/"Take Out Some Insurance on Me, Baby"
11. **July 6**   "Ain't She Sweet"/"Nobody's Child"
12. **July 13**   "A Hard Day's Night"/"I Should Have Known Better"

13. **July 20**   "I'll Cry Instead"/"I'm Happy Just to Dance With You"
14. **July 20**   "And I Love Her"/"If I Fell"
15. **August 10**   "Do You Want to Know a Secret?"/"Thank You Girl" (also October 11, 1965)
16. **August 24**   "Slow Down"/"Matchbox"
17. **November 23**   "I Feel Fine"/"She's a Woman"

1965

18. **February 15**   "Eight Days a Week"/"I Don't Want to Spoil the Party"
19. **April 19**   "Ticket to Ride"/"Yes It Is"
20. **July 19**   "Help!"/"I'm Down"
21. **September 13**   "Yesterday"/"Act Naturally"
22. **October 11**   "Roll Over Beethoven"/"Misery"
23. **October 11**   "Boys"/"Kansas City" and "Hey Hey Hey Hey" Medley
24. **December 6**   "We Can Work It Out"/"Day Tripper"

1966

25. **February 21**   "Nowhere Man"/"What Goes On"
26. **May 23**   "Paperback Writer"/"Rain"
27. **August 5**   "Eleanor Rigby"/"Yellow Submarine"

1967

28. **February 13**   "Strawberry Fields Forever"/"Penny Lane"
29. **July 17**   "All You Need Is Love"/"Baby You're a Rich Man"
30. **November 27**   "Hello Goodbye"/"I Am the Walrus"

1968

31. **March 18**   "Lady Madonna"/"The Inner Light"
32. **August 26**   "Hey Jude"/"Revolution"

1969

33. **May 5**   "Get Back"/"Don't Let Me Down"
34. **June 4**   "The Ballad of John and Yoko"/"Old Brown Shoe"
35. **October 6**   "Something"/"Come Together"

1970

36. **March 11**   "Let It Be"/"You Know My Name (Look Up the Number)"
37. **May 11**   "The Long and Winding Road"/"For You Blue"

NOTE: This list looks at the Beatles singles during their heyday, that time when all four Fabs were alive and working together. However, in 1996, the world was treated to two brand-new Beatles singles and we acknowledge this rare event here.

"Free as a Bird" was released as a CD single in November 1995 after its first airing during *The Beatles Anthology* on ABC. The single contained four songs: "Free

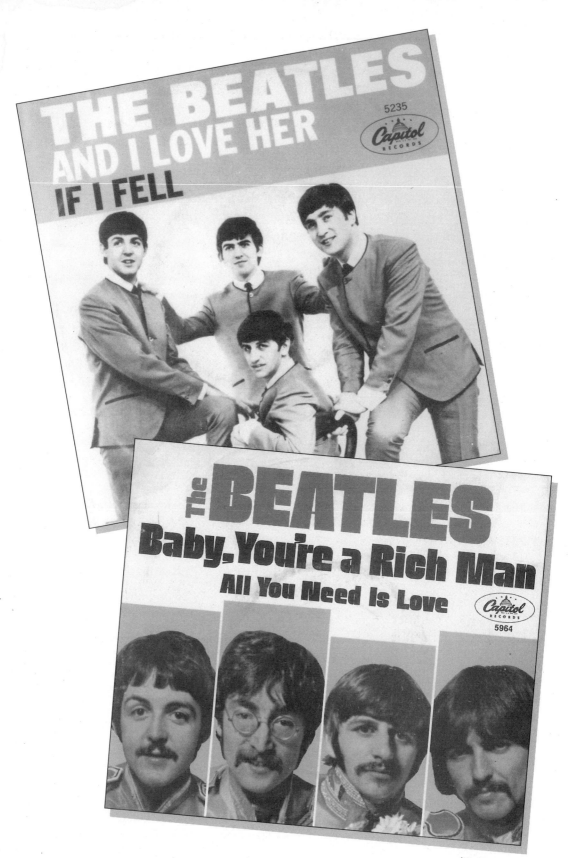

(Photofest)

as a Bird," "I Saw Her Standing There," "This Boy," and "Christmas Time (Is Here Again).'"

"Real Love" was released as a CD single in February 1996 and included four songs: "Real Love," "Baby's in Black" (Live), "Yellow Submarine," and "Here, There, and Everywhere."

"Free as a Bird" did better than "Real Love" on the charts, although both singles ultimately sold over 500,000 copies each and earned gold records.

51. 23 Songs Written by John, Paul, or George That Were Recorded by Other Musicians

The Beatles were truly productive. They wrote so many songs that there was no way they could record and release everything they came up with. (Stephen King had the same problem in his early years and several of his novels were ultimately published as "by Richard Bachman," just so he could get them off his desk and into the stores.)

Thus, the Beatles gave away some of their songs and this feature looks at what songs they blessed others with and who recorded and released the songs.

Song	Written By	Recorded By	U.K. Release Date	U.S. Release Date
*1. "I'll Be on My Way"	Paul and John	Billy J. Kramer and the Dakotas	April 26, 1963	June 10, 1963
2. "Bad to Me"	John	Billy J. Kramer and the Dakotas	July 27, 1963	September 23, 1963
3. "Tip of My Tongue"	Paul	Tommy Quickly	July 30, 1963	No U.S. release
*4. "Hello Little Girl"	John	The Fourmost	August 30, 1963	November 15, 1963
5. "Love of the Loved"	Paul	Cilla Black	September 27, 1963	No U.S. release
6. "I'll Keep You Satisfied"	Paul	Billy J. Kramer and the Dakotas	November 1, 1963	November 11, 1963
7. "I'm in Love"	John	The Fourmost	November 15, 1963	February 10, 1964
8. "A World Without Love"	Paul	Peter and Gordon	February 28, 1964	April 27, 1964
9. "One and One Is Two"	Paul	The Strangers with Mike Shannon	May 8, 1964	No U.S. release
10. "Nobody I Know"	Paul	Peter and Gordon	May 29, 1964	June 15, 1964
*11. "Like Dreamers Do"	Paul	The Applejacks	June 5, 1964	July 6, 1964
12. "From a Window"	Paul	Billy J. Kramer and the Dakotas	July 17, 1964	August 12, 1964
13. "It's for You"	John and Paul	Cilla Black	July 31, 1964	August 17, 1964
14. "I Don't Want to See You Again"	Paul	Peter and Gordon	September 11, 1964	September 21, 1964
*15. "That Means a Lot"	Paul	P. J. Proby	July 5, 1965	September 17, 1965
16. "Woman"	Paul (credited as "Bernard Webb")	Peter and Gordon	January 10, 1966	February 11, 1966
17. "Love in the Open Air"/ "Theme From *The Family Way*"	Paul	The George Martin Orchestra	December 23, 1966	April 24, 1967 (A-side only)

Song	Written By	Recorded By	U.K. Release Date	U.S. Release Date
18. "Step Inside Love"	Paul	Cilla Black	May 6, 1967	May 8, 1968
19. "Sour Milk Sea"	George	Jackie Lomax	September 6, 1968	August 26, 1968
20. "Thingumybob"	Paul	John Foster and Songs Ltd. Black Dyke Mills Band	September 6, 1968	August 26, 1968
21. "Badge"	George (and Eric Clapton)	Cream	February 28, 1969	February 5, 1969
22. "Penina"	Paul	Carlos Mendes	July 18, 1969 (Portugal only)	No U.S. release
*23. "Come and Get It" (Paul's one-man demo version of this song appears on *The Beatles Anthology 3*)	Paul	Badfinger	December 5, 1969	January 12, 1970

*Although these songs were first released by other artists, they eventually became "Beatles recordings" with the release of the Anthology and BBC collections.

52. 17 Beatles Songs That Mention the Sun and 10 Beatles Songs That Mention the Rain

Almost 10 percent of the Beatles song catalog—17 tunes—includes songs in which there is a reference to the sun. On the other hand, there are only 10 songs (some of which also include "sun" references) that include a reference to the rain.

Interpret this piece of Beatles lore as you will.

17 "SUN" SONGS

"Any Time at All" ▪ "I'll Follow the Sun" ▪ "Rain" ▪ "Good Day Sunshine"
"Yellow Submarine" ▪ "Lucy in the Sky With Diamonds" ▪ "I Am the Walrus"
"The Fool on the Hill" ▪ "Dear Prudence" ▪ "Good Night"
"Julia" ▪ "Mother Nature's Son" ▪ "It's All Too Much" ▪ "Here Comes the Sun"
"Sun King" ▪ "I've Got a Feeling" ▪ "Two of Us"

10 "RAIN" SONGS

"Please Please Me" ▪ "I'll Follow the Sun" ▪ "I'm a Loser"
"Rain" ▪ "Penny Lane" ▪ "Fixing a Hole" ▪ "I Am the Walrus" ▪ "Hey Bulldog"
"Across the Universe" ▪ "The Long and Winding Road"

53. 4 Beatles Songs Used in TV Commercials

For me and my generation ... ["Revolution"] was an honest statement about social change, [with John Lennon] really coming out and revealing how he felt . . . It was the truth, but now it refers to a running shoe.

> —James Taylor, speaking in 1989 about the
> commercial use of Beatles songs

A low point in the history of the Beatles occurred in 1985 when Beatles songs were first used in TV commercials. So far, the four songs in this list are the only ones that have been legitimately used to sell products. Hopefully, it stops there, although I doubt it.

Even though Beatles tunes have not been sold for commercial use for almost a decade now, some local merchants will brazenly use a Beatles song as the background for their own primitively produced TV spots. I personally have seen a commercial that used the Beatles' "Birthday" as the soundtrack for a furniture store's "Anniversary Sale" commercial.

Of course, these uses are illegal but they seem to be overlooked by those who might be in a position to seek remedies on behalf of the Fabs. A local TV station in a small market is rarely if ever monitored by companies such as ATV or ASCAP and can get away with almost anything, if they don't make a practice of it.

1. **"Help!"**
   WHERE THE COMMERCIAL AIRED   United States
   PRODUCT   Lincoln-Mercury automobiles
   RENDITION   Cover version by studio musicians and singers
   FEE PAID $100,000 for a six-month run
2. **"We Can Work It Out"**
   WHERE THE COMMERCIAL AIRED   United Kingdom
   PRODUCT   Hewlett-Packard products
   RENDITION   Cover version by studio musicians and singers
   FEE PAID   £45,000
3. **"She Loves You"**
   WHERE THE COMMERCIAL AIRED   Spain
   PRODUCT   Schweppes beverages
   RENDITION   Cover version by studio musicians and singers
   FEE PAID $11,000
4. **"Revolution"**
   WHERE THE COMMERCIAL AIRED   United States
   PRODUCT   Nike products
   RENDITION   The original recording by the Beatles
   FEE PAID   not known

54. 2 Different Beatle (But Not Beatles) Songs With the Same Title

"Woman" by Paul McCartney   Paul gave this song to Peter and Gordon, who recorded it in December 1965.

"Woman" by John Lennon   John wrote this song for his and Yoko's 1980 *Double Fantasy* album.

55. 3 Beatles Songs Whose Titles Were Actually Ringo's Unique Linguistic Concoctions

These three song titles all came from one of Ringo's famous malaprops. Apparently, John and Paul were always on the alert for one of Ringo's off-the-cuff remarks, since they were always inventive, clever, and imagistically intriguing. (Just imagine the possibilities if the Beatles had known that wordsmith, Yogi Berra!)

"A Hard Day's Night"
"Eight Days a Week"
"Tomorrow Never Knows"

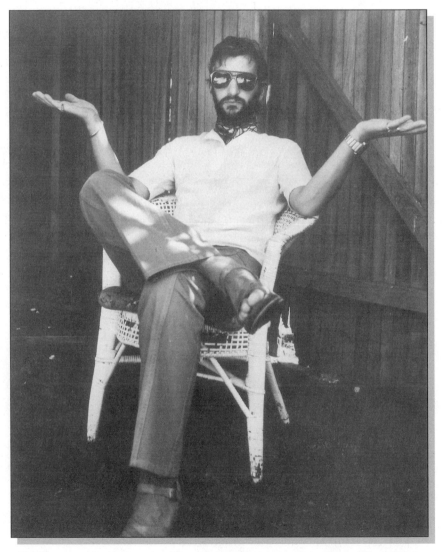

Ringo, seemingly not knowing from whence his inspiration comes. (Photofest)

They've Been Going
in and out of Style . . .

56. The 62 People on the Cover of
Sgt. Pepper's Lonely Heart's Club Band

The *Sgt. Pepper* album cover stunned the world with its boldness and creativity. The Beatles stood at a grave before a crowd of the famous and the infamous, and Beatles fans collectively scratched their heads (and had an enormous amount of fun) trying to figure out who was who and just what the hell was going on. (This was before anyone actually heard what some consider to be the Beatles' best, most important album of all time!)

Here is a listing of all 62 of the notables and notorious who grace the cover of *Sgt. Pepper's Lonely Hearts Club Band*. (The source for this listing is Nicholas Shaffner's classic book, *The Beatles Forever*, a *must* for any decent Beatles library.) Pick up the cover and try to spot them.

1. Sri Yukteswar Giri (guru)
2. Aleister Crowley (writer, mystic, drug experimenter, antichrist)
3. Mae West (American actress)
4. Lenny Bruce (American comedian)
5. Karlheinz Stockhausen (modern German atonal composer)
6. W. C. Fields (American actor)
7. Carl Jung (Swiss psychiatrist)
8. Edgar Allan Poe (American writer)
9. Fred Astaire (American actor and dancer)
10. Merkin (American artist)
11. Drawing of a pretty girl
12. Huntz Hall (Bowery Boy)
13. Simon Rodia (American folk artist, creator of *Watts Towers*)
14. Bob Dylan (American singer-songwriter)
15. Aubrey Beardsley (British artist)
16. Sir Robert Peel (pioneering British policeman and politician)
17. Aldous Huxley (British writer and philosopher)
18. Dylan Thomas (Welsh poet)
19. Terry Southern (American writer)
20. Dion (American pop singer)

21. Tony Curtis (American actor)
22. Wallace Berman (American artist)
23. Tommy Handley (World War II comedian)
24. Marilyn Monroe (legendary sex symbol)
25. William Burroughs (American writer)
26. Sri Mahavatara Babaji (guru)
27. Stan Laurel (American comic actor)
28. Richard Lindner (American artist)
29. Oliver Hardy (American comic actor)
30. Karl Marx (communist)
31. H. G. Wells (British writer)
32. Sri Paramahansa Yogananda (guru)
33. Stuart Sutcliffe (dead ex-Beatle)
34. Julie Adams (American actress)
35. Max Miller (British comedian)
36. Drawing of a nurse
37. Marlon Brando (American actor)
38. Tom Mix (American cowboy film star)
39. Oscar Wilde (British writer)
40. Tyrone Power (American actor)
41. Larry Bell (modern painter)
42. Wax statue of Dr. David Livingstone (English explorer)
43. Johnny Weismuller ("Tarzan")
44. Stephen Crane (American writer)
45. Issy Bonn (British comedian)
46. Wax statue of George Bernard Shaw (British playright)
47. Albert Stubbins (Liverpool football player)
48. Sri Lahiri Mahasaya (guru)
49. Albert Einstein (genius)
50. Lewis Carroll (English writer)
51. Sonny Liston (American boxer)
52. Wax statue of George Harrison
53. Wax statue of John Lennon
54. Wax statue of Ringo Starr
55. Wax statue of Paul McCartney
56. Unknown guru
57. Marlene Dietrich (American actress)
58. Diana Dors (American actress)
59. Shirley Temple (American actress and foreign ambassador)
60. Bobby Breen (British singing prodigy)
61. T. E. Lawrence (British author of *Lawrence of Arabia*)
62. Unknown American legionnaire

It was primarily Paul's idea to do the collage of famous figures for the cover of *Sgt. Pepper* and everyone involved in the production of the album—from photographer Michael Cooper to the Beatles themselves—weighed in on who should be included. They attempted to contact everyone they wanted to depict on the cover but with time running short, at least half of the images on the cover were published without permission. (Nobody sued, though, something Paul was positive about from the start. "Everybody will be delighted," he was quoted as saying.) At first, legendary film sex siren Mae West refused to allow her image to be used. "What would *I* be doing in a lonely hearts club band?" she asked when approached for permission. All four of the Beatles wrote personal letters to Ms. West and she ultimately relented and allowed her picture to be used on the cover. It was a different story with Leo Gorcey of the Bowery Boys. Gorcey insisted on being paid a fee for use of his picture. The Beatles refused, Gorcey stood firm, and they went with Huntz Hall instead.

57. 7 Lyrical "Lifts" From an 1843 Circus Poster That John Lennon Used in the Song "Being for the Benefit of Mr. Kite!"

John Lennon found inspiration everywhere. He could see something—such as an apple, for instance—and glimpse lyrical potential that he would eventually shape into a memorable song. When the Beatles were filming their "Penny Lane" video, John came across an antique circus poster dated February 14, 1843, that he promptly stole ("liberated" is what he called it) from the cafe wall where it hung. This poster later served as the source for one of his most memorable and musically accomplished songs, "Being for the Benefit of Mr. Kite!"

Here is a rundown of the lines from the poster and the lines of lyric from the song into which it eventually metamorphosed. This side-by-side comparison gives us a rare glimpse into the genius of John Lennon's songwriting abilities and, of course, his sense of humor.

1. POSTER "Pablo Fanque's Circus Royal"
   SONG "Late of Pablo Fanques Fair—what a scene"

2. POSTER "Being for the Benefit of Mr. Kite"
   SONG "For the Benefit of Mr. Kite" and the song's title

3. POSTER "Messrs. KITE & HENDERSON, in announcing the following entertainments, assure the Public that this Night's Productions will be one of the most Splendid ever produced in this Town, having been some days in preparation."
   SONG "Having been some days in preparation, a splendid time is guaranteed for all," "Messrs. K & H assure the public their production will be second to none."

4. POSTER "MR. KITE will, for this Night only, introduce the CELEBRATED HORSE, ZANTHUS! Well known to be one of the best Broke Horses IN THE WORLD!"
   SONG "And of course Henry the Horse dances the waltz."

5. POSTER "MR. HENDERSON will undertake the arduous task of THROWING TWENTY-ONE SOMERSETS ON THE SOLID GROUND."
   SONG "And Mr. H. will demonstrate ten somersets he'll undertake on solid ground."

6. POSTER   "MR. HENDERSON will, for the first time in Rochdale Introduce his extraordinary TRAMPOLINE LEAPS AND SOMERSETS!"
   SONG   "There will be a show tonight on trampoline."

7. POSTER   "Over Men & Horses, through Hoops, over Garters, and lastly, through a Hogshead of REAL FIRE! In this branch of the profession Mr. H. challenges THE WORLD!"
   SONG   "Over men and horses, hoops and garters, lastly through a hogshead of real fire. In this way Mr. K. will challenge the world."

(Photofest)

Sit Back and Let the Evening Go . . .

58. 8 Classic Beatles Concert Playlists from Their Peak Touring Years of 1964–1967

There was one thing that sticks in my mind. On one of the concerts, I think it was Long Beach, instead of leaving right after the show, I waited until all the audience had gone. I was just hanging around the stadium, and I watched them bulldozing. They had a bulldozer in the middle . . . and they were bulldozing all the rubble left by the audience. There were mountains of empty bottles of gin and bourbon and tequila and brassieres and shoes and coats and trash. I mean, it was unbelievable.

—George Harrison, talking in November 1987
about touring and playing live with the Beatles

The Beatles stopped touring in 1966 after a final performance at Candlestick Park in San Francisco. An important reason why they stopped performing live was because the increasing complexity of their studio recordings became almost impossible to duplicate live. Another reason was undoubtedly boredom.

This feature looks at the songs the Fabs performed when they were touring like crazy. Reviewing these playlists makes one thing extremely clear: After dozens and dozens of performances, "Twist and Shout," "I'm Down," and "Roll Over Beethoven" (to cite three Beatles live "standards") had to be a real chore to play. That thought came to me while watching Garth Brooks' live 1997 summer concert in Central Park (which was broadcast on HBO). Garth brought out special guest singer and songwriter Don McLean, most famous for the song "American Pie." Garth did the first couple of verses of "Pie" by himself and then McLean came out and completed the song. Instead of singing the song *note-perfect* to the record as Garth did, McLean played with the song's melody line, soaring and diving with the tune as though he was trying to improvise a harmony part to his classic melody. The overall effect of this was jarring and the thought occurred to me that only two things were responsible for his blatant tampering with the "American Pie" melody: Either old Don couldn't hit the notes dead on anymore (for whatever reason), or he was just so

183

bored with singing this song over and over and over for the past quarter of a century that he *had* to play with it or else he'd go nuts.

I'll bet the Beatles felt something akin to that when they started "Twist and Shout" for the gazillionth time. (By the way, the Saturday after Garth's August 6, Thursday night concert, Don McLean appeared on the *Today* show and performed live in the plaza. His repertoire? "American Pie," and, yes, he screwed around with the melody yet again. Maybe he needs some new material? Just wondering.)

1. The 12 Songs Performed by the Beatles at the Washington Coliseum and Carnegie Hall in February 1964

"Roll Over Beethoven" (sung by George)
"From Me to You" (John and Paul)
"I Saw Her Standing There" (Paul)
"This Boy" (John)
"All My Loving" (Paul)
"I Wanna Be Your Man" (Ringo)
"Please Please Me" (John and Paul)
"Till There Was You" (Paul)
"She Loves You" (John and Paul)
"I Want to Hold Your Hand" (John and Paul)
"Twist and Shout" (John)
"Long Tall Sally" (Paul)

2. The 12 Songs Performed by the Beatles on Their North American Tour in Summer 1964

"Twist and Shout" (John)
"You Can't Do That" (John)
"All My Loving" (Paul)
"She Loves You" (John and Paul)
"Things We Said Today" (Paul)
"Roll Over Beethoven" (George)
"Can't Buy Me Love" (Paul)
"If I Fell" (John)
"I Want to Hold Your Hand" (John and Paul)
"Boys" (Ringo)
"A Hard Day's Night" (John and Paul)
"Long Tall Sally" (Paul)

3. The 11 Songs Performed by the Beatles During Their 3-Week Engagement at the Hammersmith Odeon in London at Christmas 1964

"Twist and Shout" (John)
"I'm a Loser" (John"
"Baby's in Black" (John and Paul)
"Everybody's Trying to Be My Baby" (George)
"Can't Buy Me Love" (Paul)
"Honey Don't" (Ringo)
"I Feel Fine" (John)
"She's a Woman" (Paul)
"A Hard Day's Night" (John and Paul)
"Rock and Roll Music" (John)
"Long Tall Sally" (Paul)

4. The 11 Songs Performed by the Beatles During Their European Tour in Summer 1965

"Twist and Shout" (John)
"She's a Woman" (Paul)
"Ticket to Ride" (John)
"A Hard Day's Night" (John and Paul)
"Baby's in Black" (John and Paul)

"Can't Buy Me Love" (Paul)
"I'm a Loser" (John"
"I Wanna Be Your Man" (Ringo)
"Long Tall Sally" (Paul)

"Rock and Roll Music" (John)
"Everybody's Trying to Be
My Baby" (George)

5. The 12 Songs Performed by the Beatles During Their North American Tour in Summer 1965

"Twist and Shout" (John)
"She's a Woman" (Paul)
"I Feel Fine" (John)
"Dizzy Miss Lizzie" (John)
"Ticket to Ride" (John)
"Everybody's Trying to Be
My Baby" (George)

"Can't Buy Me Love" (Paul)
"Baby's in Black" (John and Paul)
"Act Naturally" (Ringo)*
"A Hard Day's Night"
(John and Paul)
"Help!" (John)
"I'm Down" (Paul)

*Alternated with "I Wanna Be Your Man," also sung by Ringo.

6. The 12 Songs Performed by the Beatles During Their British Tour in December 1965

"Dizzy Miss Lizzy" (John)
"I Feel Fine" (John"
"She's a Woman" (Paul)
"If I Needed Someone" (George)
"Ticket to Ride" (John)
"Act Naturally" (Ringo)
"Nowhere Man" (John)

"Baby's in Black" (John and Paul)
"Help!" (John)
"We Can Work It Out"
(John and Paul)
"Day Tripper" (John and Paul)
"Twist and Shout" (John)
"I'm Down" (Paul)

7. The 11 Songs Performed by the Beatles on Their World Tour in Summer 1966

"Rock and Roll Music" (John)
"She's a Woman" (Paul)
"If I Needed Someone" (George)
"Baby's in Black" (John and Paul)
"Day Tripper" (John and Paul)
"I Feel Fine" (John)

"Yesterday" (Paul)
"I Wanna Be Your Man" (Ringo)
"Nowhere Man" (John)
"Paperback Writer" (Paul)
"I'm Down" (Paul)

8. The 11 Songs Performed by the Beatles During Their Final Live Concert Performance as a Group on August 29, 1966, at Candlestick Park in San Francisco, California

"Rock and Roll Music" (John)
"She's a Woman" (Paul)
"If I Needed Someone" (George)
"Baby's in Black" (John and Paul)
"Day Tripper" (John and Paul)
"I Feel Fine" (John)

"Yesterday" (Paul)
"I Wanna Be Your Man" (Ringo)
"Nowhere Man" (John)
"Paperback Writer" (Paul)
"I'm Down" (Paul)

59. The 18 Songs Performed by John and Yoko at the One-to-One Benefit in New York City on August 30, 1972

"It's So Hard" (John)
"Instant Karma" (John)
"Mother" (John)
"Well, Well, Well" (John)
"Woman Is the Nigger Of
   the World" (John)
"Sisters, O Sisters" (Yoko)
"Attica State" (John)
"Power to the People" (John)

"Imagine" (John)
"We're All Water" (Yoko)
"Now or Never" (Yoko)
"Cold Turkey" (John)
"New York City" (John)
"Born in a Prison" (Yoko)
"Come Together" (John)
"Hound Dog" (John)
"Give Peace a Chance" (John)

60. The 22 Songs Performed by Paul McCartney and Wings During the Summer 1972 Leg of Their European Tour

"Smile Away"
"The Mess"
"Hi Hi Hi"
"Mumbo"
"Bip Bop"
"Say You Don't Mind"
   (Denny Laine)
"Wild Life"
"Sea Side Woman"
   (Linda McCartney)
"I Would Only Smile"
"Blue Moon of Kentucky"
"Give Ireland Back to the Irish"

"Henry's Blues"
   (Henry McCullough)
"1882"
"I Am Your Singer"
"Junk"
"Eat at Home"
"Maybe I'm Amazed"
"My Love"
"Mary Had a Little Lamb"
"Soily"
"Best Friend"
"Momma's Little Girl"

61. The 14 Songs Performed by Paul McCartney and Wings During Their Spring 1973 British Tour

"Big Barn Bed"
"Soily"
"When the Night"
"Wild Life"
"Sea Side Woman"
   (Linda McCartney)
"Go Now" (Denny Laine)
"Little Woman Love"/"C Moon"

"Live and Let Die"
"Maybe I'm Amazed"
"Say You Don't Mind"
   (Denny Laine)
"My Love"
"The Mess"
"Hi Hi Hi"
"Long Tall Sally"

62. The 13 Songs Performed by George Harrison During His November and December 1974 North American Tour

"Hari's on Tour Express"

"The Lord Loves the One"

"For You Blue"

"Something"

"Sue Me, Sue You Blues"

"Maya Love"

"Sound Stage of My Love"

"Dark Horse"

"Give Me Love"

"In My Life"

"While My Guitar Gently Weeps"

"What Is Life"

"My Sweet Lord"

63. The 28 Songs Performed by Paul McCartney and Wings During Their September 1975 British Tour

This concert was a significant one in the annals of post-Beatles performances. Why? It was one of the first concerts by Paul and Wings that included *five* old Beatles songs, something Paul had not previously done.

"Venus and Mars"

"Rock Show"

"Jet"

"Let Me Roll It"

"Spirits of Ancient Egypt" (Denny Laine)

"Little Woman Love"/"C Moon" (Medley)

"Maybe I'm Amazed"

"Lady Madonna"

"The Long and Winding Road"

"Live and Let Die"

"Picasso's Last Words"

"Richard Corey" (Denny Laine)

"Bluebird"

"I've Just Seen a Face"

"Blackbird"

"Yesterday"

"You Gave Me the Answer"

"Magneto and Titanium Man"

"Go Now" (Denny Laine)

"Call Me Back Again"

"My Love"

"Listen to What the Man Said"

"Letting Go"

"Junior's Farm"

"Medicine Jar" (Jimmy McCulloch)

"Band on the Run"

"Hi Hi Hi"

"Soily"

I Saw a Film Today, Oh Boy . . .

64. 16 Non-Beatle Movies in Which a Beatle Appears

This feature looks at movies that are not Beatles movies or music documentaries in which a Beatle appears. I think you'll agree that the Beatles' choices of movies in which to appear has been "eclectic" and interesting to say the least. Most of these are available on home video for purchase or rental.

1. *Blindman* (1972)   Ringo plays a "slimy Mexican bandit" named Candy in this Italian feature that stars Tony Anthony as the title character. Anthony seeks revenge on a thief who stole fifty mail-order brides from him. Film critic Leonard Maltin describes this as "mindless entertainment."
2. *Candy* (1968)   This film, based on the sexy Terry Southern novel, should be better than it is. It boasts a screenplay by the talented Buck Henry and hopes were high before its release. Our Ringo plays Emmanuel the gardener, one of the many men who can't resist the blond sex kitten Candy, played by Ewa Aulin.
3. *Caveman* (1981)   Ringo plays a hapless caveman in this dialogueless feature film in which he costarred with his wife Barbara Bach.
4. *Dynamite Chicken* (1970)   John appears (along with Jimi Hendrix, Joan Baez, Lenny Bruce, and others) in this hodgepodge of skits, songs, and terribly dated "hippie" satire.
5. *Elbert's Bad Word* (1991)   This is a Shelley Duvall "Bedtime Story" that is narrated by Ringo.
6. *How I Won the War* (1967)   Richard Lester directed John in this alleged comedy about an inept officer who must lead his troops out of England into Egypt to capture a cricket field. The film itself bombs as a comedy but critics were unanimous in praising John's clever Private Gripweed performance. This was John's only actual feature film role.
7. *Lisztomania* (1975)   Like *Tommy,* this is supposed to be a rock opera, but about the classical composer Franz Liszt, and like Tommy, it stars Roger Daltrey. Written and directed by Ken Russell, Ringo appears in this unsuccessful fantasy extravaganza as the Pope.

John in his memorable performance as Private Gripweed in *How I Won the War*. (Photofest)

8. *The Magic Christian* (**1969**) Ringo plays Youngman Grand, a millionaire's adopted heir, in this Peter Sellers film that also has appearances by John and Yoko, and a soundtrack that includes Badfinger's version of Paul's song "Come and Get It."

9. *Monty Python's Life of Brian* (**1979**) This naughty spoof of Christianity boasts an appearance by George.

10. *The Point* (**1971**) Ringo narrates this made-for-TV cartoon, which is available on video.

11. *Princess Daisy* (**1983**) Ringo appears in this TV miniseries based on the Judith Krantz novel.

12. *Rupert and the Frog Song* (**1986**) Paul does a character's voice and wrote songs for this animated children film.

13. *The Rutles: All You Need Is Cash* (**1978**) As brilliant (almost) as *This Is Spinal Tap*, this satirical documentary about the rise of a group *awfully* similar to the Fab Four boasts a cameo by a heavily disguised George. A must-see.

14. *Sextette* (**1978**) Mae West came out of retirement to make this comedy about a retired sex star who is constantly interrupted by exlovers while on her honeymoon with her sixth husband. One critic described this as "exquisitely embarrassing to watch." (He's right.) Ringo plays one of Mae West's ex-husbands.

15. *Shanghai Surprise* (**1986**) Executive producer George has a brief cameo in this Sean Penn/Madonna disaster.

Ringo, in a publicity still from *The Magic Christian*. (Photofest)

16. *200 Motels* (1971) Ringo appears in this extremely bizarre film written by Frank Zappa. Ringo plays Zappa and a character known as the Dwarf.

65. Who Would Play Whom in The Film Adaptation of J. R. R. Tolkien's *Lord of the Rings* Trilogy

A live action version of J. R. R. Tolkien's *The Lord of the Rings* starring the Beatles? I and millions of other Beatles fans would certainly pay to see that! *The Lord of the Rings* (and its prequel, *The Hobbit*), is my single favorite work of literature. I have read the entire trilogy over a dozen times. (If you have yet to read this fantasy classic . . . well, what are you waiting for?) Unfortunately, the project never got off the ground, but the Beatles did, however, give some thought to the casting (which, if you're familiar with the trilogy and Tolkien's characters, you'll agree is *perfect*). This is the lineup for the four main characters in *The Lord of the Rings*.

> **Frodo Baggins:** Paul
> **Sam Gamgee, Frodo's servant and companion:** Ringo
> **Gandalf the Wizard:** George
> **Gollum:** John

66. The 29 Cover Versions of Beatles Tunes in the Less-Than-Loved Film, *Sgt. Pepper's Lonely Hearts Club Band*

What were they thinking? The film adaptation of what many consider to be the greatest pop album of all time plays like a *Saturday Night Live* skit. A *bad Saturday Night Live* skit, for that matter: Steve Martin singing "Maxwell's Silver Hammer,"

Alice Cooper singing "Because," George Burns—*George Burns*—singing "Fixing a Hole"?

If there was worldwide legislation protecting Beatles fans from crimes against Beatledom, then the entire creative team that put this travesty together would be found guilty and sentenced to life in prison with nothing to listen to but John Tesh and Neil Diamond records.

This is a look at the twenty-nine Beatles tunes (sixteen of which are actually not *Sgt. Pepper* songs) covered in the *Sgt. Pepper's* film and the musical defiler of same. (The songs are listed in the order they appear on the four-album *Sgt. Pepper* soundtrack released with the film.)

DESECRATED BEATLES SONG	THE GUILTY PARTY(S)
Side 1	
1. "Sgt. Pepper's Lonely Hearts Club Band"	The Bee Gees, Paul Nicholas
2. "With a Little Help From My Friends"	Peter Frampton, the Bee Gees
3. "Here Comes the Sun"	Sandy Farina
4. "Getting Better"	Peter Frampton, the Bee Gees
5. "Lucy in the Sky With Diamonds"	Dianne Steinberg, Stargard
6. "I Want You (She's So Heavy)"	The Bee Gees, Dianne Steinberg, Paul Nicholas, Donald Pleasance, Stargard
Side 2	
7. "Good Morning, Good Morning"	Paul Nicholas, Peter Frampton, The Bee Gees
8. "She's Leaving Home"	The Bee Gees, Jay MacIntosh, John Wheeler
9. "You Never Give Me Your Money"	Paul Nicholas, Dianne Steinberg
10. "Oh! Darling"	Robin Gibb
11. "Maxwell's Silver Hammer"	Steve Martin
12. "Polythene Pam"	The Bee Gees
13. "She Came in Through the Bathroom Window"	Peter Frampton, the Bee Gees
14. "Nowhere Man"	The Bee Gees
15. "Sgt. Pepper's Lonely Hearts Club Band"	Peter Frampton, the Bee Gees
Side 3	
16. "Got to Get You Into My Life"	Earth, Wind and Fire
17. "Strawberry Fields Forever"	Sandy Farina
18. "When I'm Sixty-Four"	Frankie Howard, Sandy Farina
19. "Mean Mr. Mustard"	Frankie Howard
20. "Fixing a Hole"	George Burns
21. "Because"	Alice Cooper, the Bee Gees
22. "Golden Slumbers"	Peter Frampton
23. "Carry That Weight"	The Bee Gees

The Bee Gees in the bad-idea-film *Sgt. Pepper's Lonely Hearts Club Band.* (Photofest)

All the Children Sing . . .

67. 4 Beatle Offspring Who Went Into the "Family Business"

You can't turn on the television without seeing something to do with the Beatles, can you? As I was just saying to somebody earlier, kids pick up on the Beatles through the old movie Yellow Submarine. *See, I made a point of not saying anything about [the Beatles] to [Dhani]. But by the time he was five he wanted to know how the piano part to "Hey Bulldog" went, which completely threw me because I didn't understand where he'd heard a song like that. . . . Then I realized it was in* Yellow Submarine.

—George Harrison in 1988

1. **Julian Lennon, son of John** (born April 8, 1963)   It was probably kismet that Julian would go into the music business. After all, having a song of such historical importance as "Hey Jude" written especially for you had to do *something* to stimulate the creative juices flowing through Julian as he was growing up. Julian was in a couple of bands in his teens, including the Lemon Drops and Quasar but it wasn't until his incredible 1985 debut album, *Valotte* (Atlantic Records), that the world let out a collective "Whoa!" and began to take notice of John Lennon's eldest son.

   I can remember the first time I heard the title song, "Valotte" (Julian's first single), from the album. I immediately thought that Yoko had okayed the release of some lovely lost John Lennon ballad. I was floored when the disk jockeys came on after the song ended and started rapping about how much Julian "sounded like his father." Julian followed *Valotte* with three albums of varying quality and success: *The Secret Value of Daydreaming* (Atlantic Records, 1986), *Mr. Jordan* (Atlantic Records, 1989), and *Help Yourself* (Atlantic Records, 1991).

   In December 1996, Julian Lennon made news around the world by paying $39,030 at a London auction for Paul McCartney's recording notes for "Hey Jude." I guess he wanted to keep it in the family, eh? Lately Julian has not been very active in the music business but it is likely that we undoubtedly will hear from "Jules" again.

2. **Zak Starkey, son of Ringo** (born September 13, 1965)   Zak is probably the second most successful musician in the clan of Beatles progeny after Julian. Zak is a very busy professional drummer who received precisely one drum lesson from his famous dad. (See the feature "6 Famous Musicians and Bands With Whom Ringo's Son Zak Starkey Has Played Drums" following this list for much more information on Zak's musical career.)

3. **Sean Lennon, son of John** (born October 9, 1975)   Sean has embraced music with a passion and has been in several bands (including the Pits and IMA) and has also recorded professionally. Sean sang his father's song "It's Alright" on a 1990 "50th anniversary tribute to John" album and also sang on his mother's song "Never Say Goodbye," which was released on her 1983 solo album, *It's Alright*. In 1991, Sean recorded a version of his father's "Give Peace a Chance" with new lyrics that he wrote especially for the new release.

   In the winter of 1995, Yoko and Sean visited Paul McCartney and his family at Paul's home in England. During their visit, Yoko and Sean recorded Yoko's song "Hiroshima, Sky Is Always Blue" in Paul's elaborate recording studio, The Mill. Paul and members of his family also performed on the song.

   Also in 1995, Sean and Yoko released an album called *Rising,* which featured songs by Yoko recorded with Sean's band, IMA. Yoko toured with IMA the following year. Often musically daring, it seems Sean has artistically taken after his father a little more than Julian.

4. **James McCartney, son of Paul** (born September 12, 1977)   James initially wanted to become a drummer but lately seems to be more interested in playing the guitar. His first professional recording gig was playing guitar on his father's 1997 album *Flaming Pie*. During a "Town Hall" interview on VH-1 in the spring of 1997, Paul revealed that he and James had recorded together privately at home quite a lot over the years, but that James's guitar work on "The World Tonight" was the first time he had ever appeared on one of Paul's records.

PUT ON SPECIALLY BY THE CHILDREN FOR A LARK

Jason Starkey, son of Ringo (born August 19, 1967) started out in the music business as a drummer but it didn't really work out. When he was in his teens, he was quoted as saying, "Being Ringo's son is the biggest drag in my life. It's a total drag." Jason has never recorded professionally and in 1995, it was reported that he was playing drums in an unknown bar band.

Mary McCartney, daughter of Paul (born August 29, 1969) has a tangential connection with the music biz via the camera: She directed the music video for her dad's song "The World Tonight" from his 1997 album *Flaming Pie*. "She takes after her mum," Paul said during a "Town Hall" interview on VH-1 in the spring of 1997. (Linda McCartney is a highly regarded professional photographer who has published books of her work.)

Dhani Harrison, son of George (born August 1, 1978) has influenced his father's musical taste by turning the Quiet Beatle on to some contemporary artists including, according to George, the Black Crowes. In 1992 George invited Dhani onstage to play guitar during a concert in support of the Maharishi but other than that isolated appearance, Dhani does not seem to have much interest in becoming a professional musician. Recent reports have him studying design technology.

68. 6 Famous Musicians and Bands With Whom Ringo's Son Zak Starkey has Played Drums

[I]t was such a joy for me to see [Zak] play with the Who. They have always been one of his favorite bands. To see one of your children fulfill your dreams is beautiful.

—Ringo, in the July 1997 issue of *Modern Drummer*

Zak Starkey was a mere lad of five when his dad's band, the Beatles, broke up. Thus, all of Zak's knowledge of his father's contributions to the world of music is after the fact. Nonetheless, Zak took to the drums immediately after his father "introduced" him to a drum kit when he was ten and gave him what he has described as the only drumming lesson he ever received. From that single lesson a career bloomed. Zak is now in his early thirties and has been playing drums ever since, professionally for almost two decades.

The list of musicians Zak has played with is impressive and is evidence that he took to his heart a lesson his father taught him at an early age. "The greatest musical lesson I ever learned from my dad," he told *Modern Drummer*, "was to play with as many people as I could." His lesser-known work includes drumming with the bands Next, Nightfly, and Ice. This list is a compilation of a few of the world-renowned musicians and bands Zak "Ringo's son" Starkey has played with.

1. **Roger Daltrey**   Zak began playing with the Who's front man when he was only nineteen. He also toured with Daltrey while in his twenties.
2. **The Spencer Davis Group**   Zak did some studio work with this English group (remember "Gimme Some Lovin'"?) when he was in his mid-teens.
3. **John Entwhistle**   The same year Zak began playing with Daltrey, he also began working with Entwhistle, another Who band member. They worked together on an album that never came out. Entwhistle had seen Zak perform with a local band when Zak was sixteen and had asked him to work with him then, but Zak declined, citing loyalty to his bandmates. "I was in a band with these guys from the age of fourteen," he told *Modern Drummer*. "I had been in bands with the bass player since I was a kid, and I had been with the other guys for something like three years. You don't just drop everything."
4. **Ringo's All-Starr Band**   As of 1997, Ringo has mounted four "All-Starr Band Tours." He toured in 1989, 1992, 1995, and 1997 and his son Zak was the drummer (along with his father of course) on the 1992 and 1995 tours. "We were just having a lot of fun," Zak told *Modern Drummer* when asked what "double drumming" with Ringo was like. "Nothing was written in stone, and we were

Drummer, "I don't play what Keith [Moon] played note-for-note on everything. Probably 70 percent of the parts are changed, but there are certain things within every song that Keith did that *have* to be there. Otherwise it's just not *Quadrophenia,* to me or to people who are Who fans."

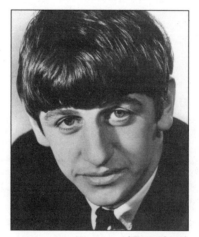

(Photofest)

Imagine . . .

69. The 5 Members of Paul McCartney's Imagined Supergroup

In a three-part interview with Matt Lauer on NBC's *Today* show that aired during the week of July 7, 1997, Paul McCartney touched on a wide range of subjects, ranging from his relationship with John to the latest state of his wife's health. What makes Matt Lauer such a terrific interviewer and engaging TV presence is that he often allows his enthusiasm to bubble through when the occasion warrants. It is supremely evident that he is not ashamed to be a fan of some of the people he gets to talk to as part of his job. This willingness to "subtly gush" often results in Lauer asking exactly the question a serious fan of the artist might ask if he or she had the chance. This happened during the third part of Matt's McCartney chat when he asked Paul who he'd choose if he ever put together a supergroup.

The conversation began:

MATT LAUER Do you have a supergroup?

PAUL MCCARTNEY Who would I put together as a supergroup? They're all dead, my supergroup. Are we allowed to get them from heaven?

MATT LAUER Okay, let's do it that way.

Paul then thought a bit and constructed the McCartney Band which, incredibly, is actually the Beatles with a guest guitarist. I guess when you were once a member of the band that is the indisputable gold standard of bands, then why fix what ain't broken, eh?

Here is the lineup of Paul McCartney's supergroup, in the order in which he picked them.

1. John Lennon
2. Jimi Hendrix
3. Ringo Starr
4. Paul McCartney ("I'll play bass.")
5. George Harrison

After naming George, Paul acknowledged that there were many musicians he'd love to play with but then he smiled and said, "That'd be a pretty good band right there [though]."

Yes it is.

In the March 1997 issue of *Guitar World* magazine, rock journalist Vic Garbarini interviewed George Harrison for a feature titled "60 Minutes." Garbarini described George as "the man who practically invented modern rock guitar as we know and fear it". He asked the former Beatle to compile a hypothetical one-hour cassette tape containing a bunch of songs he really likes and that he thinks influenced him.

George was not at a loss for choices and the following list looks at the songs he selected. There are a couple of expected tunes, but also some surprises. In any case, if you're a serious fan of rock guitar, you should probably get to work putting together this tape and keeping it in your car or Walkman for ready reference!

1. **"If You're Going to Make a Fool of Somebody" by James Ray**
   WHY HE LIKES IT   This became a fave of George's when the Beatles used to perform this "brilliant" R and B single in their early years.

2. **"Blue Suede Shoes" by Carl Perkins**
   WHY HE LIKES IT   According to George, "They don't come more perfect than this in terms of recording quality and atmosphere." George also said that he and the other Beatles could never figure out how Perkins and company created the perfect "live slap" sound of the bass and drums on this recording.

3. **"Roll Over Beethoven" by Chuck Berry**
   WHY HE LIKES IT   George, who calls Chuck Berry one of the Beatles' "guitar heroes," used to sing this song live after John gave it up and thus, it became a favorite. George told *Guitar World* that when the Beatles were performing in Tokyo, the crowds cheered when he did this song and he suspected they thought *he* was the one who wrote it.

4. **"The Bells of Rhymney"—from the *Mr. Tambourine Man* album by the Byrds**
   WHY HE LIKES IT   George remembers that this chiming, 12-string guitar Byrds song directly inspired the creation of his own *Rubber Soul* song, "If I Needed Someone."

5. **"Call of the Valley" by Brij Bhushan Kabra**
   WHY HE LIKES IT   George likes this piece by the classical Indian musician Kabra (whom George met in the sixties when Ravi Shankar brought him to his house) because of the speed and precision with which Kabra plays. George explained that Kabra used a slide guitar but modified it and added strings, making it more like a sitar. George also told Garbarini that it would be "precocious" to attempt to compare himself with Kabra, describing the musician as "incredible."

6. **"Badge"—from the *Goodbye* album by Cream**
   WHY HE LIKES IT   This one is obvious: George likes "Badge" because he cowrote it with Eric Clapton and it has some great guitar work by Eric in it.

7. **"Back on the Chain Gang"—from the *Learning to Crawl* album by the Pretenders**
   WHY HE LIKES IT   Believe it or not, Mr. Harrison likes this song because it contains one specific chord, a combination he describes as the "frustration" chord: an E7 with an F on top. He remembers that he invented the chord for his song "I Want to Tell You" on the *Revolver* album and that the Pretenders are the only group he's come across who "borrowed" it for their own song.

8. **"Brothers in Arms"**—from the ***Brothers in Arms*** album by Dire Straits

    WHY HE LIKES IT   George claims that Dire Straits doing this song was the last time he *really* enjoyed listening to any music beyond the stuff of the fifties and sixties. (If you're a musician who has recorded *anything* from 1970 through this year . . . ouch.)

9. **"Cold Day in Hell"**—from the ***After Hours*** album by Gary Moore

    WHY HE LIKES IT   George considers Moore "brilliant" and admits to admiring guitarists who can play really fast because "I can't put together more than four notes in a run."

10. **"Remedy"**—from ***The Southern Harmony and Musical Companion*** album by the Black Crowes

    WHY HE LIKES IT   George's teenage son Dhani (whom George says has lately been influencing him quite a bit musically) turned him on to this Black Crowes track and George really liked the song and the band.

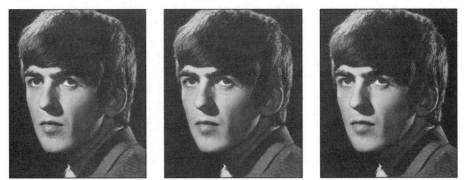

(Photofest)

It's Getting Very Near the End . . .

71. 15 Beatles Web Pages

This is a selection of some popular Beatles web pages. As with anything on the Internet, you never know if a site will still be there when you attempt to visit it, but in most cases, if a site has moved (as opposed to shutting down), it will usually provide you with a link to its new address at its *old* address.

Some of these Beatles web sites are amazing in their thoroughness and in the amount of information they offer. Many of them offer links to hundreds of other Beatles-related sites. So, happy surfing, and just be sure you don't tie up the phone line for hours at a time, okay??

John Lennon Web Page	http://www.missouri.edu/~c588349/john-page.html
Paul McCartney: The Solo Years	http://www.halcyon.com/mariegpaul.html
George Harrison Portfolio	http://www.primenet.com/%7Edhaber/bgeorge.html
Ringo Starr Page	http://web2.airmail.net/gshultz/
Pete Best Forever, Ringo Never!	http://students.vassar.edu/~dafine/petebest.html
May Pang	http://jack.clarku.edu/~RKneeland/Pangweb1.htm
The Internet Beatles Album	http://www.primenet.com/~dhaber/beatles.html
The Beatles Are Back!	http://www.nj1.aae.com/~phenry/beatles.html
Abbeyrd's Beatles Page	http://www.best.com/~abbeyrd/
The Beatles Internet Underground Page	http://www.primenet.com/~shears/beatles/
A Summary of the Beatles on Video	ftp://bobcat.bbn.com/pub/beatles/misc/video.lst
All Together Now (books)	ftp://bobcat.bbn.com/pub/beatles/welcome/allbooks
The Best Beatles Bootleg CDs	ftp://bobcat.bbn.com/pub/beatles/misc.gudboots
The Beatles Covers List	http://www.wmin.ac.uk/~clemenr/covers/covers.htm
Mike's Beatles List (links to 100 Beatles sites)	http://www.neca.com/~mikem/beat.html

72. Lee Mandato's 3 Favorite Beatles Songs

Lee Mandato is my mother and these are the three songs she immediately mentioned when I asked her what her favorite Beatles songs were. To Lee, a Beatle is a Beatle is a Beatle, and thus, she insisted on including a solo John Lennon song among her favorites. Since I was raised never to argue with me mum, I include her choices as she gave them to me.

"Hey Jude"
"Imagine"
"Yesterday"

73. Paul's Letter to John

The following is the letter Paul McCartney wrote to the late John Lennon and delivered as a speech on the occasion of John's induction into the Rock and Roll Hall of Fame on January 19, 1994. Okay, this is not technically a "list" (although it could be a one-item list, right?) but we felt it was so significant that it should be included in *The Beatles Book of Lists.*

In this touching and poignant letter, Paul writes to his old friend. In a series of fascinating anecdotes, he tells some of the history of the Beatles. This, my friends, is priceless stuff.

Dear John,

I remember when we first met, at Woolton, at the village fete. It was a beautiful summer day and I walked in there and saw you on stage. And you were singing "Come Go With Me," by the Dell Vikings, but you didn't know the words so you made them up. "Come go with me to the penitentiary." It's not in the lyrics.

I remember writing our first songs together. We used to go to my house, my Dad's home, and we used to smoke Ty-Phoo tea with the pipe my dad kept in a drawer. It didn't do much for us but it got us on the road. We wanted to be famous.

I remember the visits to your mum's house. Julia was a very handsome woman, very beautiful woman. She had long, red hair and she played a ukulele. I'd never seen a woman that could do that. And I remember having to tell you the guitar chords because you used to play the ukulele chords.

And then on your 21st birthday you got 100 pounds off one of your rich relatives up in Edinburgh, so we decided we'd go to Spain. So we hitchhiked out of Liverpool, got as far as Paris, and decided to stop there, for a week. And eventually got our haircut, by a fellow named Jurgen, and that ended up being the "Beatle haircut."

I remember introducing you to my mate George, my schoolmate, and getting him into the band by playing "Raunchy" on the top deck of a bus. You were impressed. And we met Ringo who'd been working the whole season at Butlin's camp—he was a seasoned professional—but the beard had to go, and it did.

Later on we got a gig at the Cavern Club in Liverpool, which was officially a blues club. We didn't really know any blues numbers. We loved the blues but we didn't know any blues numbers, so we had announcements like "Ladies and gentlemen, this is a great Big Bill Broonzy number called "Wake Up Little Suzie." And they kept passing up little notes—"This is not the blues, this is not the blues. This is pop." But we kept going.

And then we ended up touring. It was a bloke called Larry Parnes who gave us our first tour. I remember we all changed names for that tour. I changed mine to Paul Ramon, George became Carl Harrison and, although people think you didn't really change your name, I seem to remember you were Long John Silver for the duration of that tour. Bang goes another myth.

We'd been on a van touring later and we'd have the kind of night where the windscreen would break. We would be on the motorway going back up to Liverpool. It was freezing so we had to lie on top of each other in the back of the van, creating a Beatle sandwich. We got to know each other. These were the ways we got to know each other.

We got to Hamburg and met the likes of Little Richard, Gene Vincent . . . I remember Little Richard inviting us back to his hotel. He was looking at Ringo's ring and said, "I love that ring." He said, "I've got a ring like that. I could give you a ring like that." So we all went back to the hotel with him. (We never got a ring.)

We went back with Gene Vincent to his hotel room once. It was all going fine until he reached in his bedside drawer and pulled out a gun. We said "Er, we've got to go, Gene, we've got to go . . ." We got out quick!

And then came the USA—New York City—where we met up with Phil Spector, the Ronettes, Supremes, our heroes, our heroines. And then later in L.A., we met up with Elvis Presley for one great evening. We saw the boy on his home territory. He was the first person I ever saw with a remote control on a TV. Boy! He was a hero, man.

And then later, Ed Sullivan. We'd wanted to be famous, now we were getting really famous. I mean imagine meeting Mitzi Gaynor in Miami!

Later, after that, recording at Abbey Road. I still remember doing "Love Me Do." You officially had the vocal "love me do" but because you played the harmonica, George Martin suddenly said in the middle of the session, "Will Paul sing the line 'love me do?' the crucial line. I can still hear it to this day—you would go "Whaaa whaa," and I'd go "loove me doo-oo." Nerves, man.

I remember doing the vocal to "Kansas City"—well I couldn't quite get it, because it's hard to do that stuff. You know, screaming out the top of your head. You came down from the control room and took me to one side and said "You can do it, you've just got to scream, you can do it." So, thank you. Thank you for that. I did it.

I remember writing "A Day in the Life" with you, and the little look we gave each other when we wrote the line "I'd love to turn you on." We kinda knew what we were doing, you know. A sneaky little look.

After that there was this girl called Yoko. Yoko Ono. She showed up at my house one day. It was John Cage's birthday and she said she wanted to get hold of manuscripts of various composers to give to him, and she wanted one from me and you. So I said, "Well it's ok by me. But you'll have to go to John."

And she did . . .

After that I set up a couple of Brennell recording machines we used to have and you stayed up all night and recorded "Two Virgins." But you took the cover yourselves—nothing to do with me.

And then, after that there were the phone calls to you. The joy for me after all the business shit that we'd gone through was that we were actually getting back together and communicating once again. And the joy as you told me about how you were baking bread now. And how you were playing with your little baby, Sean. That was great for me because it gave me something to hold on to.

So now, years on, here we are. All these people. Here we are, assembled, to thank you for everything that you mean to all of us.

This letter comes with love, from your friend Paul.

John Lennon, you've made it. Tonight you are in the Rock 'n' Roll Hall of Fame.

God bless you.

Paul

The Final Word

If the Beatles or the sixties had a message,
it was learn to swim.
Period.
And once you learn to swim,
swim.

●

John Lennon
September 1980

(Author's collection)

(Photofest)

See You at Beatlefest

Beatles fans Mark and Carol Lapidos and their staff, run several "Official Beatles Conventions" every year, in New York, Chicago, and Los Angeles, and they've been running them for more than twenty years. At Beatlefest, you can hear special guests from throughout Beatles' history speak and/or perform (past guests have ranged from original Quarrymen Len Garry, Beatle brother Mike "McGear" McCartney, and Beatles archivist Mark Lewisohn, to the Rutles, Harry Nilsson, and Badfinger. You can also view rare Beatles promotional clips, visit the Beatles museum, vote for your favorites in a Battle of the Beatles Bands competition, groove to cover band par excellence Liverpool, and record your own Beatles CD, as well as pick up the latest Beatles memorabilia and collectibles in the massive Beatles marketplace—and much more. Beatlefests are weekends for Beatles fans, by Beatles fans. For Beatlefest convention information, call 1-888-9BEATLES

Index

About the Author

Stephen J. Spignesi specializes in popular culture subjects, including television, film, contemporary fiction, and historical biography.

He has written several authorized entertainment books and has worked with Stephen King, Turner Entertainment, the Margaret Mitchell Estate, Andy Griffith, Viacom, and other entertainment industry personalities and entities on a wide range of projects. Mr. Spignesi has also contributed essays, chapters, articles, and introductions to numerous books.

In addition to writing, Mr. Spignesi lectures on a variety of popular culture subjects, teaches courses on writing and publishing, and is the founder and editor in chief of the small press publishing company, the Stephen John Press. He is a graduate of the University of New Haven and lives in New Haven with his wife, Pam.

Spignesi's other books include:

Mayberry, My Hometown (Popular Culture, Ink.)

The Complete Stephen King Encyclopedia (Popular Culture, Ink.; Contemporary Books)

The Stephen King Quiz Book (Signet)

The Second Stephen King Quiz Book (Signet)

The Woody Allen Companion (Andrews and McMeel; Plexus London; Popular Culture, Ink.)

The Official "Gone With the Wind" Companion (Plume)

The V. C. Andrews Trivia and Quiz Book (Signet)

What's Your "Mad About You" IQ? (Citadel Press)

What's Your "Friends" IQ? (Citadel Press)

The "ER" Companion (Citadel Press)

The J. F. K. Jr. Scrapbook (Citadel Press)

The Robin Williams Scrapbook (Citadel Press)

The Italian 100: A Ranking of the Most Influential Cultural, Scientific, and Political Figures, Past and Present (Citadel Press)

The Lost Work of Stephen King (Citadel Press)

The Gore Galore Video Quiz Book (Signet)

The Odd Index: The Ultimate Compendium of Bizarre and Unusual Facts (Plume)

The Celebrity Baby Name Book (Signet)

Stephen King A to Z (forthcoming, Popular Culture, Ink.)